Reclaiming the Radical Economic Message of Luke

Reclaiming the Radical Economic Message of Luke

David D. M. King

PICKWICK *Publications* · Eugene, Oregon

Pickwick Publications
An Imprint of Wipf and Stock Publishers
199 W. 8th Ave., Suite 3
Eugene, OR 97401

www.wipfandstock.com

PAPERBACK ISBN: 978-1-6667-3339-6
HARDCOVER ISBN: 978-1-6667-2800-2
EBOOK ISBN: 978-1-6667-2801-9

Cataloguing-in-Publication data:

Names: King, David D. M., author.

Title: Reclaiming the radical economic message of Luke / by David D. M. King.

Description: Eugene, OR: Pickwick Publications, 2022 | Includes bibliographical references.

Identifiers: ISBN 978-1-6667-3339-6 (paperback) | ISBN 978-1-6667-2800-2 (hardcover) | ISBN 978-1-6667-2801-9 (ebook)

Subjects: LCSH: Bible. Luke—Criticism, interpretation, etc. | Economics in the Bible.

Classification: BS2595.2 K564 2022 (print) | BS2595.2 (ebook)

05/11/22

Contents

List of Figures and Tables

Acknowledgments

THIS BOOK IS A revised version of my PhD dissertation in the Joint Doctoral Program at the University of Denver and the Iliff School of Theology. As such, my first thanks go to my advisor, Dr. Gregory Allen Robbins, for guiding me through the process from coursework to completion. He doesn't always say much, but when he does speak, it is always profound and insightful. He set exams that not only tested my knowledge but also opened my mind. Every suggestion he offered made this project better.

Thanks to the members of my dissertation committee. Dr. Pamela Eisenbaum, my MA advisor, guided me in numerous courses and in individual meetings and was hugely formative in my development as a scholar. Dr. Miguel De La Torre pushed me ever to the margins, and I am grateful and better for it. Dr. Katherine Turpin, my MDiv advisor, was gracious enough to chair my committee. She was there at the beginning and at the end, and for many of the bumps along the way.

Thanks to my compatriots in study, Albert McClure and Patrick Stefan. They were often my first readers and helped me conceive and shape this project. Thanks to the New Testament World section of the Pacific Northwest SBL, who helped me refine several sections of this book. Thanks to Rev. Canon Dr. Anna Carmichael for the friendship and motivation as we both pushed to finish our programs.

Nearly all of this was written while I was pastor of Spirit of Grace Church in Hood River, Oregon. The people of this blended congregation of the Evangelical Lutheran Church in American and The United

Methodist Church offered so much support and encouragement. They also offered me two months of study leave, without which, I never could have finished. Thanks also to Rev. Dr. Rob Sachs for covering for me and to St. Mark's Episcopal Church in Hood River for providing me with an office in which to write during my leave.

Thanks to the amazingly diverse and collegial clergy of the Columbia River Gorge, including those of Gorge Ecumenical Ministries and the Mt. Adams Ministerial Association. I've never known another ecumenical community like it. Thanks especially to the clergy of Reflectionary, who gathered each week to chew over scripture and support one another.

To my parents, Mardean and Horace King, thanks for supporting me in every endeavor, from the beginning until now. I would not be here without you.

Thanks especially to my amazing wife, Melissa Mimier King, and to our remarkable children, Karthik, Kiahla, and Kaylah. They inspired me when I was defeated and picked me up when I fell down. I would be lost without them. This book, and everything good I do, is down to their love and care.

Abbreviations

ACCS	*Ancient Christian Commentary on Scripture*, ed. Thomas C. Oden
BTB	*Biblical Theology Bulletin*
CBQ	*Catholic Biblical Quarterly*
CEB	Common English Bible
ChrCent	*Christian Century*
CurTM	*Currents in Theology and Mission*
De div.	*De divitiis*
Int	*Interpretation*
JBL	*Journal of Biblical Literature*
JRE	*Journal of Religious Ethics*
JRS	*Journal of Roman Studies*
JSNT	*Journal for the Study of the New Testament*
LCL	Loeb Classical Library
LSJ	Liddell, Henry George and Robert Scott. *A Greek-English Lexicon*
loc.	Kindle location, when no page number is available
NA 28	*Nestle-Aland Novum Testamentum Graece*, 28th ed., ed. Aland et al
NovT	*Novum Testamentum*

NRSV	New Revised Standard Version
PRSt	*Perspectives in Religious Studies*
Quis div.	Clement of Alexandria, *Quis dives salvetur*
RevExp	*Review and Expositor*
ResQ	*Restoration Quarterly*
SBL	Society of Biblical Literature
STRev	*Sewanee Theological Review*
SV	Scholars Version
s.v.	*sub verso*, according to the verse
TynBul	*Tyndale Bulletin*
ZNW	*Zeitschrift für die neutestamentliche Wissenschaft und die Kunde der älteren Kirche*

CHAPTER 1

Introduction

None of you can become my disciple if you
do not give up all your possessions.

—LUKE 14:33 NRSV

SHORTLY BEFORE HIS ASSASSINATION, Rev. Dr. Martin Luther King Jr. focused his work on a Poor People's Campaign.

> The contemporary tendency in our society is to base our distribution on scarcity, which has vanished, and to compress our abundance into the overfed mouths of the middle and upper classes until they gag with superfluity. If democracy is to have breadth of meaning, it is necessary to adjust this inequity. It is not only moral, but it is also intelligent. We are wasting and degrading human life by clinging to archaic thinking.
>
> The curse of poverty has no justification in our age. It is socially as cruel and blind as the practice of cannibalism at the dawn of civilization, when men ate each other because they had not yet learned to take food from the soil or to consume the abundant animal life around them. The time has come for us to civilize ourselves by the total, direct and immediate abolition of poverty.[1]

These are radical words demanding sweeping changes in society for the benefit of the poor. But when King's holiday rolls around every January, it

1. Quoted in Weissman, "Remembering Martin Luther King," para. 13–14.

is not these words that are quoted. It is not even the words from the beginning of his famous speech from the Lincoln Memorial in August of 1963:

> In a sense we've come to our nation's capital to cash a check. When the architects of our republic wrote the magnificent words of the Constitution and the Declaration of Independence, they were signing a promissory note to which every American was to fall heir. This note was a promise that all men, yes, black men as well as white men, would be guaranteed the unalienable rights of life, liberty, and the pursuit of happiness. It is obvious today that America has defaulted on this promissory note insofar as her citizens of color are concerned. Instead of honoring this sacred obligation, America has given the Negro people a bad check, a check which has come back marked insufficient funds.
>
> But we refuse to believe that the bank of justice is bankrupt. We refuse to believe that there are insufficient funds in the great vaults of opportunity of this nation. And so we've come to cash this check, a check that will give us upon demand the riches of freedom and the security of justice.[2]

No, it is not these words. The words we hear each year are always the same: "I have a dream." All of Dr. King's work gets boiled down to those four words. And in that distillation, the radical King is lost and forgotten. The radical King is so completely lost that critics of the Black Lives Matter movement can suggest that BLM should tone things down, be less in-your-face, just like, they say, Dr. King kept things calm and reasonable, not remembering that King was remarkably controversial and unpopular during his lifetime.[3]

> As often happens in history, however, time cools political passions, and leaders once damned as radicals or traitors—and King was frequently called both—are absorbed into a patriotic narrative that stresses consensus rather than conflict. Abstracted from the specific circumstances of their history, they come to function as symbols of the nation as a whole.[4]

As the story of Dr. King is passed down again and again, he is made less revolutionary, less radical, and more respectable. In the end, he is seen as an idealist who just wants everyone to get along instead of a crusader for justice and for real, material change.

2. King, "I Have a Dream," para. 4–5.

3. Dupuy, "Most Americans Didn't Approve"; Newport, "Martin Luther King Jr."

4. Fairclough, "Foreword," xiii.

Nevertheless, the King of American civil religion is a highly selective version of King the historical actor. This is why conservatives can commemorate King with as much sincerity as liberals. Judging people "not by the color of their skin but by the content of their character" is entirely consistent with the individualism that provides the ideological underpinning of American capitalism. Conveniently forgotten is the man who berated America for its excessive materialism and militarism, who stated qualified admiration for Karl Marx and who regarded Sweden's social democracy as a model that the United States of America would do well to follow.[5]

Phillip Esler notes a similar process of domestication in the reception of the economic themes in the Gospel of Luke and its sequel, the Acts of the Apostles.

> The ingrained disregard among scholars for the social and economic setting of Luke-Acts, and their corresponding enthusiasm . . . for its alleged spiritual and individualistic approach to salvation, originate in a clear middle-class bias. Generations of scholars, in their seminaries and universities, have been so successful in making Luke's message on possessions palatable for bourgeois tastes that its genuinely radical nature has rarely been noted.[6]

The rough edges of Luke's economic message are sanded down with each new interpretation. Every time that the radical elements are ignored or explained away, it becomes that much easier for interpreters and believers to harmonize Luke with the prevailing economic practices of the culture.

Luke has long been known for having more material concerning wealth and poverty than any other gospel. In light of this, many have undertaken to set down an orderly account of the theology of poor and rich found in Luke or in Luke-Acts, notably the following: Luke Timothy Johnson, Walter Pilgrim, David Peter Seccombe, Kyoung-Jin Kim, Thomas E. Phillips, James A. Metzger, and Christopher M. Hays.[7] As Johnson summarizes, "The problem we face is that although Luke consistently

---

5. Fairclough, "Foreword," xiv.

6. Esler, *Community and Gospel*, 170.

7. Johnson, *Literary Function*; Pilgrim, *Good News to the Poor*; Seccombe, *Possessions and the Poor*; Kim, *Stewardship and Almsgiving*; Phillips, *Reading Issues*; Metzger, *Consumption and Wealth*; Hays, *Luke's Wealth Ethics*.

talks about possessions, he does not talk about possessions consistently."[8] Most commonly, this inconsistency is identified as the presence in Luke-Acts of calls both (1) to total renunciation or communal property and (2) to mere almsgiving.[9] Are all disciples required to renounce possessions? Who exactly is required to renounce, and how much are they required to give away?

I argue that this categorization is insufficient; it accounts for a relatively small amount of Lukan economic material and distracts from the overwhelming thrust of Luke's radical economic message. It suggests the most important question to ask is, "What is the least a person of means must do to avoid running afoul of the Lukan Jesus?"[10] That is to say, whether it is intended or not, focus on the discrepancies between renunciation and almsgiving serves to distract from, discredit, and defang Luke's radical economic message.

My primary thesis is that *Luke's message about wealth and poverty proposes a radical, prophetic way to understand the economy in religious terms.* In particular, it suggests a radical contrast of the world's economy with God's economy. This contrast in Luke illustrates that religion can serve a prophetic function in relation to economic injustice rather than an opiating function.[11]

This thesis can be broken up into three subsidiary claims. First, *the Gospel of Luke has a radical message about wealth and poverty.* That is, there is a radical economic message to be found within the literary bounds of the text of Luke. Specifically, it suggests that God has a preferential option for the poor, that Jesus demands a renunciation of wealth from his followers, and that wealth is generally dangerous.

This leads to a second claim: *it was radical then.* That is to say, Luke's message was radical in relation to the Greco-Roman and early Christian

---

8. Johnson, *Literary Function*, 130.

9. Donahue, "Two Decades," 135; Fitzmyer, *Luke I–IX*, 249; Johnson, *Literary Function*, 10; Metzger, *Consumption and Wealth*, 2.

10. See in particular Phillips, *Reading Issues*, 181.

11. By "radical," I mean simply something that is thoroughgoing, that promises to disrupt the established order, that gets to the roots of the issues. A radical message might be contrasted with a measured or moderate message. I do not mean the ideology identified by Hayden White as "Radicalism" in *Metahistory*, 21–24. Identification of such an ideology with Luke would be anachronistic since, by definition, it must appeal to "'science' or 'realism.'" One could imagine a modern scholar taking a Radical, Liberal, or Anarchist approach to Luke's economic message, but I am not taking claim to any of these approaches.

contexts in which it was first heard. Luke's message stood in stark contrast to the economic elements of Rome's system of imperial domination. Early Christian ascetic practice, following Luke, was understood as a radical break with normal behavior. Also, evidence can be seen in the manuscript tradition of Luke that some of Luke's most radical claims were troubling to the scribes who were assigned to copy them.

The third claim is: *it is radical now*. In particular, Luke has radically different assumptions about wealth than does modern capitalist society. A God who "lifts up the lowly" and "pulls down the mighty from their thrones" (Luke 1:52 NRSV) is no less disquieting now than it was in the first century. If anything, Luke's claim that money or market can be a rival god (Luke 16:13) seems even more apt now than in the ancient Near East. It also follows that interpretations which seek to moderate or subdue the radicalness of Luke's message serve to disfigure that message. It is perfectly acceptable to claim that Luke's demands are impractical or overly-utopian; however, it is not acceptable to then assert that to the degree Luke's message seems radical, Luke must not have meant it—a claim all too common among modern interpreters. The power of Luke's economic message is found precisely in its radicalism. It leaves no Christian alone. It cannot be easily brushed off or laid aside. Given this, how might Christians take Luke's message seriously in a capitalistic world, neither watering it down nor dismissing it entirely? Can it stand as a radical, prophetic critique of political economy and of the economic practice of individual Christians and corporate Christian bodies?

My claims about Luke's radical message are by no means unproblematic. As we have already noted, Luke is more interested in issues of poverty and wealth than is any other gospel. It is more interested in these issues than any other New Testament writing, with the possible exception of the Epistle of James. At the same time, though, Luke shows signs of being produced in a higher-class context than the other canonical gospels. It is composed with the most sophisticated Greek in the New Testament. It is careful to place its narrative within the greater context of the Roman Empire (Luke 1:5; 2:1–2). It seems to have the support of a well-to-do patron (Luke 1:1–4). Luke is clearly not the work of a peasant. How, then, can it contain a radical economic message?

Two scholars in particular—Itumeleng Mosala and Craig Nessan—criticize Luke for not being radical enough, for co-opting the radical peasant message of the historical Jesus in order to suit the needs of the elite.[12] Nessan states the problem clearly:

> The radicality of Jesus' teachings begins to be softened already within the narrative of Luke's Gospel insofar as Luke's message becomes one of exhorting wealthy Christians to be benevolent and generous to the poor, whereas the position of Jesus summons forth a response far more exacting. Such a domestication of the message of Jesus is the constant temptation, not only of Luke but of all approaches based solely on literary criticism insofar as the presuppositions of the present situation become the filter through which the teachings of Jesus are strained. This means that a legitimate literary approach to the Bible requires a grounding in the conclusions of historical-critical interpretation, lest the particularity and radicality of the incarnation of God in Jesus of Nazareth in first-century Galilee be compromised. To put the matter provocatively: the story of Jesus told apart from the social, economic, political, and religious context of first century Galilee becomes docetic.[13]

Jesus had a radical economic message, but when Luke adapts it to a more urban, more cosmopolitan context, he disfigures it, in the service of the wealthy. Mosala is even harsher, suggesting that Luke is not merely a softening of Jesus's radical message, it is a betrayal of that message:

> Given the fact, therefore, that Luke's audience is undoubtedly composed of the dominant groups of first-century Palestine—even though the subject matter is the conditions and struggles of the poor—there seems little doubt that his invocation of the Davidic royal connection [in the birth narrative] was meant to suppress Jesus' unacceptable low-class origins. From the point of view of the oppressed and exploited people of the world today, Luke's ideological co-optation of Jesus in the interests of the ruling class is an act of political war against the liberation struggle.[14]

Both Nessan and Mosala suggest that a liberationist interpreter must read behind the text of Luke in order to find the radical message of Jesus.

I take these critiques very seriously. It is entirely plausible, even likely, that Luke's economic message represents a domestication of a more

---

12. Mosala, *Biblical Hermeneutics*; Nessan, "Luke and Liberation Theology," 130–38.

13. Nessan, "Luke and Liberation Theology," 130–31.

14. Mosala, *Biblical Hermeneutics*, 171.

radical stance by the historical Jesus. I would argue, though, that even if Luke is less radical than the historical Jesus might have been, it is still far more radical than many Lukan interpreters allow. In fact, the possibility of a more radical Jesus behind the text of Luke makes it all the more important to reclaim the radical elements of Luke. Luke is our best evidence of Jesus's views and actions related to economic themes; without Luke we would have hardly any testimony to a radical historical Jesus at all.[15] If, as Nessan suggest, Luke is the first step in an ongoing process of toning down the gospel for the poor, it is important that we give as little ground to accommodation as is absolutely necessary. I make no claims about Luke's relationship to the historical Jesus; I am not trying to uncover a more radical gospel behind Luke. My task, given the Lukan document that we do have, is to make a reading that is as resistant as possible to the elite bias of nearly all of Luke's professional interpreters.

Of course, I am not free from the same bias. I am neither a first-century Palestinian peasant, nor do I come from the most marginalized classes of my country or of the world. Like most who have the leisure and resources to pursue graduate studies, I am susceptible to the same middle-class bias of which Esler warns. What is more, I share none of the experience of oppression that would make for a credible liberationist reading of the Bible. There is something problematic about someone with my background and station attempting to interpret a text like this one. As Halvor Moxnes warns:

> How can the affluent evaluate social and economic activity in our world from the viewpoint of the poor and the powerless? The uncomfortable truth is that we cannot. Only the poor and the powerless can do that. Thus, the only hope for a reversal comes from their being empowered to act on their insights. It is when we recognize the force of "the moral economy" of black women in the United States, of miners in South Africa, or of Indian peasants in Latin America, to name only a few examples, that we really understand the force of Luke's narratives.[16]

And yet, this text will not let me go. It pokes and prods at me. It haunts me, even. I cannot escape it. And so, I can do no more than to do my best. It is with a sense of humility and an awareness of my own

---

15. Schottroff and Stegemann, *Jesus and the Hope of the Poor*, 67.

16. Moxnes, *Economy of the Kingdom*, 168–69.

limitations that I approach this project and attempt to add what illumina-
tion I can to the study of economic themes in Luke.

Main Conversation Partners in Lukan Economic Studies

I am by no means the first to take up this work. Studies of poverty and
wealth in Luke or Luke-Acts are legion. Whenever one reads another,
one seems to find references to three more. I will, therefore, focus on the
following influential monographs on wealth and poverty in Luke as my
primary conversation partners.[17]

17. The following are occasionally referenced but not explored here: Hans-Joachim
Degenhardt, in *Evangelist der Armen*, distinguishes between μαθητής (disciples), who
must divest, and λάος (people), who do not, arguing that complete divestiture was only
for church leaders in Luke's time. Robert Karris, especially in "Poor and Rich," is most
known for arguing that Luke-Acts is addressed to the rich in Luke's community. Richard Cassidy argues a message of good news for the poor and warnings against wealth
and says that Jesus's radical teachings constituted a sort of nonviolent resistance to
Roman imperial systems, but his treatment is rather brief and thin. See Cassidy, *Jesus*.
Phillips uses him as a sort of straw man for arguments like mine. Friedrich Horn's
Glaube und Handeln argues that Luke contained but resisted material from Ebion-
ite, anti-wealth Christianity. For Luke, dispossession is limited to the time of Jesus,
and his real wealth ethic is found in chapters 2 and 4 of Acts. Donald Kraybill and
Dennis Sweetland say in "Possessions" that the inconsistency Johnson sees between
dispossession and communal property is best understood as a function of group dynamics; when the movement is young, it is important for everyone to divest so that
everyone is equal, but when it starts to institutionalize, the community is strengthened
by sharing ownership. They suggest that the Acts model of community property is
more normative for Luke. Luise Schotroff and Wolfgang Stegemann are distinctive
for suggesting in *Jesus and the Hope of the Poor* that the πτωχοι (poor), to which Jesus
offers beatitude, are specifically the disciples who have become poor in order to follow
him. Halvor Moxnes is strong on the importance of liberation for the poor in Luke's
gospel. However, his main aim is to learn about Palestinian peasant society by reading
Luke, and so I pass him over as a primary conversation partner. See Moxnes, *Economy
of the Kingdom*. Hans-Josef Klauck's "Die Armut" compares poverty and celibacy to
argue that Luke favors asceticism but does not force it on all (160–94). John Gillman
is right to insist that Luke-Acts proclaims a privileged position for the poor, warns
against wealth, and encourages sharing, though his *Possessions and the Life of Faith*
infrequently cited. Vincenzo Petracca suggests that the radical gospel applied to the
eyewitnesses of Jesus's ministry, while later disciples owned property. See Petracca,
Gott oder das Geld. Yang Yan makes a fascinating argument in his 2013 unpublished
dissertation, only available in Chinese. He believes that Luke softens some of the material condemning the rich in order to avoid having Rome shut the church down as an
association that was detrimental to the order of society. Specifically, Luke, in contrast
to the prophets of the Hebrew Bible, teaches the rich that they are not doomed, they
can repent. Furthermore, they can contribute to the smooth functioning of society by

Luke Timothy Johnson (1977)

All English-language studies of wealth and poverty in Luke after 1977 stand in the shadow of Luke Timothy Johnson's influential dissertation, *The Literary Function of Possessions in Luke-Acts*. As suggested by the title, he parts from earlier redactional studies to take a literary approach, treating Luke-Acts as a coherent, finely-crafted, literary whole. He begins with the examples of communal possessions found in the beginning of Acts and argues that possessions in Luke-Acts serve the literary function of creating a direct line of authority from Jesus, to the twelve, to the rest of the early church. All the protagonists of Luke-Acts are portrayed as prophets, people who are accepted by God but rejected by the people. The use of possessions exemplifies the attitudes of people to the prophet. The poor and those who give up or hand over their possessions are also those who accept the prophet; the rich and those who hold back their possessions are also those who reject the prophet. By developing this theme first with Jesus and then with the apostles, Luke provides for a transfer of authority from Jesus to the apostles to the early church. Using possessions symbolically, Luke discredits the authority of priests, scribes, and Pharisees while establishing the church as the new Israel, God's own people.

Johnson is perhaps best known for his assertion that the wealth-poverty material in Luke is inconsistent. This insight comes from Degenhardt, but it is Johnson who gives us the pithy and oft-quoted "The problem we face is that although Luke consistently talks about possessions, he does not talk about possessions consistently."[18] Johnson says the inconsistency is between texts which suggest the holding of communal possessions and texts which promote the practice of almsgiving, in contrast to the more commonly recognized distinction between disciples who renounce their possessions and those who seem to keep them.

Johnson largely avoids the ethical implications of Luke's wealth-poverty material. His focus on their symbolic value in establishing the theme of the prophet and the people allows him simply to be silent about what example Jesus-followers might take. It is not that Johnson's thesis is incorrect; it simply misses the point. Its unwavering focus on the symbolic meaning of possessions serves to distract from any ethical implications of the gospel whatsoever. At times, the distraction seems willful.

---

providing for the needs of the most vulnerable. See Yang, "Warning and Exhortation," 208–10.

18. Johnson, *Literary Function*, 130; Degenhardt, *Evangelist der Armen*.

Johnson returns to wealth and poverty in Luke-Acts in three later works.[19] Even in these later writings, he soft-pedals the economic themes and brings out non-economic themes, like healing and inclusion of the marginalized. For Johnson, the ethics come from the concept of prophecy, not from the specific economic details of the account in Luke-Acts.

Walter Pilgrim (1981)

In contrast to Johnson's symbolic approach, Walter Pilgrim shows an overwhelming interest in ethics in his 1981 study, *Good News to the Poor*. His primary aim is to address how the economic themes in Luke-Acts are instructive for modern Christians. He presents his conclusions as more radical than the interpreters with whom he is in conversation and guards against their spiritualizing tendencies which subvert the plain message of rich and poor.[20]

Pilgrim begins with the observation that the Hebrew Bible (and later Christian tradition) contains two different strands of economic material: one which advocates the renunciation of wealth and another which sees wealth as a gift of God.[21] In the face of this discrepancy, Pilgrim seeks to turn to Luke-Acts for guidance for a Christian wealth ethic for his time. Rather than a look to the historical Jesus, Pilgrim wants to analyze Luke's particular construction of the gospel materials in order to find how one might live as a Christian in a time of increasing wealth inequality.[22]

Pilgrim identifies three strands of wealth ethic in Luke-Acts: calls to total renunciation of possessions, warnings against wealth, and instructions on the right use of wealth. He understands the first of these as being binding only on the Twelve, failing to explain why Jesus gives a general command to renunciation for all his disciples in Luke 14:33.[23] He does, however, believe that the example of the renunciation of the Twelve stands as a critique to later wealthy Christians. He believes that wealth has a corrupting power, that it needs to be resisted. He puts forward Zacchaeus as the best example of what one should do with wealth. Zacchaeus gives a sacrificial amount of his wealth away, and he does it for the benefit of the

19. Johnson, *Prophetic Jesus*; Johnson, *Luke*; Johnson, *Sharing Possessions*.

20. Pilgrim, *Good News to the Poor*, 13–14.

21. Pilgrim, *Good News to the Poor*, 11.

22. Pilgrim, *Good News to the Poor*, 12.

23. Kim, *Stewardship and Almsgiving*, 22.

poor. "The rich cannot be saved with their riches intact."[24] They must give radically of their wealth, and they must do it for the benefit of the poor.

That is perhaps the most important part of Pilgrim's stand: the Lukan wealth ethic is ultimately about the poor. It is the yawning gap between those who are fabulously wealthy and those who struggle to survive that prompts Pilgrim's study in the first place. The idea that wealthy and comfortable Christians can go about their lives as if poverty is not a problem is scandalous to Pilgrim. The church should be leading the way toward equality and liberation for the poor. Jesus's disciples should not be lagging behind the disciples of Marx when it comes to advocacy for the poor. What Luke demands is a radical economic ethic of blessings for the poor and woes against the rich.[25]

David Peter Seccombe (1982)

In his influential 1982 dissertation, published as *Possessions and the Poor in Luke-Acts*, David Peter Seccombe argues strongly against applying Luke's economic message directly to a Christian wealth ethic. Instead, wealth-poverty themes should be understood as a way of addressing the salvation of Israel as a nation. Poverty should not be idealized, and renunciation is in no way called for.

Seccombe defines the inconsistency in Luke's treatment of wealth and poverty in a way quite similar to my assessment, as between a radical ethic and the seeming acceptance of wealth:

> How is it possible to reconcile the existence in Luke-Acts of two apparently contradictory pictures? For on the one hand there is material which appears to glorify poverty, condemn the rich, and demand the renunciation of all possessions, but on the other the well-to-do are shown receiving favour from Jesus, and in Acts the Christian movement is portrayed making its way among socially and economically advantaged people.[26]

He also argues, like I do, that this inconsistency is no real inconsistency. His findings, however, are opposite to mine. He finds no justification for grounding a radical wealth ethic in Luke-Acts.

---

24. Pilgrim, *Good News to the Poor*, 170.

25. Pilgrim, *Good News to the Poor*, 174.

26. Seccombe, *Possessions and the Poor*, 12.

Seccombe starts his argument by defining rich and poor in non-economic terms. The poor (πτωχοί) should be interpreted in light of Hebrew Bible usage of עניים as referring not to the actual poor, nor to the so-called pious poor, but to the nation of Israel as a whole.[27] The economic themes in Luke-Acts are thus not economic, but soteriological. There is no economic reversal, no call to renounce wealth, no privileged position for the poor. In fact, "there is nothing socio-economic or socio-religious about Luke's use of 'poor' terminology" at all.[28] What is more "To seek to ground a liberation theology, or an ethic of poverty, upon these texts would be to misunderstand and misuse them."[29] What there is instead is "the story of the way salvation came to all Israel, and then to the nations, in the person of Jesus."[30]

Seccombe promotes an ethic of limitless discipleship. What is most important is belief in Jesus. Should something get in the way of faith in Jesus, the disciple must be willing to give it up, whether it be possessions, family, or even life. However, this situation is relatively rare. Most disciples will never find themselves in a situation where such costly discipleship is required.[31] So long as wealth does not impede belief, and it rarely ever does, one need not change one's lifestyle.

Seccombe frames the problem correctly. He is right that Luke does not idealize poverty. His conception of limitless discipleship has merit. However, his decision to apply a "more subtle and thoughtful application" of Luke's economic themes—one that rejects the "over readiness to make direct ethical applications"—completely misses the point.[32] It is a concession to the Mammon that Luke warns against.

Phillip Francis Esler (1987)

Though Phillip Esler's *Community and Gospel in Luke-Acts* is infrequently cited in the literature, and though wealth and poverty are the subject of only one of its chapters, it is included here because its approach and conclusions

27. Seccombe, *Possessions and the Poor*, 24–43.

28. Seccombe, *Possessions and the Poor*, 95.

29. Seccombe, *Possessions and the Poor*, 95.

30. Seccombe, *Possessions and the Poor*, 95.

31. Seccombe, *Possessions and the Poor*, 226.

32. Seccombe, *Possessions and the Poor*, 228.

are so essential to my own.[33] This book might well be understood as an expansion and test of the argument set forth by Esler. His socio-redactional approach seeks to understand Luke's particular composition of the gospel materials within the context of Luke's own community, which Esler contends was made up both of the poor and the rich.

Esler argues not only that Luke has a radical economic message, but also that Luke's radical message has been systematically blunted by professional interpreters, nearly all of whom, by definition, identify more with the rich than with the poor. Esler insists that Luke-Acts must be interpreted with clear attention to the situation of the actual poor in the Roman Empire, an imperative that we will fulfill in chapter 5.[34]

Esler reads against the grain of Lukan scholarship by placing the poor at the center of interpretation, a privileged position, he argues, where Luke also places the poor:

> One of the most remarkable aspects of Luke's vision of the Christian community is that, although it contained wealthy and influential members, the privileged places in it were reserved for the very dregs of Hellenistic society, especially the beggars and the physically disabled. For this reason, it is appropriate to speak of a 'theology of the poor' in Luke-Acts. There is abundant evidence in the text of the Lucan emphasis on the priority accorded to the utterly destitute in the scheme of salvation.[35]

For Esler, Luke is not simply for the rich with occasional reference to the poor. The poor are not just some literary trope used for the edification of the rich. The concerns of the poor are central. God is on the side of the poor and will bring about justice, a reversal on their behalf. Even when addressing how the rich should divest themselves, Esler is careful to make clear that such divestiture must be for the benefit of the poor. The rich cannot, as some suggest, "set themselves right with God by bringing their riches to a bottomless pit and throwing them in, while the starving poor looked helplessly on."[36]

---

33. Of the other studies described here, the only to fully treat Esler is Kim, *Stewardship and Almsgiving*, 28–32.

34. Esler, *Community and Gospel*, 169–70. Esler calls out Luke Timothy Johnson in particular for "proceed[ing] full-speed in the opposite direction, by arguing that Luke's material on possessions is really just a metaphor in telling his story 'of the Prophet and the People.'"

35. Esler, *Community and Gospel*, 187.

36. Esler, *Community and Gospel*, 196.

Esler insists that Luke's message against wealth is both radical and systemic. It is not a message that is satisfied with mere almsgiving, nor is it a message that is solely about the salvation of individual rich persons.

> Even granted that the reversal of the socio-economic advantages of the rich might not occur until the next life . . . , the Lucan Gospel questioned the propriety and therefore the legitimacy of the entire system of social stratification in the Hellenistic cities. This was a radical challenge to the prevailing social arrangements. In practical terms, Luke was not advocating the revolutionary overthrow of those arrangements; but he was insisting, as we shall see, that they be eschewed by any of the rich and influential who wished to be members of the Christian community. Luke may not have been entirely successful in this, but that by no means mitigates the radical nature of his case.[37]

In short, Esler warns against any attempt to explain away, side-step, or discount Luke's radical gospel. Luke's message of good news for the poor and "grim news for the rich" may be difficult to take, it may be utopian, it may strain the ability of most Christians to perform, but that does not strip it of its power or its importance.[38] In stark contrast to what we have seen from Johnson and Seccombe, and to what we will see momentarily from Phillips, Esler's work insists on guarding against any interpretive moves that distract from or diminish Luke's radical gospel.

Dario López Rodriguez (1997, English 2012)

First published in 1997 as *La Misión Liberadora de Jesús: El Mensaje del Evangelio de Lucas*, Dario López Rodriguez's *The Liberating Mission of Jesus* homes in on two "non-negotiable themes" contained in the Gospel of Luke: "the universality of mission and the special love of God for the poor and the excluded."[39] It does not focus exclusively on economic issues, nor does it present a comprehensive analysis of economic themes in Luke. It is included here, though, because it comes from a marginal perspective and it takes seriously Luke's message for the poor and marginalized.

Unlike many of the other works detailed here, López Rodriguez writes from an explicitly pastoral perspective, though with no less

---

37. Esler, *Community and Gospel*, 189.

38. Esler, *Community and Gospel*, 188.

39. López Rodriguez, *Liberating Mission*, xiv.

academic rigor. He is concerned not only with what Luke might say in the abstract, but particularly with how it should be lived by those who seek to follow Jesus, and specifically by his own community of Latin American evangelicals. While López Rodriguez's position is comparatively radical, he presents it as a simple, clear reading of the gospel, a gospel that insists on liberation:

> The proposal highlighted in this study of the message of Luke's gospel is that this gospel presents the liberating mission of Jesus of Nazareth as a paradigm for the individual and collective witness of believers on all social frontiers and in all cultural contexts. It is a proposal based in a specific temporal context in which millions of human beings of all ages are treated as social trash or disposable items by the global North, and as waste and human leftovers that are not worth anything that the invisible hand of the market expels. The central thesis is that a series of theological themes intersect and converge in Luke's gospel, which together articulate an understanding of mission in terms of integral liberation.[40]

López Rodriguez's paired themes organically avoid the Johnsonian "inconsistency" obsessed over by so many other interpreters. He fully embraces a preferential option for the poor, grounded in the Nazareth manifesto (Luke 4:16–21) and embodied in the life, preaching, and ministry of Jesus.[41] At the same time, this liberative message is not undermined by the presence of faithful rich persons, because López Rodriguez finds ways to identify most of them as marginalized characters. Levi and Zacchaeus are part of a hated class of tax collectors.[42] Jesus's female patrons, though wealthy, are women.[43] The wealthy centurion whose slave was healed by Jesus is a Gentile.[44] Because López Rodriguez has defined marginality in two different ways—economically and socially—inconsistency is largely avoided. Jesus calls his disciples to cross societal boundaries and stand in solidarity with the marginalized, regardless of which societal forces create that marginalization. This attention to the poor and marginalized infuses his exegetical methodology in a way that seems completely consistent with the radical message of Luke's gospel.

40. López Rodriguez, *Liberating Mission*, 2.
41. López Rodriguez, *Liberating Mission*, 8–9.
42. López Rodriguez, *Liberating Mission*, 45.
43. López Rodriguez, *Liberating Mission*, 18–19.
44. López Rodriguez, *Liberating Mission*, 11.

The analysis of social or political events from a tranquil academic position or from the balcony, beyond being limited by its meager connection with reality and its unconcern for real human beings, cannot claim to be a xerox copy of what occurs in the historical present. Speaking from within, connected to critical experiences of human beings of flesh and bone, has the advantage of providing us with a more genuine picture—beyond the cold statistical charts or the opinion polls—of the problems that the marginalized have to face every day. In order to know the world of the marginalized of our time, we must first come out of the tunnel of indifference, leaving aside all of the prejudices that limit the establishment of more inclusive social relations. Missional practice, in order to be contextual, and therefore committed, must sink its roots into the temporal setting in which the marginalized experience their joys and sorrows, construct their dreams and hopes, fight for each day's bread, create new forms of social communication, and express their incorruptible faith in the God of life, defending the cause of the destitute and the needy.[45]

I find López Rodriguez quite convincing. His reading of Luke from the margins is greatly to be preferred, though it is not an approach that I can credibly replicate. At times, his ability to find marginality in characters who are quite powerful seems a bit too neat, and his wider-lens focus on marginality leaves several economic verses and themes unaddressed. He is strong on good news for the poor, but less consistent on resistance to wealth. Still, among the scholars treated here, López Rodriguez has perhaps the best understanding of God's preferential option for the poor and marginalized.

Kyoung-Jin Kim (1998)

In his 1998 dissertation, published as *Stewardship and Almsgiving in Luke's Theology*, Kyoung-Jin Kim uses stewardship as an interpretive lens for understanding the wealth-poverty material in Luke.[46] By doing so, he is able to find a middle ground between fully accepting calls to renunciation and completely ignoring them. The reader of Luke should use their possessions in a way befitting the understanding that those possessions actually belong to God.

45. López Rodriguez, *Liberating Mission*, 49.

46. Kim, *Stewardship and Almsgiving*, 33.

Kim revisits Degenhardt's claim that disciples in Luke can be divided into two groups: itinerant disciples and sedentary disciples.[47] Itinerants—like Peter, James and John, but not limited to them—are called to full renunciation in order to fulfill a particular call to ministry. Sedentary disciples—like Mary, Martha, Levi, Zacchaeus and Jesus's female patrons—can practice a modified form of renunciation while still retaining most of their possessions by giving alms and practicing good stewardship.[48]

Kim understands the ideal of stewardship as best defined by the master-slave relationship. Earthly disciples own no possessions, they simply dispose of God's possessions in a way that would be pleasing to God. His treatment of one parable summarizes his argument.

> In narrating the parable of the faithful and wise steward [Luke 12:13–49], Luke, first, appears to define the duty and role of a steward as a unique sort of slave who is entrusted with material possessions by a master and takes charge of them; secondly, with respect to the attitude of a steward, he describes one whose belongings are not his own but his master's. A steward is not to dispose of them at his own will and for his own sake, but to use them entirely according to the will and order of his master. Thirdly, bearing in mind an eschatological crisis which may happen all of a sudden, a steward is to carry out his duty with alertness, because his position as steward does not continue for good but can be put under examination at any time. Fourthly, a judgment will come eventually but will vary according to the conduct of the stewards. Finally, as regards the matter of the addressees of this parable, it has been argued that it is more likely that the steward does not represent the Apostles or church leaders, but all disciples. However, as Luke's interest lies in those who are given or entrusted much, it is concluded that this parable is intended especially for the rich members of Luke's community.[49]

Kim so fully accepts the master-slave framing that he uses the Parable of the Pounds (Luke 19:11–27) as an example of good stewardship. It does not matter what the ethics are, the slave must always do what the master wills.[50]

While he generally takes total renunciation off the table, Kim still admits that Luke contains a radical wealth ethic. He notes that the sort of

47. Degenhardt, *Evangelist der Armen.*
48. Kim, *Stewardship and Almsgiving,* 107–10.
49. Kim, *Stewardship and Almsgiving,* 145.
50. Kim, *Stewardship and Almsgiving,* 163.

care for the poor *qua* poor promoted in Luke was essentially unknown in the Greco-Roman world, a serious departure from the culture of patronage. This novel approach to care for the poor "enables us to claim that Luke's exhortation of almsgiving towards the wealthy was so radical as to surprise the rich members of his community."[51] Luke is willing to take this risk, Kim argues, because of the injustice of extreme wealth imbalance, an imbalance that left the poor in constant insecurity.[52]

While Kim and I differ both in method and in conclusions, his study at least takes seriously the radicality of Luke's economic content. His bi-vocational solution softens but does not banish Luke's radical gospel, as one might first suppose. His handling of the material is both subtle and insightful.

Thomas E. Phillips (2001)

Thomas Phillips employs reader-response criticism in his 2001 dissertation, published as *Reading Issues of Wealth and Poverty in Luke-Acts*, to try to avoid the failings he finds in previous studies. He judges these studies unsophisticated in that they "deal inadequately with the diversity of perspectives within the third gospel and Acts."[53] To address this, Phillips applies the theories of Wolfgang Iser on how a reader navigates and processes inconsistencies in a text. He asks, "How is the reader's understanding of and behavior related to issues of wealth and poverty affected by reading the third gospel?"[54] The ethic that emerges, based on John the Baptist's advice in Luke 3:10–14, is one that encourages generosity and warns against greed but offers no radical challenge to wealthy readers, no hope of liberation for the poor, and no significant critique of economic systems or structures. Phillips suggests that only this reading is consistent with John's wealth ethic at the beginning of Luke and with the characterization of Peter and Paul at the end of Acts.[55]

Phillips makes an early decision to interpret language of wealth and poverty metaphorically and finds that decision validated as he continues to read the gospel. Noting that the narrative and song of Mary

51. Kim, *Stewardship and Almsgiving*, 282.

52. Kim, *Stewardship and Almsgiving*, 282–83.

53. Phillips, *Reading Issues*, 2.

54. Phillips, *Reading Issues*, 83.

55. Phillips, *Reading Issues*, 2–3.

are packed with Jewish imagery, when he reads the language of reversal in the Magnificat, Phillips makes a "tentative selection of meaning in favor of a metaphorical reading of 'rich' and 'hungry,'" suggesting that themes of reversal in the Jewish scriptures are meant to be interpreted metaphorically.[56] This tentative decision becomes determinative for the rest of Phillips's reading of Luke-Acts. For example, when reading Jesus's mission statement in Luke 4, Phillips finds:

> The language of preaching good news to the poor is, along with the language of releasing captives, giving sight to the blind and liberating the oppressed, therefore, quickly taken metaphorically in light of the gestalt formed by reading earlier portions of the narrative.[57]

And so it is with the rest of Luke-Acts. Any radical economic language is taken metaphorically and is thus irrelevant to any wealth ethic the reader forms.

That is not to say that Phillips finds no wealth ethic at all. Readers are encouraged to practice generosity, but not in any systematic way. Generosity should be regulated by "the presence or absence of persons in need."[58] Greed is understood to be sinful, but not wealth. Phillips finds nothing that encourages radical change either of the individual or of society. Instead, he finds a message that is consistent with his reading of Jewish texts and Stoic philosophers, a message consistent with the worldviews of Seneca, Philo of Alexandria, and Clement of Alexandria.[59] One's attitude to wealth is much more important than one's disposition of wealth. So long as one's attitude toward wealth does not distract from one's relationship with God, one need not change one's life, and the implication is that wealth only rarely creates such a distraction.

As one might guess, Phillips is one of my primary opponents. His reader-response approach, grounded in the presupposition that radical economic themes in scripture are best understood metaphorically, is a perfect embodiment of the aforementioned middle-class bias that Esler warns against. He provides a ready example of precisely what a reading of Luke drained of its radical power looks like: a message that conforms perfectly to the economic norms of its time.

56. Phillips, *Reading Issues*, 91.
57. Phillips, *Reading Issues*, 96–97.
58. Phillips, *Reading Issues*, 182.
59. Phillips, *Reading Issues*, 243–66.

James A. Metzger (2007)

Like Phillips, James Metzger uses reader-response methodology in his 2007 dissertation, published as *Consumption and Wealth in Luke's Travel Narrative*, to interpret the economic material in Luke. Metzger, though, comes to a drastically different, and far more radical, conclusion. Metzger's analysis is limited in scope; it primarily treats four parables in Luke's Travel Narrative: the Parable of the Wealthy Landowner (Luke 12:16–21), the Parable of the Father and his Two Sons (Luke 15:11–32), the Parable of the Unjust Steward (Luke 16:1–13) and the Parable of the Rich Man and Lazarus (Luke 16:19–31).[60]

Metzger notes how readers can domesticate the gospel by emphasizing themes of almsgiving. Regarding interpreters like Pilgrim and Phillips, he says,

> For those who conclude that readers are not asked to divest themselves of property and possessions, Luke's almsgiving traditions naturally assume center-stage. Therefore, John's counsel to crowds, tax collectors, and soldiers in 3:10–14 and Zacchaeus's vow in 19:8 will become paradigmatic, exemplary texts, and passages that portray a complete break with one's past and possessions will recede into the background.[61]

By foregrounding these more palatable themes, the reader is able to discount entirely the more radical parts of Luke's gospel. When rich and poor are understood metaphorically, the gospel loses its power as criticism of oppressive economic practices and systems. Metzger emphasizes the radical message found in these four parables and finds a thoroughgoing critique of Mammon.

Metzger does not think that the different attitudes toward wealth contained in Luke can be fruitfully harmonized. He does not think that the radical message he finds in his study can be extended to the rest of Luke-Acts. Instead, he emphasizes the need to hear all of the different voices in Luke and to show "that a more subversive reading of these traditions is both plausible and defensible."[62] Importantly, Metzger also applies his reading to the world of advanced, global capitalism, finding that "Jesus' call for the elimination of wealth coupled with his emphasis on

60. Metzger, *Consumption and Wealth.*

61. Metzger, *Consumption and Wealth*, 6.

62. Metzger, *Consumption and Wealth*, 190.

consuming only what one needs . . . is fundamentally incompatible with capitalism as currently practiced" and identifying concrete steps that can be taken in light of Luke's radical economic message.[63]

Christopher M. Hays (2010)

In his well-argued 2010 dissertation, published as *Luke's Wealth Ethics: A Study in Their Coherence and Character*, Christopher Hays rejects the conclusion that Luke's economic material is inconsistent. Instead, he suggests that Luke clearly calls for renunciation, but that renunciation might look different in different contexts. Influenced by liberation theology, Hays wants to resist the temptation to overly spiritualize Luke's economic themes.[64]

Hays argues that Johnson's pithy statement about the inconsistency of Lukan wealth-poverty material has had an outsized place in the conversation, that "later scholars have regularly pointed to Johnson as having decisively proven the insurmountable heterogeneity in Lukan teaching."[65] This leads scholars to treat the response of various Jesus-followers as fundamentally different from one another, rather than as variegated expressions of the same principle of renunciation. Hays instead concludes that:

> Luke possesses a coherent ethical principle with a range of contingent applications. The crucial principle is stated explicitly, at the climax of series of Luke's three most stringent criteria for discipleship: "Nobody can be my disciple who does not renounce all their possessions" (14.33; my translation). The sundry applications of this principle are not left to whim, as if Luke endorses an ethical free-for-all guided only by an individual's arbitrary sense of morality. In Luke's Gospel, renunciation of possessions takes multiple forms depending upon two factors specific to the individual disciple: vocation and wealth. One's vocation in the Kingdom of God and relative affluence determine the particular expression one gives to renouncing all possessions.[66]

While renunciation does not always mean the complete abandonment of all possessions for an itinerant lifestyle on the road with Jesus, it always

---

63. Metzger, *Consumption and Wealth*, 195.
64. Hays, *Luke's Wealth Ethics*, 2–24.
65. Hays, *Luke's Wealth Ethics*, 18.
66. Hays, *Luke's Wealth Ethics*, 185.

requires a radical reordering of one's life, not a simple nod to the preexisting standard of almsgiving.[67]

> Happily, it does seem to be [the] case that each of the modes of life endorsed in Luke's Gospel can justly be described as renouncing πάντα. The itinerant of limited means leaves behind his or her home and livelihood, carries only basic supplies, and trusts God for daily provision; that is one way to renounce all. The more affluent itinerant cannot just keep her money stowed away in a safety deposit box, but might well renounce her possessions by giving most everything to the poor, or by continuously using her resources to provide for her basic needs and those of her fellow itinerants.
>
> For the non-itinerants, the same command to renounce all obtains, but is manifested differently owing to their local fixity. The rich localized disciples are called to justice in their conduct, to extend hospitality to the itinerants, and to engage in generosity to the fullest extent permitted by their considerable resources; in this way, without leaving everything behind, they still renounce all their possessions. The poor localized disciples, with their relatively meager means, are also to extend hospitality to the itinerants, to share whatever they have with those in greater need than themselves, and to give every penny they can squeeze from their already meager means.
>
> Luke hardly propounds a single, monolithic form of discipleship; he approvingly describes multiple practices which vary according to an individual disciple's vocation and wealth. Still, in whatever form it takes, nobody can follow Jesus who does not renounce all of their possessions.[68]

Hays rejects the *interim* solution (Seccombe), which says that renunciation was only for Jesus's own time, and attempts to build a synthesis between the *bi-vocational* solution (Degenhardt, Kim), which suggests that different disciples are called to different ethics, and the *personalist* solution (Johnson, Metzger), which suggest that Luke offers several different wealth ethics from which the Jesus-follower must choose.

Hays also spends two chapters placing Luke within the contexts of Jewish and Greco-Roman wealth ethics, and another chapter showing the continued consistency of the renunciation ethic in the Book of Acts.[69]

---

67. Hays, *Luke's Wealth Ethics*, 180.

68. Hays, *Luke's Wealth Ethics*, 186.

69. Hays, *Luke's Wealth Ethics*, 264–67.

His work is one of the most thoroughgoing, comprehensive, incisive, and well-argued in the field. I consider him an ally and hope to build on his work with the integration of the Parable of the Pounds, attention to the theme of good news for the poor, and application of Lukan economic ethics in the ancient and modern worlds.

Rachel Coleman (2018)

A recent, as-yet-unpublished dissertation on wealth and poverty in Luke-Acts deserves our attention. Rachel Coleman's "The Lukan Lens on Wealth and Possessions: A Perspective Shaped by the Themes of Reversal and Right Response" offers a fresh look on the matter. She largely avoids the distinctions argued over by the above authors and instead posits that the key to understanding wealth and poverty in Luke-Acts is using Luke 1:5—4:44 as the lens through which the rest of the work is understood. Following the suggestion of Robert Morgenthaler, Robert Tannehill, and Fearghus Ó Fearghail that these first four chapters represent a unified introduction, she suggests that they function as a "theological *preparation*" for the two-volume work.[70]

Across three "panels" of the introduction, Luke establishes that "the motif of wealth and possessions is intimately connected to the theme of reversal (the nature of God's saving work)" and "the theme of right response (the nature of discipleship)."[71] In the first (Luke 1:5–56), Mary's lowliness is contrasted with the relative prestige of Zechariah and Elizabeth, and it is the unexpected character from the powerless margins, Mary, who makes the fullest response and proclamation of radical faith in God's salvation.[72] In the second (Luke 1:57—2:52), Luke portrays lowly characters like Mary, shepherds, Simeon, and Anna making a radical response to God's action.[73] In the final panel (Luke 3:1—4:44), the early ministry of John the Baptist and Jesus is characterized by good news for the poor leading to concrete action, and both figures are opposed by the

---

70. Coleman, "Lukan Lens," 2, 9; Morgenthaler, *Die lukanishce Geschictsschreibung als Zeugnis*; Tannehill, *Luke*, 17–22; Ó Fearghus, *The Introduction to Luke-Acts*.

71. Coleman, "Lukan Lens," 96–97.

72. Coleman, "Lukan Lens," 37–61.

73. Coleman, "Lukan Lens," 61–73.

wealthy and powerful.[74] This firmly establishes the twin themes of reversal and right response in the beginning of the gospel.

Those themes carry through the rest of Luke-Acts and establish a coherent message about wealth and possessions that can be neatly summarized in five points. First, the proper response of disciples to Jesus is leaving what they have and following him. Second, this leaving and following is a requirement for all disciples, not only for a special class of disciples. Third, Jesus's disciples carry the values of the eschatological kingdom, values that are a reversal of the values of the world. Fourth, Luke uses "poor" to refer both to the actual poor or marginalized and to those who welcome Jesus's message, but he uses "rich" only to refer to the materially wealthy. Finally, God intends all surplus wealth to be used for almsgiving and for hospitality, a hospitality that incorporates marginalized people into the community.[75]

Coleman is refreshing in her nonconformity to the theory of Lukan inconsistency. She dispenses with it in the introduction and proceeds to make her own argument about a consistent message of God's reversal and the faithful response of God's (marginalized) people. Interestingly, even though her interpretation focuses on the prominent role of the poor and marginalized as fully realized agents in Luke's first four chapters, her subsequent reading of Luke-Acts tends to focus on the perspective of the wealthy and how they can discharge their possessions for the benefit of the poor.

Method and Outline

The structure of this book follows its three sub-theses. It is, however, divided into more than three chapters. Chapters 2–4 cover the sub-thesis *Luke has a radical economic message.* Chapters 5–6 address *it was radical then.* Finally, chapters 7–8 deal with *it is radical now.* Correspondingly, the project employs three different methodologies.

My exegetical approach in the first section combines literary-critical and redaction-critical methodologies. I share with other narrative and literary critics the assumption that a text like Luke is authored, that it is, at least to some useful extent, a coherent whole.[76] Therefore, I am not

74. Coleman, "Lukan Lens," 73–95.

75. Coleman, "Lukan Lens," 150–54.

76. See, for example Johnson, *Literary Function*; Talbert, *Reading Luke*; Fitzmyer, *Luke I–IX.*

particularly interested in a historical project that values Luke only insofar as it can reveal the traditions that are behind it. I assume that Luke is constructed, using previous sources, in a way that makes sense to the author. It is the Luke that we have that I am interested in, not in some ideal pre-Luke, for example, the sayings of the historical Jesus. However, I am interested in how Luke uses sources, deploying and tweaking them to put forward a particular view of Jesus and a particular message for the Christian community.

In chapter 2, "A New Accounting," I apply a statistical approach to the economic material in Luke. After cataloguing and analyzing every reference in Luke to economic matters, I identify four main themes, two of which suggest a radical economic message and two of which seem to undermine that message. I show that the radical message of good news for the poor and resistance to wealth is much stronger than the detracting message of accommodation to wealth. I show that Luke deploys and changes material to present a more radical message than Mark or Matthew. I also show that the greatest threat to that radical message comes from parables and Q material.

In chapter 3, "Luke's Clear Message of Liberation," I take a closer look at the two themes that constitute the radical message: good news for the poor and resistance to wealth. Applying redaction and literary criticism, I make the affirmative case for Luke's radical economic message. Pericope by pericope, I document just how Luke constructs that message and engage with the interpretations of other Lukan scholars.

I apply a similar approach in the fourth chapter, "Challenges to Liberation," this time to the Lukan material that seems to undermine its radical message. I show that much of it is not as problematic as it first seems. In particular, the Parable of the Shrewd Manager and the Parable of the Pounds can be fitted into a consistent reading of Luke that promotes a message of good news for the poor and resistance to wealth. While there is some ambiguity in Luke's message, its overall thrust is toward liberation.

The project then turns from exegesis to history, using the basic historical-critical tools of Early Christian Studies (Patristics) and History. Chapter 5, "Roman Economic Domination and Luke's Radical Alternative," engages with historians of ancient Roman economy to put Luke in context and explore its impact in early Christian economic ethics. I apply and improve the Friesen-Longenecker economic scale to add nuance to the binary terms "rich" and "poor." Then I track the shift in Roman society, influenced by Luke, from civic benefaction to care for the poor. Finally, I explore the story of the Rich Young Man (Luke 18:24–30), its manuscript history, and two early Christian interpretations; Clement of Alexandria deploys several techniques to defang the radical message of Luke, while *De Divitiis* embraces Luke's radical message but is deemed unorthodox. Within the context of the ancient world, Luke's message was threatening to established economic systems.

In chapter 6, "Lukan Accommodation to Roman Economic Domination," I engage with a new study that takes quite a different view. Roland Boer and Christina Petterson's *Time of Troubles* suggests that Christianity, including writings like Luke, acted as a form of *régulation* that supported and justified economic exploitation. In particular, they argue that the parables of slavery in the gospels normalize slavery as a form of economic extraction. While acknowledging that there is some ambiguity in Luke, I argue that it still has liberative power.

In a final turn, this project shifts from history to constructive theology, engaging with theology, ethics, and economics. The seventh chapter, "Modern Mammonism," explores the idea, suggested by Luke 16:13, that the market can act as if it were a rival god. I argue against Michael Novak—and along with several other theologians—that the market is not always providential, that faith in the market is contrary to faith in God, and that God works against the negative consequences of market capitalism. I also return to two parables—the Parable of the Shrewd Manager and the Parable of the Pounds—and show how their traditional interpretations reveal the worst abuses of capitalism. The metaphor of market as god provides a useful lens for a theological critique of market capitalism.

In chapter 8, "Reclaiming the Radical," I attempt to responsibly apply Luke's wealth ethics to the modern world. With liberation theologians like Gustavo Gutierrez, I argue that God prioritizes the voices and concerns of the poor. In its words against wealth, Luke suggests a skepticism in the benevolence of markets, a call to a thoroughgoing solidarity with the poor (Rebecca Todd Peters), and a special concern for the environment that is threatened by uncontrolled economic growth (Pope Francis). Luke provides a useful utopia that calls Christians to continuous conversion from faith in the market to faith in God and to the praxis that that faith entails.

In a final, short chapter, I reflect on the course of the argument, the prophetic voice of Luke, and my roles as reader, interpreter, author, and disciple. Neither my work nor Luke's escapes the flaw of coming from a position of privilege. Nevertheless, God-willing, the radically liberative gospel of Jesus Christ may shine through.

CHAPTER 2

A New Accounting

Be on guard against all kinds of greed; for one's life
does not consist in the abundance of possessions.

—LUKE 12:15 NRSV

IN THIS CHAPTER I will take a fresh look at the totality of the economic material in Luke's gospel in order to get a sense of just how radical Luke's message really is, that is, how disruptive it is to the normal economic order.[1] I conclude that Luke contains a radical economic message that is characterized by good news for the poor and resistance to wealth. I propose that the more interesting inconsistency in Luke's wealth ethic is not, as many interpreters claim, the distinction between renunciation and almsgiving, but the distinction between the radical message of economic upheaval and a thread of seeming endorsement of acquisition as usual. The most interesting economic question suggested by the data of Luke is not "How can the same Jesus who demands total renunciation be happy with almsgiving"? but "How can the same Jesus who says 'some are last who will be first and some are first who will be last'" (Luke 13:30) also say, "to all those who have, more will be given; but from those who have nothing, even what they have will be taken away" (Luke 19:26 NRSV)?

---

1. A shorter version of this chapter published as King, "A New Accounting," 90–107.

Methodology

My methodology is intentionally simple, the sort of thing I learned as an MDiv student: just make a list and count.[2] Is there a way of putting some numbers to the issue of Luke's complicated relationship with money? Can we quantify Luke's economic material in a way that brings some clarity to the whole?

I begin by making a list of every reference in Luke to poor, rich, wealth, poverty, money, greed, and other related topics.[3] For consistency, each reference is one and only one verse. The advantage of removing some subjectivity from the process outweighs the possible disadvantage of losing a sense of which verses are chocked full of economic material and which are only glancing references. For each verse, I take note of several pieces of data: (1) who is speaking, whether a character, the narrator, or in the case of Luke 1:3 the author; (2) the type of speech, e.g., narration, dialog, teaching, or parable; (3) the setting of the reference; (4) the pericope name and number; (5) the redactional source; and, out of curiosity, (6) the Jesus Seminar rating.[4]

Having collected this basic information, I record whether each reference touches on any of several economic themes, which are not mutually exclusive. They are: God favors the poor, the heroes of Luke favor the poor, villains are against the poor, heroes are in solidarity with the poor, almsgiving, voluntary dispossession or renunciation, God is against the

---

2. Specifically, it is the kind of exercise suggested by Barr, *New Testament Story*.

3. The appendix to this study, the complete catalogue with statistical tools, can be found in King, "Appendix."

4. The types of speech are as follows: *dedication*, which applies only to the opening verses; narration, when we hear the voice of the Lukan narrator; *dialog*, when characters are engaged in conversation; *teaching*, when Jesus has an extended monologue; *prayer*, when Jesus is praying; *reading*, when Jesus reads from the scroll in the synagogue; *song*, when Mary and Zechariah break into ecstatic, poetic prophecy; and *parable*, which includes all parable material whether it is Jesus's narration or the voice of the characters inside the parable. The setting is normally the place where the action is happening, to the degree that Luke includes that detail. Within a parable, the setting refers to the internal setting of the parable, not the external setting of where Jesus is telling it. The pericope names and numbers come from Aland, *Synopsis of the Four Gospels*. The redactional source is figured very simply, verse by verse: if there is a parallel in Mark, it is Mk; if there is a parallel with Mt but not Mark, it is Q; if there is no parallel in Mark or Matthew, it is L. I am not making any claims about the contents of Q, but simply using a shorthand to indicate whether or not there are parallels in Mark and Matthew. Jesus Seminar ratings only apply to Jesus's speech and come from Funk and Hoover, *Five Gospels*.

rich, heroes are against the rich, warnings against wealth, villains love wealth, villains favor the rich, some acceptance of wealth, words against the poor, descriptions of oppression or hardship, reciprocity or patronage, and reversal.[5]

While these categories can be analyzed individually, they can also be summarized into four broad themes. Expressed in the basest terms, they are: (A) the poor are good, that is, God has good news for the poor; (B) wealth is bad, it is dangerous and should be gotten rid of; (C) wealth is okay, synonymous with the "some acceptance of wealth" category; and (D) the poor are bad, synonymous with "words against the poor." By color coding these themes—dark blue for A, light blue for B, orange for C, and red for D—it is possible to see at a glance which themes and categories show up over the course of the gospel. In this book, those colors are transformed to grayscale textures.

The last phase of categorization is the most subjective. Any given verse might be aligned with several of the different categories and might address more than one of the four themes. In order to compare the four themes in a meaningful way, it is necessary to choose for each verse which of the four themes is strongest. That is to say, I assign each verse one of the four themes on a mutually exclusive basis so as not to overinflate the number of economic references in Luke by counting some verses more than once.

Once all of this data has been collected, it can be sorted in various configurations to develop a sense of the contours of economic material in Luke. The following analysis begins with the totality of Lukan economic material. Next, it compares the Lukan economic material derived from different sources, that is, from Mark, from Q, or from L. Material from L best embodies the radical economic message, while material from Q is the most problematic for that message. Finally, we compare Lukan economic material based on voice. The radical economic message is strongest in Jesus's teaching and weakest in the parables.

5. Heroes include figures like Jesus and the disciples. Villains include people like Pharisees and cruel masters. "Some acceptance of wealth" refers to times when Jesus or the narrator do not seem to have any problem with wealth or interact favorably with wealthy persons without demanding repentance. "Words against the poor" include material that seems contrary to the usual theme in Luke that God favors the poor.

Overall Outlook

Out of the 1151 verses of Luke, 359 (31 percent) have some kind of reference to economic themes and 312 (27 percent) have a meaningful enough reference that they could be assigned to one of the four main themes. That is a full quarter of the gospel that has economic implications. We can see already that economic issues are a significant theme in Luke.

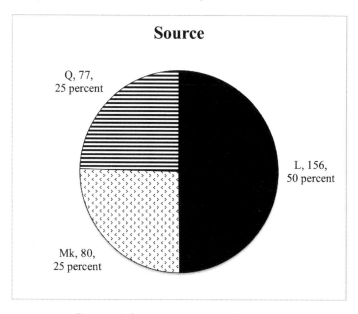

Figure 1. Lukan economic material by source

Of those 312 verses having a meaningful economic reference, half have no parallel in Mark or Matthew. About a quarter each come from Mark or Q. Luke inherits a significant amount of economic material from Mark and Q. Remarkably, Luke takes that Mark and Q material and matches it with equal amount of economic material from L.[6] It is little wonder that Luke has a reputation as the gospel most concerned with economic issues.

---

6. For comparison, about 42 percent of all Lukan material is sourced in Mark, 23 percent in Q, and 35 percent in Lukan special material. Honoré, "Statistical Study," 96. Though it is not the point I am trying to make here, this would indicate that L material has a higher density of economic content than does the material Luke derives from Mark and Q. I am not trying to prove here that Luke has more economic material than do Mark or Q, I am only trying sketch out the landscape of Luke's economic material and from where it is derived.

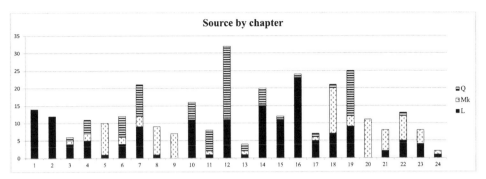

Figure 2. Lukan economic material by source and chapter

A quick look at the category totals reveals that, while many interpreters may find the distinction between almsgiving and renunciation captivating, Luke spends very little time on it. Only twenty-nine verses contain even the faintest allusion to almsgiving while forty-one verses relate in some way to voluntary dispossession. This compares with, for example, seventy-four verses which attest God's favor for the poor and seventy-three verses which contain warnings against wealth. What is more, many of the clearest calls to almsgiving are paired with calls for renunciation in the same verse (Luke 12:33; 18:2; 19:8; 21:4). Modern persons of relative means might be quite concerned with how much a faithful Christian is required to give away, but it does not seem to present a problem for Luke, who seems to make no effort whatsoever to make a distinction between the two practices. In fact, trying to carve out a difference between renunciation and almsgiving does more to distract from Luke's radical message than it does to elucidate a better understanding of the gospel's wealth ethics.

Luke contains a significant amount of material that proclaims good news for the poor (A). Seventy-four verses make the point that God shows favor to the poor. An example is Jesus's statement: "Blessed are you who are poor, for yours is the Kingdom of God." (Luke 6:20 NRSV) Another fifty-two verses describe the heroes of the gospel showing favor to the poor, for example the Good Samaritan who cares for a man who has been robbed (Luke 10:33–38). In a negative proof of God's care for the poor, 16 verses show the villains of Luke's gospel speaking or acting against the poor, such as the scribes who devour widows' houses (Luke 20:47).

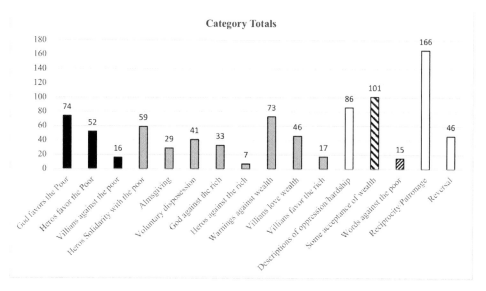

Figure 3. Number of verses in each economic category

Another significant chunk of Luke shows solidarity with the poor or warnings against wealth (B). In the largest category, seventy-three verses present warnings against wealth, like the thorns of riches that choke the word the sower sows (Luke 8:14). Forty-five describe villains loving wealth, such as the money-loving Pharisees of Luke 16:14. Fifty-nine verses describe the heroes showing solidarity with the poor, such as the disciples who go out on missionary work without provisions (Luke 9:3). As mentioned above, twenty-nine verses refer to almsgiving and forty-one to voluntary dispossession. One of the verses that contains both themes is Jesus's simple command, "Sell your possessions, and give alms" (Luke 12:33 NRSV). Thirty-three verses explicitly place God in opposition to the rich, such as God pulling down the mighty from their thrones (Luke 1:52). In addition, seven verses show the heroes opposing the rich and seventeen show the villains favoring the rich.

But there is material in Luke that brings into question this radical message of favor to the poor and warnings against wealth. A full 101 verses contain material in which wealth is in some way accepted (C). This could be as simple as the presence of a rich person who is not chastised for wealth, such as the centurion of Luke 7:2. I am intentionally generous in assigning verses to this category, because I do not want to ignore or overlook any material which might run counter to my thesis. As we will see later, most of these verses offer little or no challenge to Luke's overall radical message.

However, a very important fifteen verses do offer a significant challenge to that radical message (D). These include statements like Luke 19:26, "To all those who have, more will be given; but from those who have nothing, even what they have will be taken away." These verses will require special attention if we are to argue that Luke has a relatively consistent, radical message.

A few other categories are present which do not fit neatly into the four larger themes. Significantly, forty-six verses contain the theme of reversal, that is, the poor being lifted up and/or the rich being brought low. Eighty-six verses describe some kind of material hardship, many without providing an immediate moral judgment about that hardship. And a large, though not shocking, number of verses—166—have something to do with the common ancient themes of patronage or reciprocity.

If we assign a single theme to each verse in order to count each verse only once, we can get a sense of the overall thrust of the economic material in Luke. Of those 312 verses with meaningful economic material, the overwhelming majority (71 percent) promote the radical economic message. The smaller part of these (29 percent) offers good news to the poor (A). The larger part (42 percent) contains solidarity with the poor or warnings against wealth (B). This is a significant finding. It shows clearly that the default position for Luke is the radical economic message in favor of the poor and against wealth.

However, there is some material in Luke which seems, at least on some level, to challenge or contradict that radical economic message. One quarter of Luke's economic material offers a soft critique (C), such as the presence in the story of faithful rich people. These will need to be addressed if I am to demonstrate a relatively consistent, radical message. Much more challenging, though, is the 4 percent of material that seems to go directly against Luke's radical message (D). This is the interesting contradiction in Luke's economic material: the contradiction between the radical message and the voice of the powerful *status quo*. And this is the contradiction that will be explored in detail in chapters 3 and 4.

Before we turn to a deeper analysis of the text, there is still more we can learn from the numbers. Specifically, much is revealed when we sort the data for source and for voice. We will quickly see where the most radical and the most problematic material comes from.

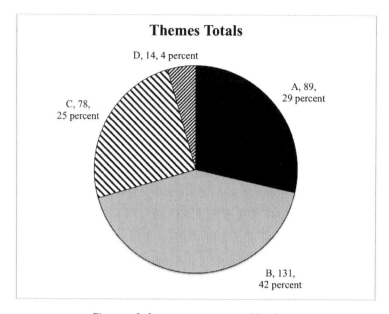

Figure 4. Lukan economic material by theme

Source Analysis

Analyzing the data with source in mind reveals that Luke is working the material to give it a more radical edge. We saw above that about a quarter of Luke's economic material comes from Mark, about a quarter comes from Q, and half is found only in Luke. Luke sets the scene with a fair amount of L material, and hardly a chapter goes by in which we do not find some L material. There is a particularly large cluster of L material in chapters 14–16. The chapters with the most overall economic material are 7, 12, 14, 16, 18, and 19.

If we look at the economic material derived from L on its own, we see that it is more radical than is the gospel as a whole. More than three quarters of the L material supports the radical economic message; 78 percent of L compared with 71 percent of Luke. The message of good news for the poor (A) accounts for 36 percent of the L material, while solidarity with the poor and resistance to wealth (B) account for 42 percent. On the other hand, in L only 22 percent of economic material challenges the radical message. Light challenges (C) add up to 19 percent and significant challenges (D) to 4 percent. When Luke has complete control of the material, the radical economic message is intensified.

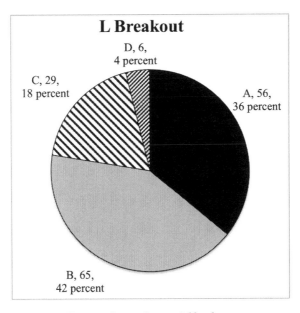

Figure 5. Source L material by theme

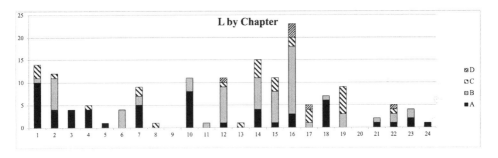

Figure 6. Source L material by theme and chapter

Looking chapter by chapter at the L material, we can see how the four themes are distributed over time. The chapter with the most L economic material is chapter 16. It is also the chapter with the most problematic (D) material. This is the Parable of the Unjust Steward and the Parable of the Rich Man and Lazarus, along with material that connects the two.

Looking at what Luke borrows from Mark, we see that the picture is quite different. There is roughly the same percentage of material calling for solidarity with the poor and warnings against wealth (B). However, there is significantly less about good news for the poor (A)—22 percent for Mk vs. 40 percent for L—and significantly more soft challenges to the radical message (C)—32 percent for Mk vs. 19 percent for L.

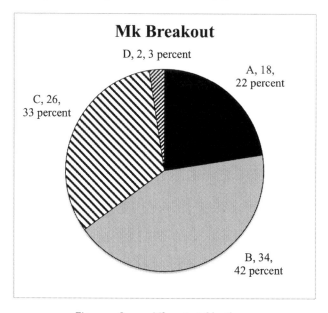

Figure 7. Source Mk material by theme

The material Luke inherits from Mark is not as radical as the material Luke writes or derives from proprietary sources. It still has a message in favor of renunciation, found most clearly in the call of Levi in Luke 5 and the story of the rich young man in Luke 18. And it still has some material in which God favors the poor, like the apothegm "Some are last who will be first, and some are first who will be last" in Luke 13:30. But that message is muted when compared to the L material. And Mark provides the problematic Parable of the Wicked Husbandman (Luke 20:9–16) and one of the two instances when Jesus says, "To those who have, more will be given; and from those who do not have, even what they seem to have will be taken away." (Luke 8:18 NRSV)

There are also sixteen verses in which Luke edits Markan material in order to intensify its economic message or make it more radical. When Jesus calls disciples, Luke specifies that they left "everything" to follow him (Luke 5:11, 28). Jesus's anointing is moved to the house of a Pharisee in Luke, where the Pharisee is portrayed as rich in contrast to the anointing woman's poverty. The episode is also edited so as to avoid the comparison of the ointment with its equivalent value in care for the poor

(Luke 7:36, 38, 46; see Mark 14:5, 7). Where Mark says only that Jesus is teaching, Luke reintroduces the liberative empire of God's message (Luke 8:1). Luke makes two of the people Jesus heals—the Gerasene demoniac and the hemorrhaging woman—more explicitly economically desperate (Luke 8:27, 43). When Jesus sends out the twelve, they are allowed fewer provisions than in Mark (Luke 9:3). When discussing greatness, Luke adds the phrase, "the least among all of you is the greatest" (Luke 9:48 NRSV). In an exchange with a lawyer, Luke frames the question in terms of inheritance rather than the simpler framing of Mark (Luke 10:25). Luke sets Jesus's confrontation with Pharisees over ritual purity in the house of a Pharisee, adding to the intensity of the conflict (Luke 11:37). In an apocalyptic speech, Luke makes it more explicit that people should not stop to save possessions while they are running in fear (Luke 17:31). When Jesus confronts the rich young man, Luke specifies that he must sell "all" his possessions (Luke 18:22). When Jesus compares his disciples with Gentile rulers, Luke includes the detail that powerful people like to be called "benefactors" (Luke 22:25). In the same discourse, Luke makes more stark the comparison between servant and master when Jesus claims his own identity as servant (Luke 22:27).

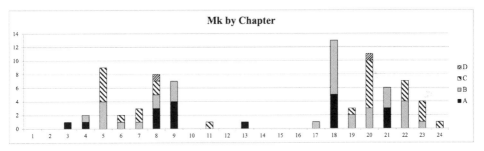

Figure 8. Source Mk material by theme and chapter

There are an additional twenty-one verses in which Luke makes changes to Mark that are not clearly more or less radical. Nowhere does Luke edit Mark to be less radical, with the possible exception of Luke 18:28, in which Mark's Peter declares the disciples have left everything (παντα) to follow Jesus, while Luke's Peter, in most manuscripts, says they left their own (ἴδια). Thus we can see that Luke has a tendency, when using material from Mark, to preserve its economically radical message and sometimes to intensify that message, but never or very seldom to soften it.

Turning next to the Q material in Luke, we see a similar pattern to what we saw with Markan material. The Q material is not as radical as is the L material or Luke as a whole. Just as we saw with Mark, Q has about the same percentage (42 percent) of material that warns against wealth or shows solidarity with the poor (B) as does L. This is a constant across all three sources. However, Q has significantly less good news for the poor (A), with only 20 percent compared to L's 36 percent. Like Mark, Q also has many more soft critiques of the radical message (C), with 31 percent compared to 19 percent in L. Most striking of all, Q has more than a small percentage of strong critiques to the radical message (D). Theme D accounts for only 3.8 percent of L but totals 7.8 percent of the Q material found in Luke.

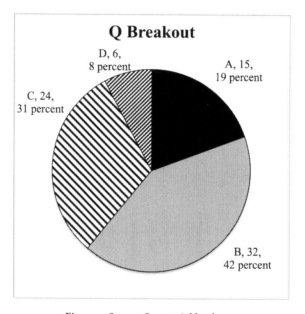

Figure 9. Source Q material by theme

The material Luke has in common with Matthew is far less radical than the material he gets from his own sources. There are still a significant number of warnings against wealth and solidarity with the poor (B). Jesus goes hungry and eschews worldly power when tempted in the wilderness (Luke 4:3–7); he sends out the seventy with scanty provisions (Luke 10:2–7); he engages in several discourses on the meaninglessness of wealth and what disciples must give up in order to follow (Luke 11:39–46; 12:22–34; 14:26–27); and he tells the Parable of the Great Supper (Luke

14:18–24), the Parable of the Lost Sheep (Luke 15:7), and the Parable of the Pharisee and the Tax Collector (Luke 18:14). Luke also draws some key apothegms from Q, including "you have hidden these things from the wise and the intelligent and have revealed them to infants" (Luke 10:21 NRSV), "no slave can serve two masters. . . . You cannot serve God and Mammon" (Luke 16:13 NRSV), and "those who try to make their life secure will lose it, but those who lose their life will keep it" (Luke 17:33 NRSV). However, there is markedly less good news to the poor (A) drawn from Q, most notably in the Beatitudes (Luke 6:20–21) and in a long section of teaching in chapter 12 (Luke 12:6–7, 24–32).

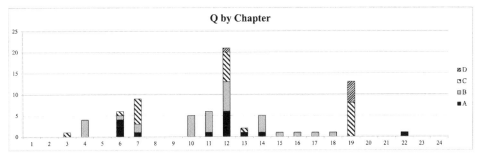

Figure 10. Source Q material by theme and chapter

At the same time, the material Luke draws from Q is far more problematic for the radical message than is the material from L and Mark. Most of the offending material is in just three chapters. In chapter 7, Jesus interacts with a wealthy and powerful centurion without directing him to dispossess himself or give alms (Luke 7:2–10). In chapter 12, he goes on at length comparing his followers to slaves (Luke 12:39–59). Finally, the Parable of the Pounds seems to endorse the business-as-usual of economic exploitation (Luke 19:13–27). As we will see in chapter 4, these are among the most problematic verses in the gospel in terms of their challenge to the radical economic message.

As we saw with the material Luke borrows from Mark, Luke reworks parts of Q, often intensifying the economic message or making it more radical.[7] There are twelve such verses in which the Lukan version is more radical than the version found in Matthew. The beatitudes on the poor and hungry are less spiritualized and are spoken directly to the poor, not about them (Luke 6:20–21). In Luke, Jesus criticizes the Pharisees and

---

7. For the purposes of this study, I am simply comparing Luke with the parallel passages in Matthew. I am not trying to compare Luke with a re-constructed Q.

lawyers to their faces, whereas Matthew's Jesus only speaks about them (Luke 11:43–46). Jesus commands the crowd to "be compassionate as your Father is compassionate" rather than the Matthean "perfect" (Luke 6:36). Matthew's Jesus declares that prophets and righteous ones desired but did not see what the disciples see, but Luke's Jesus says prophets and kings (Luke 10:24). In the Parable of the Great Supper, Luke has the host explicitly invite the poor and marginalized and excludes the well-to-do—an economic message in contrast to Matthew's political message (Luke 14:21–24). Matthew's Jesus wants disciples to love him more than relatives and possessions, but Luke's Jesus demands that his followers hate those things (Luke 14:26). Luke frames the gaining and losing of one's life in more economic terms than does Matthew (Luke 17:33). When promising the disciples that they will one day sit on judge's thrones, Luke makes explicit that they will also be provided with food and drink (Luke 22:30). But most dramatic of all, when speaking about treasures in heaven, Matthew warns that earthly treasures are fleeting, while Luke instead directs listeners to sell their possessions and give alms. He also directly connects these actions with gaining heavenly treasure, suggesting that they are cause and effect (Luke 12:33).

Luke also has some variances with Matthew that do not promote a more radical economic message. Fifteen verses have changes that cannot easily be classified as more or less intense than Matthew. But unlike what we saw with Luke's Markan material, there are six Q verses in which the Lukan version is worse for the radical message than is the Matthean version. They are all intensifications of the economic message, but they are intensifications of a regressive economic message, that is, material from category C. All six of these verses are contained in the Parable of the Pounds. As mentioned before, this is the most problematic pericope for my thesis that Luke presents a message of liberation, and it will require special attention in chapter 4.

By cross-referencing our data on economic themes in Luke with information on which sources Luke is drawing from, we can make a few basic conclusions. First, to all of the verses with economic themes that Luke draws from Mark and Q, he adds an equal number of verses from L. Luke is more interested in economic themes than either Mark or Q/Matthew. Furthermore, the L material is more unambiguously radical and liberative than is the material drawn from Mark and Q. All three sources have about the same amount of material warning against wealth and showing solidarity with the poor (B). However, L has much more good news for the poor (A) while Mark and (especially) Q have more challenges to the radical economic message (C & D). Luke's version of shared material often has a more radical or more explicitly economic perspective than the parallel passages in Mark and Q. Specifically Luke intensifies 20 percent of the economic verses he draws from Mark, and 16 percent of the verses taken from Q are more radical than their parallels in Matthew. Thus Luke consistently adds to, amplifies, and intensifies the liberative economic themes found in Mark and Q, with only one exception: the Parable of the Pounds. In general, though, we can say that Luke has a stronger and more encompassing message in favor of the poor and against wealth than do either Mark or Q/Matthew.

Voice Analysis

Just as we cross-referenced data on Luke's economic content with data on their source, we can also cross-reference them with data on their voice. Voice is divided into four major categories. Narration is the voice of the narrator and accounts for 18 percent of Luke's economic material. Dialog is when characters are engaged in conversation and adds up to 26 percent. Teaching, at 24 percent, is when Jesus engages in normal speech in monologue. Finally, parables, which account for 28 percent, are a special type of monologue. There are also four minor categories. Prayer, with only one verse, which will be treated along with teaching as a single category: teaching and prayer. Song (2.2 percent), reading (0.6 percent), and dedication (0.3 percent) all contain very few references and will be treated briefly now.

Songs, readings, and the dedication account for only 10 verses of Luke, and they all appear in the first four chapters. The dedication to "most excellent Theophilus" (Luke 1:3 NRSV) suggests a patron for Luke's work who comes from the equites, and is thus theme C. Mary's song contains 4 theme A verses and one theme B (Luke 1:47–48, 52–54) and sets the early tone of the gospel with a strong, radical economic message. Zechariah's song has two verses of good news for the poor (A; Luke 1:68–69). Finally, Jesus's reading in the synagogue contains two verses of theme A material (Luke 4:18–19) and serves as Jesus's mission statement.

With that brief bit of prologue, let us begin now with the narrative voice. It is most conspicuous for having no hard challenges to the radical economic message (D). The warnings against wealth and solidarity with the poor (B) account for 40 percent, about the same as what we saw in all three sources above. Good news for the poor (A) adds up to 26 percent, close to the 29 percent in Luke overall. Suggestions that wealth might be acceptable (C) account for the remaining 33 percent of narration. That is a bit more than C material in Luke (25 percent), but close to C and D together in Luke (29 percent). Narration, then, is a fairly close parallel to the statistics we see in Luke as a whole.

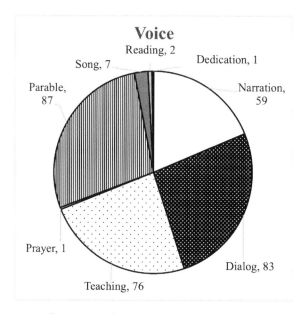

Figure 11. Lukan economic material by voice

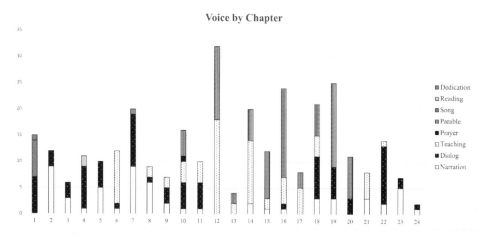

Figure 12. Lukan economic material by voice and chapter

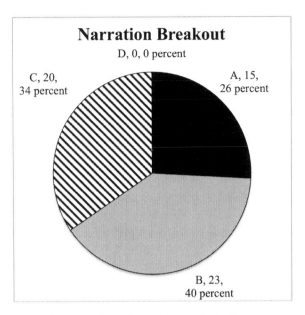

Figure 13. Narration voice material by theme

The narrator provides a variety of good news for the poor (A). Three characters—the prophet Anna, John the Baptist, and Jesus—are described proclaiming God's empire in economic terms (Luke 2:38; 3:18; 8:1). In three cases, Jesus offers healing or intervention for the poor: with the widow of Nain (Luke 7:13–15), the Gerasene demoniac (Luke 8:27), and the blind beggar near Jericho (Luke 18:40). In two other cases he offers food, first with a miraculous catch of fish (Luke 5:6), and second with the miracle of the loaves and fish (Luke 9:16–17). In Luke 10:38, Martha, a hero in the story, welcomes poor Jesus into her home. Both poor shepherds (Luke 2:18) and a poor widow giving alms (Luke 21:2) are held up as models and favored by God. Finally, in Luke 3:20, a villain of the story, Herod, acts to silence the liberative message of John the Baptist.

There are also many places where the narrator advances the message against wealth and in solidarity with the poor (B). Some events covered in the A material also appear here, such as the shepherds being graced as holders of God's message (Luke 2:9), the prophet Anna who lives in poverty in the temple (Luke 2:37), and the blind beggar by the roadside (Luke 18:35). In addition to these three, many other verses narrate heroes having solidarity with the poor. Jesus is laid in a manger (Luke 2:7, 16), his parents make the poor-person's offering of turtledoves and pigeons at the Temple (Luke 2:24), he goes without food for forty days (Luke 4:2), he and his followers pluck heads of grain from the field to eat (Luke 6:1), and John the Baptist's witness of solidarity with poor is acknowledged by the crowd following Jesus (Luke 7:29). James, John, and Levi all leave "everything" in order to follow Jesus (Luke 5:11, 28). There are four verses in which the narrator describes Jesus in opposition to various rich people: when he sends a huge herd of pigs running off a cliff to their death (Luke 8:33),[8] when he drives sellers out of the temple (Luke 19:45), when we see rich people putting money in the treasury (Luke 21:1), and in his conflicts with the Pharisees, whom the narrator describes as "lovers of money" (Luke 16:14 NRSV). This last verse and two others move forward Jesus's warnings against wealth: the moment when the rich young man goes away sad because he has many possessions (Luke 18:23) and in the temple when the disciples' admiration of the great buildings sets up Jesus's retort (Luke 21:5). Several verses show villains being enamored of wealth or of the rich, some we have already mentioned above. The emperor loves his taxes (Luke 2:1), Pharisees and lawyers are too caught up in their wealth to accept John's baptism (Luke 7:30), a Pharisee's guests squabble over places of honor at a meal (Luke 14:7), Pharisees love money and reject Jesus (Luke 16:14), and the authorities mock Jesus with symbols of wealth and power (Luke 23:11, 38). All these show the narrator taking a stand in favor of the liberative message.

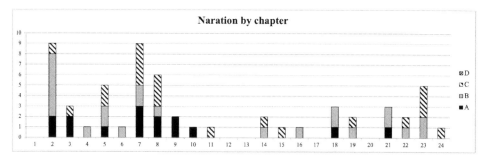

Figure 14. Narration voice material by theme and chapter

However, the narrator also mentions many ways in which Jesus seems to be chummy with the wealthy (C). He comes from a notable lineage (Luke 2:4; 3:23–38). He shares meals with the well-to-do (Luke 5:27–29; 7:36; 11:37; 14:1). He performs healings for a centurion (Luke

8. That is to say, Jesus destroys the property of a large-scale owner.

7:2, 10) and a synagogue leader (Luke 8:41, 55). He is followed by tax collectors (Luke 5:27; 15:1; 19:2). He is supported in some extravagance by
the anointing woman (Luke 7:38), his female patrons (Luke 8:3; 23:56),
his disciples (Luke 22:13), and Joseph of Arimathea (Luke 23:50, 53). The
narrator does not show Jesus actively on the side of wealth, but there are
several moments in which Jesus seems to interact with wealth and the
wealthy without criticizing such wealth. Overall, though, the voice of the
narrator has a message quite similar to the message of Luke as a whole,
with the notable exception that the narrator has no strong challenges (D)
to the radical economic message.

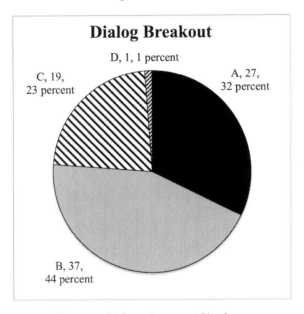

Figure 15. Dialog voice material by theme

The dialog voice shows a similar distribution of economic themes,
closely in line with the message of Luke as a whole, though slightly more
radical. Good news for the poor (A) accounts for 32 percent of dialog
material, as compared to 29 percent of Luke overall. Another 44 percent
of dialog contains warnings against wealth and solidarity with the poor
(B), slightly more than the 42 percent of Luke. While 25 percent of Luke's
economic material consists of weak challenges to the radical economic
message (C), only 23 percent of dialog material contains such challenges.
Finally, 4 percent of Luke's economic material represents strong challenges to the radical economic message (D), but only 1 percent of the

dialog material does. The dialog voice contains slightly more material sympathetic to the radical economic message (A & B) than does Luke as a whole, and slightly less material that is antagonistic to it (C & D).

There is much dialog in Luke that speaks in favor of the poor (A), including a significant amount before the start of Jesus's public ministry. Specifically, Gabriel, Mary, and Elizabeth all talk about God favoring Mary in her lowliness (Luke 1:28, 31, 38, 42). An angel shares good news of a savior with poor shepherds (Luke 2:10–11). Later, John the Baptist has a teaching which is favorable to the poor, advocating the sharing of clothing and food with the poor (Luke 3:11), the fair collection of taxes (Luke 3:13), and for soldiers to refrain from extorting the people (Luke 3:14). All of these are good news for the poor in light of contemporary conditions. Once Jesus enters the scene, he identifies himself as a proclaimer of good news to the poor (Luke 4:21, 43;, 7:22). The crowds acknowledge Jesus as a great prophet when he saves a widow from poverty by raising her only son from the dead (Luke 7:16). There is also dialog surrounding two other of Jesus's healings which bring people out of poverty: the hemorrhaging woman (Luke 8:48) and the blind beggar (Luke 18:41–42). Jesus directly exhorts his listeners to give aid to the poor at the great feeding (Luke 9:13) and after the parable of the Good Samaritan (Luke 10:36–37). He discusses a reversal in which those who have become poor to follow him will be lifted up (Luke 9:4; 18:30; 22:29–30). He discusses with the other crucified criminal that he will be brought from a lowly earthly estate into a paradisiacal kingdom (Luke 23:42–43). Finally, Cleopas and his companion identify Jesus as someone who was to redeem Israel from slavery (Luke 24:21).

Supporting this good news for the poor is dialog material that advises against wealth and shows solidarity with the poor (B). An angel tells the shepherds that the savior will be found in a lowly manger (Luke 2:12). Jesus and the Devil engage in a conversation in which the Devil offers wealth and power, but Jesus chooses renunciation (Luke 4:3–4, 6–7). Jesus says he has come to call tax collectors to repentance (Luke 5:32). He identifies John the Baptist's asceticism (Luke 7:25, 33). He identifies the anointing woman's gift of kisses in opposition to Simon the Pharisee's withholding of oil. He instructs his disciples to take no provisions for their travels (Luke 9:3). He notes that he is offering his poor disciples the things kings would like the have (Luke 10:24). He has a discussion with Martha of Bethany about the relative value of material things (Luke 10:41–42). He has another discussion in a Pharisee's house about greed and justice for the lowly (Luke 11:39, 41–43, 46). Later, he tells Pharisees that God does not value the things humans value (Luke 16:15). He has a key discussion with the rich young man and the crowds about giving up possessions and giving to the poor in order to follow in Jesus's path (Luke 18:22, 24–25, 28–29), followed by a similar discussion with Zacchaeus (Luke 19:8–10). He indicts the temple establishment for stealing from the poor (Luke 19:46). He engages in a dispute over taxes and whether true wealth belongs to the emperor or to God (Luke 20:25; 23:2). He indicts the scribes for loving wealth and neglecting the poor (Luke 20:46–47). At the last supper, he engages in a conversation with the disciples about how, in contrast to the prevailing order, God's Empire values poverty, humility, and service (Luke 22:25–28, 35). This represents a strong argument against wealth in Luke's dialogical material.

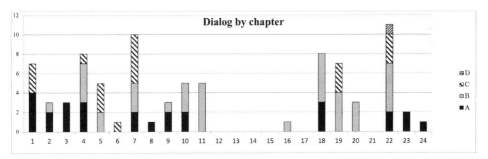

Figure 16. Dialog voice material by theme and chapter

In contrast, the dialogical material presents a fairly weak critique of the radical economic message (C & D). By far the strongest, the only verse of D material, is when Jesus changes his instructions to his disciples and tells them to take purses, bags, and swords with them (Luke 22:36), to which the disciples reply that they already have two swords (Luke 22:38). To this, we can add several soft critiques of the radical economic message (C). Gabriel and the crowd use kingly language to talk about Jesus (1:32–33; 19:38). Jesus notes that while there were many lepers in the time of Elisha, only the rich foreigner was cleansed (Luke 4:27). Jesus is seen to engage with tax collectors and be less ascetic than John (Luke 5:30, 33–34; 6:4; 7:34). He heals the servant of a rich centurion (Luke 7:4–5, 8–9). He invites himself to Zacchaeus's house before Zacchaeus repents, irritating the crowd (Luke 19:5, 7). Finally, Jesus has access to a well-appointed room for the Passover (Luke 22:11–12). In spite of these few distractions, it is plain that the voice of dialog in Luke has a strong current of the radical economic message, stronger than in Luke as a whole.

Moving on to Luke's material containing the teaching and prayer of Jesus, we find a pattern that is more divergent from the whole of Luke than was either narration or dialog. First, a full 55 percent of Jesus's economic teaching is teaching against wealth or in solidarity with the poor (B), compared to only 42 percent in Luke as a whole. This is a striking increase. It is paired with a drastic decrease in soft challenges to the radical economic message (C): 8 percent as compared to 25 percent in Luke. Strangely, though the teaching material contains a greater percentage of strong challenges to the radical economic message (D): 8 percent, double the 4 percent of Luke as a whole. Only good news for the poor (A) mirrors the percentage in the gospel, 29 percent in both the teaching material and in the gospel as a whole. So, we see that Jesus's teaching is generally more radical than the rest of the gospel, but it contains an unusually large number of serious challenges to that radicalism.

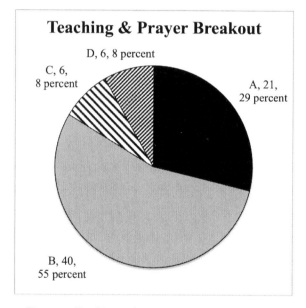

Figure 17. Teaching and prayer voice material by theme

Jesus's teaching of good news for the poor (A) begins with the Sermon on the Plain, in which he promises good for the poor and hungry (Luke 6:20–21) and exhorts his listeners to give to beggars and show mercy to debtors (Luke 6:30, 36). The Lord's Prayer also encourages forgiveness of debts (Luke 11:4). In chapter 12, Jesus repeatedly asserts that God cares for and values the poor (Luke 12:6–7, 24, 27–28, 32), a sentiment that is echoed in chapter 18 (Luke 18:7–8, 16). He teaches that the last will be first at the feast of God's Empire (Luke 13:29–30) and that those throwing banquets should also invite the poor on God's behalf (Luke 14:13–14). He teaches that the poor widow's small offering is more valuable than the large offerings of wealthy men (Luke 21:3–4). Finally, he teaches that the Son of Man is coming to redeem (Luke 21:28).

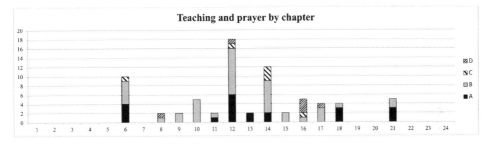

Figure 18. Teaching and prayer voice material by theme and chapter

Jesus's teachings against wealth (B) also begin in the Sermon on the Plain, in which Jesus curses the rich and full (Luke 6:24–25), encourages lending without expecting anything in return (Luke 6:34–35), and suggests that those having their coat stolen should give their shirt as well (Luke 6:29). He teaches that riches can choke faith (Luke 8:14) and that one can save one's life by losing it (Luke 9:24). He shows solidarity with the poor by having "no place to lay his head" (Luke 9:58). He teaches his disciples to take no provisions and be happy with whatever they receive (Luke 10:2, 4, 7–8). He thanks God in prayer for hiding things from the wise and disclosing them to the weak (Luke 10:21). The Lord's Prayer asks only for daily bread (Luke 11:3). Chapter 12 contains a strong indictment of greed and encourages the disciples not to seek after material things (Luke 12:15, 21–23, 26, 29–31.) It also instructs his listeners to sell their possessions and give to the poor as a way of amassing heavenly treasure (Luke 12:33–34). Jesus encourages dinner guests to humble themselves rather than seeking position (Luke 14:9–12). He gives a stinging command in which he insists that no disciple can follow him without renouncing absolutely everything (Luke 14:26–27, 33); this is one of the strongest indictments of wealth in the gospel. He teaches that heaven rejoices when tax collectors repent (Luke 15:7, 10). He has a key teaching that no one can serve both God and wealth (Luke 16:13). He suggests that possessions cannot save, that they only distract from salvation (Luke 17:28, 31, 33; 21:6, 34). He teaches that only childlike dispossession can allow access to God's Empire (Luke 18:17). This is not only a powerful anti-wealth message in terms of quantity, it also contains some of the most radical verses in the gospel, repeatedly teaching absolute disposses-sion as a condition of discipleship.

However, Jesus also has teachings that seem quite contrary (C & D) to this radical economic message. He tells his listeners to pray for those who abuse them. He encourages those who are being sued by the powerful to give in, even if they don't have enough money to pay (Luke 12:58–59). Some of his teaching on humility at meals seems to parrot the prevailing view that wealth is honorable (Luke 14:8). He seems to assume that some of his listeners have the means to build towers (Luke 14:28–29). He seems to suggest that one's management of dishonest wealth is an indicator of one's faithfulness with Godly things (16:9–12). He sug-gests that his followers think of themselves as useless slaves (Luke 17:10). Most potent of all, though, Jesus teaches: "to those who have, more will be given; and from those who do not have, even what they seem to have will be taken away" (Luke 8:18 NRSV), a seeming reversal of the teaching that the last will be first (Luke 13:29). And so, paired with Jesus's radical teaching in the dialogical material, we also have a troublesome set of anti-radical teachings which seem to endorse the economic *status quo* of the rich oppressing and extracting wealth from the poor. This, in miniature, is the problem we can see in the gospel as a whole.

While there are some strong anti-radical sentiments in the teaching material, the parables contain the most pervasive anti-radical message of all. Nearly half of the parable material speaks against the themes that God favors the poor and wealth is to be avoided. Forty percent of the parable material represents soft challenges (C), while a further 8 percent repre-sents hard challenges (D). Of all of the C material in Luke, 42 percent of it is found in the parables. Of all of the D material, a full 50 percent of it is found in the parables. Only 21 percent of economic parable material is good news for the poor, and only 33 percent of it stands against wealth or in solidarity with the poor. The parables represent by far the greatest concentration of anti-radical material in Luke.

Let us look first, though, at parables that contain good news for the poor (A). The Parable of the Good Samaritan consistently shows heroes caring for the poor and villains neglecting them (Luke 10:31–35), though

Jesus's casting of heroes and villains does not match societal norms. Another parable imagines a master swapping roles to serve his faithful servants (Luke 12:35). The Parable of the Great Supper sees a master inviting the poor and marginalized into the feast (Luke 14:21–23). Gentiles refuse to care for the Prodigal Son in his need (Luke 15:16). The Shrewd Manager lightens the weight of debts for his master's clients (Luke 16:6–7). Poor Lazarus is brought by angels to be comforted in heaven (Luke 16:22). Finally, the Unjust Judge, who self-identifies as a villain, is reluctant to grant a poor widow justice (Luke 18:2–5). This is the extent of the parables' good news for the poor.

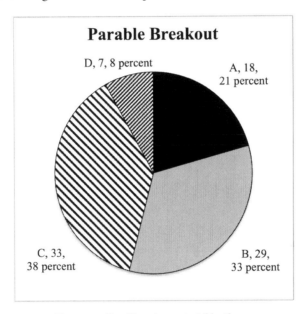

Figure 19. Parable voice material by theme

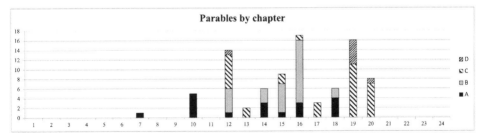

Figure 20. Parable voice material by theme and chapter

There are more parables that warn against wealth (B), though. The Parable of the Rich Fool is a good example (Luke 12:16–20). In the Parable of the Great Supper, the riches of the rich keep them from entering the feast (Luke 14:18–19, 24). The Parable of the Prodigal Son shows the dangers of seeking the pleasures of money (Luke 15:12–13, 18, 21, 29–30). The Parable of the Shrewd Manager depicts a villainous master who loves wealth (Luke 16:1–5). The Parable of the Rich Man and Lazarus likewise shows a villainous rich man who is punished by God for his inattention to Lazarus (Luke 16:19–21, 23–25, 29, 31). Finally, the Parable of the Pharisee and the Tax Collector shows an economic oppressor seeking and receiving forgiveness from God (Luke 18:13–14).

Now we can return to the parables which seem to speak against the poor or in favor of accumulation (C & D). A couple of parables on watchfulness in Chapter 12 contain some warnings against wealth, but are colored by their identification of God with an absentee landlord (Luke 12:39, 42–48). They conclude with a statement of mixed content: "But the one who did not know and did what deserved a beating will receive a light beating. From everyone to whom much has been given, much will be required; and from the one to whom much has been entrusted, even more will be demanded" (Luke 12:48). Another three parables picture God or Jesus as owners: something that is only slightly problematic (Luke 13:6–9, 24–30; 15:6). The Prodigal Son is greeted on his return with some opulence by his father (Luke 15:22). The master's approval of the Shrewd Manager is somewhat problematic (Luke 16:8). Jesus seems to accept the norm that slaves must be exploited by their masters (Luke 17:7–9). The Parable of the Wicked Tenants seems to identify God with a vengeful master to a degree that shocks the crowd listening to Jesus (Luke 20:9–16). But by far the most problematic parable is the Parable of the Pounds, which seems to endorse accumulation and exploitation while identifying God with a brutal and oppressive nobleman-king (Luke 19:12–27). The parable is summed up with the apothegm: "to all those who have, more will be given; but from those who have nothing, even what they have will be taken away" (Luke 19:26 NRSV).

Sorting for voice reveals that most of the fight over economics in Luke takes place in the teaching and parables of Jesus. There is a fair amount of introductory material that firmly establishes the theme of good news for the poor (A) before Jesus gets his stride. Also, all of the voices contain significant economic material. However, the words of Jesus have the most intense distillation of economic themes. The strongest warnings against wealth (B) are in Jesus's non-parabolic teaching, and the strongest challenges to the liberative message (C & D) come from the parables. If we are to argue that Luke has a relatively consistent message of good news for the poor and warnings against wealth, then it is the parables we will have the hardest time dealing with.

Conclusion

Counting and analyzing the references to economic themes in Luke yields a better understanding of the overall character of Luke's economic argument. We see that Luke has a greater interest in economic issues than Mark or Matthew, doubling the amount of material he takes from Mark and Q with material he provides himself. Furthermore, Luke presents economic material that is heavily weighted in favor of good news for the poor (A) and resistance to wealth (B). The main conflict in the text seems to be between this radical message and the more conventional economic message of the C and D material. Luke consistently intensifies the economic material that he takes from Mark and Q, and the material Luke gives in L is consistently more radical than the material taken from Mark and especially Q. Luke establishes the theme of good news for the poor (A) early, before Jesus really takes the stage. The most concentrated and strongest warnings against wealth (B) come from Jesus's teaching. And while there are some scattered materials which might endanger Luke's radical economic message, by far the strongest challenge comes from the parables, most especially the Parable of the Pounds. Having established this basic framework, we are now free in the next two chapters to engage more closely first Luke's radical economic message and then the possible challenges to that message.

CHAPTER 3

Luke's Clear Message of Liberation

*Blessed are you who are poor, for yours is the
kingdom of God. . . . Cursed are you who are
rich, for you have received your consolation.*

—LUKE 6:20, 24

IN THE PRECEDING CHAPTER, we took an overview of the economic material in Luke and saw how that material can be sorted into two themes of economic liberation (A & B) and two themes that call into question that liberation (C & D). In this chapter, we will focus on those first two themes: good news for the poor (A) and resistance to wealth (B). I will show that, contrary to the opinions of many of its interpreters, Luke does indeed proclaim this radical two-part message. The theme of good news for the poor is established early in the gospel, in the key texts that define what good news means in Luke and what God's empire is about. Suffused throughout the gospel is also a deep suspicion of wealth and an ethic of solidarity with the poor. Luke carefully works his sources to present this radical ethic, the most radical economic ethic we find in the gospels.

Good News for the Poor (A)[1]

In his influential 1976 article, Robert Karris argues that while Luke's community contained some poor people, the gospel is addressed primarily to the rich and their concerns regarding their own salvation and the use of their possessions.

> Luke's community clearly had both rich and poor members. Luke is primarily taken up with the rich members, their concerns, and the problems which they pose for the community. Their concerns, as evidenced in 18:18–30 and 19:1–10, revolve around the question: do our possessions prevent us from being genuine Christians?[2]

While Luke does address this concern of the rich, it does not do so at the exclusion of the concerns of the poor. Luke contains a great deal of good news for the poor, material which would make little sense if it were intended nearly exclusively for the rich.[3] It is Luke's ability to "code-switch" that allows him to address the concerns of the poor in a document read by the powerful.[4] In this section, I will make the case for Luke's message for the poor, a message of good news and liberation.

Birth Narrative

Some of the most powerful good news for the poor in Luke comes from L material in the first three chapters, setting the tone for the rest of the gospel. Economic issues are central to the origin stories of Jesus and John the Baptist. Luke sets up the gospel with a vigorous argument for God's preferential option for the poor.[5]

It begins with the person of Mary. She is a poor person who finds special favor with God, in part due to her poverty.[6] The angel Gabriel ap-

1. A version of this section was presented as King, "Luke's Good News for the Poor."

2. Karris, "Poor and Rich," 124.

3. Degenhardt, *Evangelist der Armen*, 210; Gillman, *Possessions and the Life of Faith*, 27.

4. Crowder, "Luke," 159.

5. Rachel Coleman makes this same point, although she includes Luke 4 as part of the introduction. Coleman, "Lukan Lens," 95–98. Dario López Rodriguez argues that the marginality of Zechariah, Elizabeth, Simeon, Anna, and Mary makes them more receptive to the voice of God. López Rodriguez, *Liberating Mission*, 15.

6. We know that Mary is poor because she self-identifies as poor and because when

pears to her, telling her twice that she has been favored by God (Luke 1:28, 30), while she refers to herself as God's servant (Luke 1:38). In the next scene, Elizabeth affirms the words of Mary and Gabriel, that she is blessed by God (Luke 1:42). All this culminates in Mary's song—based on the song of Hannah (1 Sam 2:1–10), though more radical—in which Mary repeatedly proclaims God's preferential option for the poor. God is a savior to the lowly servant (Luke 1:47–48). God favors the lowly over the mighty (Luke 1:52). God favors the hungry over the rich (Luke 1:53).[7] Mary is both the evidence and the prophet of God's good news for the poor.[8]

And the theme continues through the rest of the birth narrative. When Zechariah opens his mouth to sing, he sings of God's liberative action for the people: "[God] has looked favorably on his people and redeemed them. He has raised up a mighty savior for us" (Luke 1:68–69 NRSV). So too, the homeless prophet Anna declares God's redemption from slavery (Luke 2:38). And when the army of God's angels come to bring the imperial announcement of God's good news, they appear not to the powerful or to the learned, but to poor shepherds in the fields (Luke 2:9–11). As noted especially by Coleman and López Rodriguez, these are the ones to whom God's gospel is given, to God's preferred people, the

---

she and Joseph make the temple sacrifice for her purification after childbirth, they do not offer the expected lamb and dove (Lev 12:6), but rather the poor woman's option of two doves (Lev 12:8; Luke 2:24). Crowder, "Luke," 161; Coleman, "Lukan Lens," 41–47; Fitzmyer, *Luke I-IX*, 426. However, Raymond Brown suggests, based on fourth-century CE rabbinic testimony, that two birds may have been the expected offering in Jesus's time. Brown, *Birth of the Messiah*, 448.

7. Hannah's song, while praising God for lifting up the lowly and bringing down the mighty, has a more fatalist note than the Magnificat. "The Lord makes poor and makes rich; he brings low, he also exalts" (1 Sam 2:7 NRSV). In Luke's adaptation, Mary never associates God with this kind of fatalism; God is always on the side of the powerless and against the powerful. Luke's Mary also does not suggest that God lifts up the poor in order to make them more acceptable to or fit in better with the wealthy, as: "He raises up the poor from the dust; he lifts the needy from the ash heap, *to make them sit with princes and inherit a seat of honor*" (1 Sam 2:8 NRSV; emphasis added).

8. Aída Besançon Spencer takes seriously Mary's authorship of the Magnificat. She notes that its sentiments seem to form the basis for Jesus's own radical ministry and that she should continue to be a role-model for women and people from oppressed communities. God called her to be a leader, and God may well call others whom the world considers unworthy. Spencer, "Position Reversal." Amy-Jill Levine and Ben Witherington also emphasize Mary's agency and role as prophet of justice. Levine and Witherington, *Gospel of Luke*, 38–43.

poor and the marginalized.[9] And of course, all of this material is contained only in Luke.

While Thomas Phillips admits that Mary and Joseph are poor since they make the poor-person's offering at the temple, he nevertheless makes an early choice to read all of the references to wealth and poverty here as metaphorical. He makes a two-fold justification for this choice. First, the characters in this part of the story are Jewish. Presumably the Hebrew Bible only speaks of wealth and poverty in metaphorical terms, so Luke must also be metaphorical here. Second, everything in the birth narratives must be read through the lens of Luke 1:51–52: "He has scattered the proud (ὑπερήφανος) in the thoughts of their hearts. He has . . . lifted up the lowly (ταπεινός)." It contains references to pride and humility, and since those are "human attributes" and not "physical possessions or conditions," all of the explicit references to rich and poor are most likely metaphorical, says Phillips.[10]

There are several problems with this argument. First, there is no reason to think that a "Jewish milieu" suggests metaphorical language in regard to economic themes; the Hebrew Bible is packed with messages about very real economic conditions. Second, there is no reason that two adjectives in 1:51–52 should make every other reference metaphorical. Third, even if we do accept that pride and humility are keys to interpreting this entire passage, these words do not necessitate a metaphorical reading. The Greek ὑπερήφανος can refer to arrogance or pride, but it can also refer to living sumptuously. Likewise, ταπεινός can refer to humility, but it can just as easily refer to powerlessness or poverty.[11] From the very beginning of his reader-response analysis, Phillips is making the choice to read rich and poor metaphorically even when there is no particular reason to do so. He is falling into the middle-class bias of which Phillip Esler warned.[12]

Many other interpreters make this early choice to read economic themes metaphorically. David Peter Seccombe makes an extended argument that Mary's song is about God freeing Israel from Gentile rule.[13] Christopher Hays agrees that it is about nationalism rather than

9. Coleman, "Lukan Lens," 73; Gillman, *Possessions and the Life of Faith*, 38; López Rodriguez, *Liberating Mission*, 15–16.

10. Phillips, *Reading Issues*, 90–92.

11. *LSJ*, s.v. "ταπεινός."

12. Esler, *Community and Gospel*, 170.

13. Seccombe, *Possessions and the Poor*, 70–83.

economics.[14] Luke Timothy Johnson and Kyoung-Jin Kim are concerned with the symbolic value of possessions and the slave-master relationship, respectively.[15] However, these qualifications of the real, radical economic message are warned against by a large chorus of commentators—with perspectives as diverse as William Barclay and Elsa Tamez—who all insist that Mary's Magnificat not be overly-spiritualized, but accepted for it's true message of economic reversal, a message consistent with the rest of Luke and with voices in both Jewish and Christian tradition.[16] As Rachel Coleman argues effectively, Mary and her song represent radical good news for the poor and set a tone for the interpretation of the rest of the gospel.[17]

As noted in chapter 1, Itumeleng Mosala has a very different reading of Luke 1–2.[18] Rather than seeing Luke as too radical, Mosala sees Luke as hopelessly anti-radical. He believes Karris is right to identify Luke's audience as the wealthy.[19] He further sees evidence that Luke is trying to gentrify both Mary and Jesus so they can be more easily digested by the rich. Mary sees Elizabeth and Zechariah so that she can receive the blessing of the priestly class.

> Mary, probably a single mother from the ghettos of colonized Galilee, needed the moral clearing of the priestly sector of the ruling class—those who were the target of Luke's Gospel. Essentially, her class origins were too unbecoming for the eyes of the class for which Luke is writing. How can the Savior of the world come from depressed ghetto areas and not from wealthy

---

14. Hays, *Luke's Wealth Ethics*, 101–4.

15. Johnson, *Luke*, 42; Kim, *Stewardship and Almsgiving*, 122, 190.

16. Alexander, *Your Money or Your Life*, 122–23; Balch, "Mary's Magnificat," 657; Barclay, *Luke*, 19–20; Bovon, *Luke 1*, 63; Cassidy, *Jesus*, 21; Craddock, *Luke*, 29–30; Crowder, "Luke," 161; Esler, *Community and Gospel*, 187–88; Gillman, *Possessions and the Life of Faith*, 38; Levine and Witherington, *Gospel of Luke*, 42; Lieu, *Gospel of Luke*, 11; López Rodriguez, *Liberating Mission*, 5, 109; Marshall, *Gospel of Luke*, 85; Pilgrim, *Good News to the Poor*, 77–80; Ringe, *Luke*, 35; Schottroff and Stegemann, *Jesus and the Hope of the Poor*, 28–29; Stegemann, *Gospel and the Poor*, 26; Tamez, *Bible of the Oppressed*, 68; Tannehill, *Luke*, 53–57; Tiede, *Luke*, 55–56; Wright, *Luke for Everyone*, 15–16.

17. Coleman, "Lukan Lens," 41–61. Coleman especially notes how the lowly social status of Mary is highlighted by a comparison with the relatively high status of Elizabeth and Zechariah, a contrast that can be seen in terms of lineage, social-economic status, gender, physical location, response, and timing.

18. Mosala, *Biblical Hermeneutics*, 154–89.

19. Mosala, *Biblical Hermeneutics*, 162.

suburbia, like other prominent societal figures before him? Luke could not sell that kind of messiah to his ruling-class audience.[20]

That is the purpose of Mary's visit to Elizabeth and Zechariah. That is also Joseph's only role in the story: to give Jesus a royal lineage. Luke works actively to domesticate and defang the more radical economic message of the historical Jesus, says Mosala.

> From the point of view of the oppressed and exploited people or the world today, Luke's ideological co-optation of Jesus in the interests of the ruling class is an act of political war against the liberation struggle.[21]

As noted above, I am sympathetic to Mosala's argument. The sophistication of Luke's writing indicates that he is of the upper classes or at least very conversant with them. It seems entirely plausible that Luke moderates a far more radical message that lies behind him; radical movements tend to be moderated by those who come after, seeking to make them more broadly acceptable.

Nevertheless, Luke contains some of the most radical economic language in the New Testament. With all of Luke's imperfections, without Luke we wouldn't have these radical words in the tradition at all. As Schottroff and Stegemann say:

> If we did not have Luke, we would probably have lost an important, if not the most important, part of the earliest Christian tradition and its intense preoccupation with the figure and message of Jesus as hope of the poor.[22]

I will continue to address Mosala's critique, and that of Nessan, in the coming chapters. For now, though, while I acknowledge that Luke's portrayal of Mary may not be as radical as Mosala would like, it is certainly more radical than the likes of Phillips would allow.

Defining and Enacting the Mission

Once the sons of Mary and Elizabeth grow up, each has an opportunity to declare God's good news and then to clarify that that good news is

---

20. Mosala, *Biblical Hermeneutics*, 167.

21. Mosala, *Biblical Hermeneutics*, 171.

22. Schottroff and Stegemann, *Jesus and the Hope of the Poor*, 67.

in fact good news for the poor. In L material, John the Baptist paints a picture of what the good news of God's Empire actually looks like in the world. It is the person without a coat receiving one from someone who has two (Luke 3:11). It is the poor person not having to fear abusive taxes or extortion from soldiers (Luke 3:13–14). While this is also a message to the rich who must give, what is important to notice here is that all of the actions John suggests represent improvements in the real conditions of the poor.[23] John is not asked an economic question, but he gives an economic answer, because economics are at the core of the gospel.

When Jesus emerges from the desert to proclaim the good news of God's Empire, he also defines that good news as good news for the poor. In Luke, and only in Luke, Jesus takes as his mission statement the words of Isaiah; Jesus has been sent by God "to preach good news to the poor, to proclaim release to the prisoners, and . . . to liberate the oppressed" (Luke 4:18–19 CEB).[24] What is more, he also comes to initiate God's Jubilee, when all debts are forgiven and all land is returned to the peasants who first had it (Luke 4:19).[25] Luke's Jesus explicitly says that his ministry is primarily about liberation. And not just spiritual liberation. Liberation from oppression. Liberation from poverty. Liberation from debt.

---

23. Esler, *Community and Gospel*, 196–97. Johnson points out that when addressing soldiers and tax collectors, John "does not identify them as enemies or oppressors, does not demand that they leave their employment, does not enter into a condemnation of the economy or rule of the empire that they serve." Johnson, *Prophetic Jesus*, loc. 1138–42. Crowder counters, "The message of John the Baptist pushes further against the divisions caused by differences in social status. Those who have must share clothing and food with those who have not; those who have must cease cheating and extorting." Crowder, "Luke," 163. Coleman also, "The three imperatives are related to radical generosity, communality, justice, and contentment. . . . These commands are costly, especially for tax collectors and soldiers, who are likely hard-pressed to make a living wage without resorting to the kinds of exploitative strategies against which John rails." Coleman, "Lukan Lens," 78–79.

24. Esler, *Community and Gospel*, 167; González, *Faith and Wealth*, 75–76; Johnson, *Literary Function*, 92. Coleman has a particularly deft analysis that catalogues how Jesus's quotation is carefully curated to emphasize its radical message. Coleman, "Lukan Lens," 83–89. Talbert shows how Jesus's reading is enclosed in a carefully constructed chiasm. Talbert, *Reading Luke*, 54–55. Mitzi Smith notes that "African American women engaged in the civil rights movement appropriated Luke 4:18 (which cites Isa 61:1–2), 'the Spirit of the Lord is upon me,' rather than acquiesce to Pauline mandates not to suffer a woman to teach a man." Smith, "Slavery," 16.

25. See especially Ringe, *Jesus*, 36–45. Also: Alexander, *Your Money or Your Life*, 227; Rhee, *Loving the Poor*, 35. For an argument against, see Johnson, *Prophetic Jesus*, loc. 1155–58.

Liberation from alienation from the means of production. These are the principles of God's Empire. This is what gospel looks like.

Interpreters are split on whether this good news for the poor is actually good news for the poor. Focusing on Jesus's establishment as a prophet, in six pages, Johnson neither mentions that Jesus's prophecy is directed at the poor nor that it has anything to do with prisoners or the oppressed.[26] Phillips argues that since Jesus proclaims that the Isaiah passage has already been fulfilled that it cannot be anything but metaphorical.[27] Hays takes a middle ground, arguing that πτωχοίς carries both a spiritualized and a non-spiritualized sense, while Schottroff and Stegemann say it refers to the disciples who have become poor in order to follow Jesus.[28] However, many—including Esler and Kim—cite this as an explicit statement that Jesus's gospel is for the poor.[29] Tamez says regarding this passage:

> The Good News that speaks of the liberation of the oppressed cannot be pleasing to the oppressors, who want to go on exploiting the poor. But the Good News is indeed good to those who want to change and to see a more just society. For the most part, those who want to live in a society in which justice and peace reign are those who suffer hunger, oppression, poverty. For this reason the Good News is directed especially to the poor.[30]

At the beginning of his ministry, Jesus clearly states his gospel as a gospel of good news for the poor.

No one takes this more seriously than López Rodriguez, who uses the Nazareth episode as the frame for understanding the entire gospel. For him, every part of what he calls the "Nazareth manifesto" oozes with good news for the poor and marginalized. Poor Jesus, the son of a carpenter, brings the good news. He declares it in the backwater province of Galilee, in the unremarkable town of Nazareth. The message that Jesus

---

26. Johnson, *Literary Function*, 91–96.

27. Phillips, *Reading Issues*, 95–98.

28. Hays, *Luke's Wealth Ethics*, 110–11; Schottroff and Stegemann, *Jesus and the Hope of the Poor*, 90.

29. Cassidy, *Jesus*, 22; Esler, *Community and Gospel*, 180–83; Gillman, *Possessions and the Life of Faith*, 44–50; Kim, *Stewardship and Almsgiving*, 27–28; Rhee, *Loving the Poor*, 35; Pickett, "Luke as Counter-Narrative," 429.

30. Tamez, *Bible of the Oppressed*, 69.

delivers is a statement of "the Galilean Option," God's radical preference for the poor and marginalized.[31]

Once Jesus has identified the twelve disciples who are a part of his inner circle, he has another chance to clarify his message, and again he defines it in material terms. "Blessed are you who are poor, for yours is the kingdom of God. Blessed are you who are hungry now, for you will be filled" (Luke 6:20–21 NRSV). God's Empire belongs to the poor.[32] God's blessing is satisfaction for the hungry. Unlike in the Matthean parallel these beatitudes are addressed to *you* poor, *you* hungry, and Luke lacks the spiritualizing "poor *in spirit*," "hunger and thirst *for righteousness*" (Matt 5:3, 6 NRSV; emphasis added). Further, God wants loans for the poor and the forgiveness of those loans when they can't be paid back, a detail not found in the Matthean parallel (Luke 6:30–35; Matt 5:42–44). Later, when Jesus teaches his disciples how to pray, the prayer assumes that Jesus-followers forgive the debts of people who cannot repay them: "Forgive us our debts as we forgive everyone indebted to us" (Luke 11:4, variant; my translation). In both cases, the cancelling of human debts is connected to God's own forgiveness of debts (Luke 6:34; 11:4).

Schottroff and Stegemann argue that πτωχοί here refers specifically to Jesus's disciples, who have left everything to follow Jesus, and not to the poor in general. Hays shows, though, that the disciples are simply not poor enough to be "beggars," and there is no good reason to exclude the non-disciples from this group.[33] Coleman argues that the word is used in two different ways in Luke. When used descriptively it refers to those who have responded to Jesus by leaving and following, but when used prescriptively it refers to literal, socio-economic poverty along with other marginalized groups.[34] While Hays argues that Luke has edited Matthew's Beatitudes to de-spiritualize them, Phillips works hard to reverse Luke's effort and re-spiritualize them—this is about Jewish nationalism, not money.[35] Seccombe says the same, and emphasizes that Jesus's message

---

31. López Rodriguez, *Liberating Mission*, 27–43.

32. See also Luke 18:16.

33. Hays, *Luke's Wealth Ethics*, 107–10.

34. Coleman, "Lukan Lens," 110.

35. Hays, *Luke's Wealth Ethics*, 110; Phillips, *Reading Issues*, 106–9. Faustin Mahali, interestingly, sees Matthew as the more radical message here. Luke is concerned that the rich offer charity to the poor, but not with actually addressing the sources of poverty, not with achieving actual righteousness. Thus Luke discourages the poor from claiming their own agency and makes them helpless receivers of alms. Mahali, *Concept*

is not aimed especially for the poor, nor should one see any liberation-ist message in these words.[36] However, many, including Elizabeth Clark and Richard Horsley, suggest that Jesus is initiating a new age, a renewal of covenant, in which "the poor, the hungry, and the despondent would receive the rewards so frequently denied them."[37] Stephanie Buckhanon Crowder sees this is a continuation of Jesus's liberating mission: "In Luke, Jesus never strays from his messianic declaration to bring release and to set free."[38]

Jesus also intervenes to materially help the poor as he is travelling to proclaim the good news of liberation. When a widow's son dies, leaving her without any social safety net, Jesus resuscitates her son so that she is not left without support (Luke 7:12–16).[39] When a man is so plagued by demons that he is left naked and homeless in the tombs, Jesus exor-cises the demon and reincorporates the man into the community (Luke 8:27–35). When a woman has been made destitute paying doctors to heal a hemorrhage they can't heal, Jesus heals her, finally allowing her to have some peace (Luke 8:43–48). When he encounters a blind beggar on the road to Jerusalem, he heals him (Luke 18:40–42). When hungry crowds gather around him in an isolated place, Jesus feeds them (Luke 9:13–17). Whatever else these miracles may be, they are also concrete support from God for people who are needy. And when Jesus is asked if he really is the Messiah, he points to these actions as evidence. People are being healed from illnesses that make them destitute. The poor are getting good news (Luke 7:22).[40]

---

of Poverty, 93–94.

36. Seccombe, *Possessions and the Poor*, 84–96.

37. Quote from Clark, *Reading Renunciation*, 178. Renewal of covenant comes from Horsley, *Covenant Economics*, 109. See also Esler, *Community and Gospel*, 186–88; Gillman, *Possessions and the Life of Faith*, 52–53; Kim, *Stewardship and Almsgiving*, 19; Pilgrim, *Good News to the Poor*, 57–59; Rhee, *Loving the Poor*, 35; Ringe, *Jesus*, 51–54; Tamez, *Bible of the Oppressed*, 70.

38. Crowder, "Luke," 166. Levine, though, questions this. She finds no evidence that Jesus was particularly involved with the poor. Levine and Witherington, *Gospel of Luke*, 176–77.

39. López Rodriguez, *Liberating Mission*, 64.

40. As we have come to expect, Johnson focusses on how this incident identifies Jesus as prophet. Johnson, *Literary Function*, 99. Phillips denies that the poor here are the literal poor and instead focusses on the soteriological significance of the say-ing. Phillips, *Reading Issues*, 118–19. Meanwhile others see this as clear evidence that Jesus's ministry is especially for the poor: Coleman, "Lukan Lens," 113–15; Esler, *Com-munity and Gospel*, 188; Kim, *Stewardship and Almsgiving*, 187; Pilgrim, *Good News to*

In several more verses, Jesus indicates that God prefers the lowly to the powerful, the poor to the rich. Three times he says that God will lift up the last over the first. He tells his disciples that the least among them is the greatest (Luke 9:48). He says that when the nations are gathered together for a feast that the last will be first and the first last (Luke 13:29–30). Similarly, Jesus seems to indicate that God will provide for those who have been on the losing side of life: "Those who try to make their life secure will lose it, but those who lose their life will keep it" (Luke 17:33 NRSV). Jesus also says, when observing the donations being made in the temple, that the small gifts of the poor are counted by God as more valuable than the large gifts of the rich (Luke 21:2–4).[41] God prefers the poor and keeps a special place for them.

What is more, God provides for the poor in the here and now. God provides for the subsistence of birds, and God will provide also for the subsistence of the poor, because God values the poor (Luke 12:24–32).

> Consider the ravens: they neither sow nor reap, they have neither storehouse nor barn, and yet God feeds them. Of how much more value are you than the birds! Consider the lilies, how they grow: they neither toil nor spin; yet I tell you, even Solomon in all his glory was not clothed like one of these. But if God so clothes the grass of the field, which is alive today and tomorrow is thrown into the oven, how much more will he clothe you— you of little faith. (Luke 12:24, 27–28 NRSV)

Interpreters tend to focus more on the avoidance of anxiety in this passage, but this pericope also contains good news of God's care for the poor.[42]

Part of how God does this is by calling on the wealthy to invite not their friends, but the poor, to dine with them (Luke 14:13–14). Though interpretation tends to focus on the hospitality of the rich person, we also have here good news for the poor. Nearly all, including Phillips, agree that

---

the Poor, 72–73; Ringe, Jesus, 45–49.

41. López Rodriguez, Liberating Mission, 97–106; Hays, Luke's Wealth Ethics, 182–83. Gillman follows Addison G. Wright in arguing that Jesus's words are a lament of the widow's situation. She is being exploited by the establishment, and Jesus does not want her house to be devoured. This interpretation still highlights Jesus's preference for the poor. Gillman, Possessions and the Life of Faith, 61–62; Wright, "The Widow's Mites." Also, De La Torre, Politics of Jesús, loc. 2012–16.

42. See Phillips, Reading Issues, 143–44; Seccombe, Possessions and the Poor, 146–57.

real generosity to real poor persons is called for here, a radical hospitality that replaces the typical reciprocity culture of the Greco-Roman world.[43]

> What Jesus' teaching here represents is a challenge to the order-
> ing of things, persons, and patterns of exchange represented by
> "the Pharisees," in favor of a different ordering, one expressive
> of the new economy of salvation understood as "good news to
> the poor."[44]

As we can see, Jesus's words and actions define his mission as a mission that is aimed particularly at the poor and marginalized. When Jesus talks about and lives out the presence of God's Empire, it is through preferential care for the poor. This is not some metaphorical poor that only serves a literary (Johnson) or soteriological (Phillips) function. God's concern, expressed through Jesus's mission, is good news for the poor.

Parables of Samaritan, Banquet, and Unjust Judge

Four parables round out Luke's message of good news for the poor. Many of these also contain warnings against wealth. Here, however, we are exploring not so much what they say for the rich, but what they say for the poor.

In the Parable of the Good Samaritan (Luke 10:30–37), found only in Luke, a man is left injured and completely destitute when he is attacked along the road. While he is not helped by a priest or a Levite who are passing by, he does receive help from an unlikely source: a Samaritan, who ends up becoming the hero of the story. Jesus uses the Samaritan, who hands over two denarii for care of the traveler, as an object lesson for how to fulfill the commandment to love one's neighbor. When God is being followed, those who find themselves in trouble without the means to help themselves will receive help and care. Kim is clear to point out that the one being helped is in a circumstance of poverty and destitution.[45]

---

43. Coleman, "Lukan Lens," 123–24; Esler, *Community and Gospel*, 194–95; Hays, *Luke's Wealth Ethics*, 129–33; Kim, *Stewardship and Almsgiving*, 184–88; Moxnes, *Economy of the Kingdom*, 127–38; Phillips, *Reading Issues*, 146–47; Pilgrim, *Good News to the Poor*, 73–74, 139–41.

44. Barton, "Money Matters," 51.

45. Kim, *Stewardship and Almsgiving*, 177–79. Pilgrim notes that the situation is life-or-death: Pilgrim, *Good News to the Poor*, 141–43. Coleman, Hays, López Rodriguez, and Phillips see the need to respond to need with loving action. Coleman, "Lukan Lens," 174–78; Hays, *Luke's Wealth Ethics*, 117–19; López Rodríguez, *Liberating*

The Parable of the Great Supper is found also in Matthew, but only Luke's version makes it explicitly good news for the poor. After the well-to-do spurn the invitation to a dinner party, Matthew's Jesus has the host send out slaves to invite everyone they find to the feast, both good and bad. Luke's Jesus, on the other hand, has the host send slaves out with explicit instruction to invite the poor and marginalized (Luke 14:21–22; Matt 22:9–10). For Matthew, it is a political parable, but for Luke it is about class. Amanda Miller has an especially insightful reading, noting that this is not just about almsgiving to the poor, it is about a relationship between rich and poor. There is a difference between a soup kitchen that feeds only the poor and a banquet in which rich and poor eat side-by-side.[46]

Finally, the Parable of the Unjust Judge (Luke 18:1–8), found only in Luke, contributes to the message of good news for the poor through a negative example. The judge—who is clearly a villain—refuses to help a poor widow find justice. Only a godless person would deny help to the poor; this judge admits to himself that he is, in fact, godless: "I have no fear of God and no respect for anyone" (Luke 18:4 NRSV). And yet, even the unjust judge is eventually hounded into granting justice because he is afraid the widow may punch him and hurt his honor.[47] God, on the other hand, will willingly and eagerly give justice to the poor. It is part of God's character to act on behalf of the poor.[48]

These parables, along with the Parable of the Rich Man and Lazarus (16:19–31), which will be treated later in the chapter, show a consistent ethic in favor of the poor. God is on the side of the poor, as are all who seek to follow in God's way. God has a preferential option for the poor. Those who want to follow God should work to realize that preferential option in the world.

Mission, 66–77; Phillips, *Reading Issues*, 135–38.

46. Miller, "Bridge Work," 423–27. See also Coleman, "Lukan Lens," 125.

47. Robbins, "Luke 18:1–8," loc. 4832–35.

48. For an excellent treatment of this parable, see Dinkler, "Interior Monologues," 388–91.

Conclusion

While Karris claims that Luke's gospel is directed almost exclusively to the rich, we have found significant and important material in Luke that speaks to the poor. As Esler points out:

> One of the most remarkable aspects of Luke's vision of the Christian community is that, although it contained wealthy and influential members, the privileged places in it were reserved for the very dregs of Hellenistic society, especially the beggars and the physically disabled.[49]

López Rodriguez correctly points out that Luke's gospel is a gospel for the lost and the least:

> Luke is the gospel for the exiles of the earth who do not count for anything, for the needy and the marginalized of the world, for the defenseless and the ragged of society.[50]

As Coleman rightly insists, it is the poor who are consistently portrayed as the people who are able to hear Jesus's message and respond in faith.[51] Most of Luke's published interpreters do not count themselves among the poor and destitute. If we fail to see Luke's message for the poor, that does not mean it is not there. As Schottroff and Stegemann eloquently say, it is unjust "to deprive the poor of their gospel by interpreting it in such a way that it becomes our promise, a promise to the wealthy."[52] That is what has too often been done. But as we see, any account of economic themes in Luke must account for the profusion of good news for the poor.

Resistance to Wealth (B)

As we saw in chapter 2, the largest category of economic material in Luke is category B: resistance to wealth. Luke is packed with warnings against wealth and examples of solidarity with the poor. In the literary treatment of each of the other three categories in this and the following chapter, it is possible to touch on every or nearly every incidence in Luke. The category B resistance to wealth material, however, is simply overwhelming.

49. Esler, *Community and Gospel*, 187.
50. López Rodriguez, *Liberating Mission*, 40.
51. Coleman, "Lukan Lens," 97.
52. Schottroff and Stegemann, *Jesus and the Hope of the Poor*, v.

Treating it all in even a cursory manner would exceed the space available in this project. Here I will choose to give priority to four pericopes. The first two are the Parable of the Rich Fool and the Parable of the Rich Man and Lazarus. The second two are Jesus's encounters with the rich ruler and with Zacchaeus. In order to give them space, I will treat some of the remaining material briefly, and some of the material I will forgo altogether in this chapter.[53] These pericopes have all been mentioned in chapter 2, and some of them will be treated in depth when we turn to the application of Luke to the world of early Christianity and to the modern world. Here we will address several pericopes which are representative of the whole. Luke has a message of renunciation of wealth for the benefit of the poor.

Wealth Avoidance for Jesus and his Disciples

Jesus and his disciples set a clear example of wealth avoidance. Jesus seems to live a minimalist lifestyle, at least in terms of his own possessions. His disciples leave everything in order to follow him. When Jesus sends his disciples out, he sends them with nearly nothing. The behavior of Jesus and his disciples establishes a norm that is instructive for later disciples: wealth is to be avoided.

As explored earlier in the chapter, Jesus is born in poverty, and there are signs that he lives without significant possessions during his ministry. We see him engaging in ascetic practice while he is in the wilderness for

---

53. In the Sermon on the Plain, Jesus gives some radical advice. He preaches unlimited almsgiving: "Give to everyone who begs from you; and if anyone takes away your goods, do not ask for them again" (Luke 6:30 NRSV). He also seems to forbid the lending of money at interest (Luke 6:34–35). When Jesus teaches his disciples to pray, the only possession they should ask for is bread for the day (Luke 11:3). In a passage mentioned above, at a dinner party, Jesus warns against inviting to dinner those who can return the favor and instead suggests inviting only those who cannot (Luke 14:7–14). Perhaps the most important economic passage in Luke is one that we will explore in detail in chapter 7, the apothegm in which Jesus identifies wealth as a rival god (Luke 16:13). Service to the powers of wealth is idolatry. In an apocalyptic passage, Jesus warns that those who cling to possessions will lose their lives (Luke 17:28–33). When asked about taxes, Jesus says, "Give to Caesar what belongs to Caesar and to God what belongs to God" (Luke 20:25). Readers should not be fooled; all things belong to God. The parables of the Lost Sheep, Lost Coin, and Lost Son in chapter 15 and the Parable of the Pharisee and the Tax Collector will be omitted in this section. The Parable of the Great Supper (14:18–24) is addressed above. The Parable of the Unjust Steward (16:1–13) will be treated in chapter 4.

forty days; he refrains from food to the point of starvation and refuses the devil's suggestion to miraculously make bread for himself (Luke 4:2–3). More telling, though, is Jesus assertion of himself that "Foxes have holes, and the birds of the air have nests; but the Son of Man has nowhere to lay his head" (Luke 9:58 NRSV). Jesus self-identifies as homeless, and as we have seen throughout the gospel, he seems to rely almost exclusively on the hospitality of others.[54] He gives up home, family, and occupation in order to engage in ministry.

In line with his example, Jesus's early disciples give up their possessions in order to follow him. When Jesus calls Simon Peter, James, and John as his first disciples, Luke is clear that they leave everything (ἀφέντης πάντα) in order to follow him (Luke 5:11). In both Mark and Matthew, they leave their boats and father, but not everything (Mark 1:20; Matt 4:22). Again, when Jesus calls a tax collector (either Levi or Matthew) in Mark and Matthew he simply gets up from the table to follow Jesus (Mark 2:14; Matt 9:9). Luke is explicit: "He got up, *left everything*, and followed him" (Luke 5:28 NRSV; emphasis added).[55] When Pharisees and scribes complain that Jesus is consorting with a tax collector like Levi, Jesus explicitly identifies him as a sinner, presumably because of his tax collecting or wealth (Luke 5:32). López Rodriguez sees Jesus reaching across lines of exclusion to welcome a person marginalized by society, a tax-collector hated by decent Jews, but he also recognizes that in order to follow Jesus, Levi must give up his fortune and his exploitative tax-collecting practices.[56]

Most interpreters acknowledge that Luke redacts here to make the disciples' renunciation more complete.[57] In fact, this is enough for Phillips to question his earlier observation that renunciation is not required of disciples.[58] The question becomes, though, whether the example of these four disciples is one that should be followed by Jesus's later disciples.[59] Kim argues that there are two kinds of disciples, itinerant disciples and sedentary disciples, and only the few itinerant disciples are called to

54. Pilgrim, *Good News to the Poor*, 97; Gillman, *Possessions and the Life of Faith*, 65.

55. Coleman, "Lukan Lens," 105.

56. López Rodriguez, *Liberating Mission*, 44–58.

57. For example, Esler, *Community and Gospel*, 167; Gillman, *Possessions and the Life of Faith*, 68; Hays, *Luke's Wealth Ethics*, 82.

58. Phillips, *Reading Issues*, 101–2.

59. Pilgrim, *Good News to the Poor*, 87–89.

leave all.[60] Phillips argues that since Levi is seen throwing a banquet for Jesus after his supposed renunciation, the "everything" that these four disciples leave must be their occupations.[61] However many scholars, including Coleman agree with me in insisting that the renunciation of these disciples is something worth imitating, something that is applicable to all disciples.[62]

Not only do Jesus's disciples give up possessions when they come to him, they also refrain from possessions when he sends them out. Jesus sends the twelve out to extend his work, saying, "Take nothing for your journey, no staff, nor bag, nor bread, nor money—not even an extra tunic" (Luke 9:3 NRSV). This is stricter than Mark's parallel, in which the disciples are instructed to bring both a staff and sandals (Mark 6:8–9). Luke denies them a staff and avoids telling them to bring anything. Luke also duplicates this story one chapter later, with Jesus now sending seventy disciples, telling them, "Carry no purse, no bag, no sandals" (Luke 10:4 NRSV). Luke's Jesus makes it clear that this instruction is not only for the twelve, it is a model for the larger movement.

With regard to these pericopes, there are few interpreters who think they should be normative. Johnson, Kim, Phillips, Hays, Levine, and Witherington all suggest these instructions are limited only to the eighty-two persons cited in the story.[63]

> The extreme minimalism that Jesus endorses for his disciples in Luke 9 and 10 is depicted as an exception to the rule; these passages do not illustrate how all disciples are to give πάντα. . . . Only certain disciples, at two discrete points in the ministry of Jesus, express their renunciation of πάντα (cf. 14.33) in this way.

60. Kim, *Stewardship and Almsgiving*, 101. So too, Levine and Witherington, *Gospel of Luke*, 254. Gerd Theissen also distinguishes between two groups. The characteristic group within the Jesus Movement is made up of "wandering charismatics" who give up possessions and rely on the provision of others as they travel to spread the gospel. These are the most important members of the movement, even long after Jesus's death. The second group, "local sympathizers," support the work of the wandering charismatics. For Theissen, unlike for Kim, the call to renunciation is intended for all, but it is imperfectly followed. Theissen, *Sociology of Early Palestinian Christianity*, 8–23.

61. Phillips, *Reading Issues*, 104. Others suggesting these disciples are not meant to be imitated include Schottroff and Stegemann, *Jesus and the Hope of the Poor*, 81.

62. Coleman, "Lukan Lens," 101–5. Others include Alexander, *Your Money or Your Life*, 59; Hays, *Luke's Wealth Ethics*, 82; Ringe, *Luke*, 78.

63. Johnson, *Luke*, 148; Kim, *Stewardship and Almsgiving*, 101–3; Phillips, *Reading Issues*, 125–31; Hays, *Luke's Wealth Ethics*, 88–93; Levine and Witherington, *Gospel of Luke*, 254–77.

> Thus we ought to resist assertions that Luke considers exhaustive divestiture to characterize Jesus' entire public ministry.[64]

Many suggest that the divestiture here is not really about voluntary poverty, but about vulnerability and complete reliance on God.[65] Others suggest that this minimalist missionary work represented the typical practice of the early church.[66] Pilgrim, Bovon, Gillman, and Fitzmyer all suggest that this is behavior that is meant to be imitated by later Christians.[67] In general, I agree with Fitzmyer that there is no reason to think of these instructions as being separate from the overall economic message of Luke. Luke has an anti-wealth agenda, and these instructions are part of it.

Later, when Jesus describes the costs of being his disciple, Luke's version is both longer and stronger than the Matthean parallel. Matthew's Jesus simply says that if someone loves their family more than they love Jesus, they are not worthy of Jesus (Matt 10:37). Luke's Jesus is far harsher, saying, "Whoever comes to me and does not hate father and mother, wife and children, brothers and sisters, yes, and even life itself, cannot be my disciple" (Luke 14:26 NRSV). It is not just about being worthy of Jesus; no one can even be a disciple if they hold on to other relationships. Luke's Jesus goes on to tell two stories about how one must count the cost before attempting a new project (Luke 14:27–33). Potential disciples had better make sure they can pay the price before they sign on with Jesus. And what is the price? "None of you can become my disciple if you do not give up all your possessions" (Luke 14:33 NRSV). There is no parallel in Mark or Matthew to this jaw-droppingly absolute pronouncement.

As we have come to expect, Phillips finds a literal reading too implausible to accept:

> Although this saying may be read as a demand for "absolute poverty," the internal frame of reference makes that reading extremely implausible for two reasons. On the one hand, the two parallel sayings about "hating" one's family and self (v. 26) and about bearing one's cross (v. 27) are clearly not literal directives.

---

64. Hays, *Luke's Wealth Ethics*, 93. Compare to Brian Capper, who argues that this is not the norm, but that it is part of a virtuoso religion that creates a visible utopia that others can learn from. Capper, "Jesus," 71–72.

65. Johnson, *Luke*, 148; González, *Luke*, 112; Hays, *Luke's Wealth Ethics*, 88–93; Lieu, *Gospel of Luke*, 69.

66. Bovon, *Luke 1*, 345; Ringe, *Luke*, 129.

67. Pilgrim, *Good News to the Poor*, 96–98; Bovon, *Luke 1*, 345; Gillman, *Possessions and the Life of Faith*, 73; Fitzmyer, *Luke I–IX*, 754.

> Renouncing one's possessions does not necessarily result in literal poverty any more than hating one's family necessarily results in abandoned children or than bearing one's cross necessarily results in literal crucifixion.[68]

Seccombe suggests that these things might occasionally be required of disciples, but only in very extreme circumstances. One must be prepared to die; one must be prepared to leave family; one must be prepared to give up possessions.[69] In contrast, Coleman, Pilgrim, Schottroff, and Stegemann emphasize the radicalness of Jesus's demand, a demand directed not only to a few, but to all disciples. They also note that Luke's construction is meant to emphasize the leaving of possessions. Hating family is hard, expecting martyrdom is hard, but giving up all possessions is the most unimaginably difficult of all.[70]

Another set of instructions to disciples are paralleled in Mark and Matthew (Mark 10:42–45; Matt 20:25–2; Luke 22:25–28). Jesus contrasts the authoritarian leadership style of Gentiles with the servant-leadership that he demands of his followers. Only in Luke's version is it claimed that Gentile leaders like to be called benefactors. This pericope will be further explicated in chapter 5.

Like Jesus, his early disciples give up possessions and adopt an itinerant lifestyle. This renunciation is more explicit in Luke than it is in Mark and Matthew. Their mode of life suggests that wealth is either not needed or to be avoided.

Curses

The Gospel of Luke also contains several curses against wealth and the wealthy. The Magnificat, which we noted above shows God's favor for the poor, also shows God's opposition to the rich. God "has brought down the powerful from their thrones, and lifted up the lowly; he has filled the hungry with good things, and sent the rich away empty" (Luke 1:52–53 NRSV).[71]

---

68. Phillips, *Reading Issues*, 149.

69. Seccombe, *Possessions and the Poor*, 115–16.

70. Coleman, "Lukan Lens," 128; Pilgrim, *Good News to the Poor*, 90–92; Schottroff and Stegemann, *Jesus and the Hope of the Poor*, 82–83.

71. Coleman, "Lukan Lens," 60.

Significantly, Luke contains curses which parallel the beatitudes in the Sermon on the Plain. "Damn you rich! You already have your consolation. Damn you who are well-fed now! You will know hunger" (Luke 6:24–25 SV).[72] It is part of the standard theme of reversal, but it is also an acknowledgement of God's disdain for wealth. Seccombe denies both these claims, saying the passage is not economic and it implies no reversal.[73] Phillips claims that because this is in the beatitudes and woes genre that it must be soteriological rather than economic.[74] Kim, Coleman, and De La Torre, though, see this as a key part of Luke's economic message. Kim writes:

> In consequence, we could suggest that 6.24–26 does not mean that the rich are cursed only owing to their wealth, and the poor are blessed only owing to their poverty, but rather indicates a possibility which may be actualized in practice. But such a possibility, in being confirmed in the ensuing material, turns out to be an actual fact. Therefore this passage may be regarded as a suggestive prophecy at the outset of the Gospel, and at the same time can be presented as an actual fact in terms of the Gospel as a whole. Here we find once again Luke's literary artifice seen by his arranging material in a way suitable for his aim. That is to say, by placing one of his theme passages, 6.24–26, at the head of the Gospel in the form of a prophetic announcement, and then confirming it gradually in the ensuing material, Luke effectively provides his readers with his intended theme.[75]

Three times Jesus curses Pharisees and scribes for their greed. In a passage paralleled in Matthew, Jesus excoriates Pharisees for being filled with greed despite the fact that they make tithes of herbs (Luke 11:39–46; Matt 23:4, 6–7, 23, 25–28). A little later, in L material, when Jesus criticizes the Pharisees, the narrator makes it explicit that it is because the Pharisees "were lovers of money" (Luke 16:14 NRSV). Finally, Luke echoes Mark's criticism of the scribes because they "devour widows'

---

72. The SV better captures the way a curse would be expressed in contemporary language. It is hard to imagine a real person saying "Woe to you rich!"

73. Seccombe, *Possessions and the Poor*, 95.

74. Phillips, *Reading Issues*, 109.

75. Kim, *Stewardship and Almsgiving*, 204–5. See also Gillman, *Possessions and the Life of Faith*, 54–55; Coleman, "Lukan Lens," 112; De La Torre, *Politics of Jesús*, loc. 2221–26.

houses" (Luke 20:47 NRSV). Many of Jesus's chief antagonists are portrayed as opposing Jesus because they are greedy.[76]

One of the rare pericopes attested in all four gospels is the so-called Cleansing of the Temple. Luke's version is the shortest of the four, and it is scrubbed of any details that distract from the economic import of the action: "Then he entered the temple and began to drive out those who were selling things there; and he said, 'It is written, "My house shall be a house of prayer"; but you have made it a den of robbers'" (Luke 19:45–46 NRSV). There are no animals, no tables, no whip of cords. There is only selling, which is equated with robbery.[77]

These passages show a clear antagonism against wealth in Luke's gospel. Wealth is dangerous, it is cursed, it leads to ruin. This theme will be developed further in the Parable of the Rich Man and Lazarus below.

Parables

Jesus tells many parables that warn against wealth. There are so many that space prevents treating all of them in the detail that they deserve. As mentioned above, only two will be addressed here. Both the Parable of the Rich Fool and the Parable of the Rich Man and Lazarus show the peril of putting one's trust in wealth.

The Rich Fool, Anxiety, and Treasures (12:15–34)

An extended section of teaching and parable begins with Jesus's words, found only in Luke, "Take care! Be on your guard against all kinds of greed; for one's life does not consist in the abundance of possessions." (Luke 12:15 NRSV).[78] It is hard to imagine a clearer or more succinct warning against wealth than this. Seccombe describes it as "the strongest warning formula in Luke-Acts."[79] The value of life should not be mea-

76. Johnson would argue that the order here is reversed. They are portrayed as greedy because they oppose Jesus. Johnson, *Literary Function*, 109–10.

77. Surprisingly, Phillips acknowledges that this event is about actual economic themes. The temple establishment represents greed, and Jesus takes a stand against greed. Phillips, *Reading Issues*, 176–77.

78. They come in response to a request for Jesus to settle an inheritance dispute.

79. Seccombe, *Possessions and the Poor*, 139.

sured by the splendor given to it through possessions.[80] While Seccombe argues that the risk is of being distracted away from God's Word, Pilgrim sees a more general warning against wealth.[81]

Jesus next tells the Parable of the Rich Fool (Luke 12:16–21), again, found only in Luke.[82] After a particularly good harvest, a rich man decides he will tear down his current barns and build new, bigger ones to accommodate his surplus grain. Jesus gives us the internal dialogue, "I will say to my soul, 'Soul, you have ample goods laid up for many years; relax, eat, drink, be merry'" (Luke 12:19 NRSV). God appears in the parable to say, "You fool! This very night your life is being demanded of you" (Luke 12:20 NRSV), and asks the rich man who will own his possessions once he is dead. Finally comes Jesus's saying: "So it is with those who store up treasures for themselves but are not rich toward God" (Luke 12:21 NRSV).

Harkening back to verse 15, Phillips argues that this parable is a warning against the sense of security that one gets from possessions, not against the having and acquisition of possessions *per se*.

> The rich fool is not condemned for possessing, or even for amassing, wealth but rather for his foolish assumption that his wealth could secure a future for him, that the treasure which he had stored up could—in the most meaningful sense—maintain his life.[83]

Phillips thus argues that this is not a warning against wealth at all; it is simply a plea to trust in God. However, James Metzger suggests that a reading such as Phillips's is only possible if one takes the parable out of its context in Luke:

> It is primarily the parable's context that encourages readers to confirm the suggestion of overconsumption and hedonism in his final self-exhortation (v. 19) and view him both as an example of πλεονεξία [greediness, avarice] and as "one who treasures-up for himself" (v. 21) Moreover, if readers chose in v. 15 to ascribe not only greed but a rapacious and aggressive desire to

---

80. Seccombe, *Possessions and the Poor*, 141.

81. Pilgrim, *Good News to the Poor*, 109–10. Also Gillman, *Possessions and the Life of Faith*, 74.

82. There is a similar parable in the Gospel of Thomas 63. Pilgrim, *Good News to the Poor*, 109. Esler also notes similarities to 1 Enoch 97:8–10. Esler, *Community and Gospel*, 189–90.

83. Phillips, *Reading Issues*, 141. See also, Johnson, *Luke*, 201.

advance one's interest at the expense of others to πλεονεξία, the landowner may very well be associated with a class of ruthless elite who show no concern whatsoever for the poor and disen-franchised. Jesus' parable would then be an instance of dramatic irony in which readers, already set against the "rich" (see 1:53; 6:24), view the landowner as a hopelessly tragic character from the outset (v. 16), predictably formulating a plan that stands in direct opposition to Jesus' mission to the poor.[84]

This parable is actually about greed and possessions. As Coleman suggests, this parable insists that "right response to Jesus includes an inescapable reordering of economic priorities and practices."[85] Possessions are not just a cipher for lack of faith.[86]

That might not be clear if we were given the following sayings on anxiety on their own (Luke 12:22–32). "Do not worry about your life, what you will eat, or about your body, what you will wear" (Luke 12:22 NRSV). For the most part, Luke is very close to the Matthean parallel (Matt 6:25–34). The hearers are reminded that the birds do not work for their food, the lilies do not work for their beautiful clothing, but God still provides. However, Matthew and Luke give different morals to the lesson. Matthew closes by emphasizing freedom from anxiety: "Do not worry about tomorrow, for tomorrow will bring worries of its own. Today's trouble is enough for today" (Matt 6:34 NRSV). Luke deflects that message with "Do not be afraid, little flock, for it is your Father's good pleasure to give you the kingdom," before rolling immediately into more explicitly economic material: "Sell your possessions, and give alms. Make purses for yourselves that do not wear out, an unfailing treasure in heaven, where no thief comes near and no moth destroys. For where your treasure is, there your heart will be also" (Luke 12:32–34 NRSV). Matthew can talk about anxiety and faith, but Luke carefully crafts the same Q material to make sure we know that this really is about posses-sions.[87] It really is about renunciation and almsgiving. It is the freedom from anxiety that leads to dispossession and almsgiving.

---

84. Metzger, *Consumption and Wealth*, 83–84.

85. Coleman, "Lukan Lens," 121.

86. As in Johnson, *Literary Function*. Seccombe argues that this is about greed, but that there is no condemnation for acquiring. Seccombe, *Possessions and the Poor*, 144–45.

87. Kim acknowledges this, as well. Kim, *Stewardship and Almsgiving*, 182–83.

Both Seccombe and Phillips correctly note this while still trying to downplay the call to renunciation. Seccombe argues that the command to sell and give cannot possibly be a command because, if it were, it could only cause anxiety:

> These folk are already in the path of discipleship, and are being encouraged to enter more fully into the freedom of complete trust in God and attachment to his Kingdom. It would be strange if Luke (or Jesus) had sought to free disciples from anxiety, only, immediately, to lay upon them a demand which could not but have generated in them the utmost anxiety.[88]

Phillips correctly states, "Only the person who is freed from the mistaken notion that security may be obtained via material possessions is able to practice generosity, to sell possessions and give alms."[89] He then immediately goes on to argue that there cannot be a command here, unless it is only a command about understanding "the relative value of material possessions and about securing treasures in heaven."[90] Seccombe and Phillips must summon all of their powers to try to side-step this most clear of commands. It is a feat even Luke Timothy Johnson—who generally ignores the non-symbolic meaning of Luke's economic material—cannot manage:

> The point is not simply that they should "not worry" about food and clothing, but that they should *far more radically* "sell their possessions. Give alms." . . . The teaching to the disciples on lack of fear before death and this teaching on a lack of anxiety about possessions are all of a piece, and *profoundly challenging.*[91]

The Parable of the Rich Fool is part of a full chapter of economic material that Luke artfully crafts so as to emphasize its economic themes. It contains some of the clearest calls to renunciation and warning against wealth in the gospel. These themes continue in another parable—the Parable of the Faithful Servants—which will be treated in chapter 4.

---

88. Seccombe, *Possessions and the Poor*, 154.

89. Phillips, *Reading Issues*, 143.

90. Phillips, *Reading Issues*, 144.

91. Johnson, *Luke*, 202; emphasis added.

The Rich Man and Lazarus (16:19–31)

There is perhaps no parable that lays out the twin economic themes of Luke—good news for the poor and resistance to wealth—as starkly as the Parable of the Rich Man and Lazarus (Luke 16:19–31), a parable attested only in Luke. It comes at the end of a chapter stuffed full of economic material, including the Parable of the Unjust Steward (treated in chapter 4) and one of the gospel's key apothegms: "No household slave is able to slave for two masters . . . you cannot serve God and Mammon" (Luke 16:13; my translation).

The parable juxtaposes an extremely rich man, finely dressed, who feasts extravagantly every day with a poor man, hungry, covered with sores, plagued by dogs, who lives outside the rich man's gate. Strangely for a poor person, and for a parabolic character, the poor man is named: Lazarus, my God helps.[92] When both characters die, they find their conditions reversed in the afterlife, with Lazarus comforted in heaven and the rich man tortured in Hades. The rich man engages in a dialogue with Abraham regarding his condition and is told that the condition is only fair on account of what the two men experienced in life. Abraham also says that the message of the law and prophets is sufficient warning for anyone to understand this consequence.

But why is Lazarus elevated? Why is the rich man punished? Some see a pure eschatological reversal. The rich man goes to Hades because of his wealth; Lazarus goes to heaven because of his poverty. So says Metzger:

> Even when almsgiving is practiced widely and with regularity, it cannot really be received by the poor as good news (4:18), for it offers only a mirage of resource redistribution and fails to provide any lasting, structural changes. Almsgiving, in effect, does not challenge the existing social order: the rich retain their wealth, power, and privilege while the poor struggle to subsist. For the rich man, then, the first (and most important) step to meriting entrance into Abraham's chamber would have been disposal of excess resources so that he could no longer be called "rich" (v. 19). . . . Neither Jesus nor Abraham cares how the rich man acquired or sustained his wealth. The mere fact that he possessed excess and used it to fund a life of decadence and overconsumption accounts for his present locale opposite

92. De La Torre, *Politics of Jesús*, loc. 1976–77. While the rich man is not given a name in this parable, in some readings he acquires the name "Dives," simply the latin for "rich one."

Abraham. This parable therefore confirms and reinforces Jesus' final statement in his nimshalim on the preceding parable: personal wealth, however it may be obtained or sustained, is totally incompatible with service to God (16:13).[93]

It has nothing to do with care for Lazarus. It is simply the rich man's wealth that condemns him.

Alternatively, some say that the rich man is not condemned for his wealth but for his inattention to Lazarus. Seccombe and Phillips argue in this vein.

> Once again we have failed to find poverty ideal, renunciation ethic or reversal doctrine. Nevertheless we are clearly dealing with an extremely far-reaching demand for charity to the needy which could have afforded little comfort to any of Luke's well-off readers. Luke is saying in no uncertain terms that the Kingdom is forever closed to those who close their hearts against the needy.[94]

For Phillips, it is particularly important that Lazarus is in proximity to the rich man. It is not about a general ethic of charity. What condemns the rich man is that he was in the presence of clear suffering and failed to respond to it.[95] This is a key point for Phillip's overall reading of economic issues in Luke.

The best readings do not insist on making a false choice between the two; the rich man can be guilty both of holding on to wealth and of not caring for Lazarus. Coleman, Hays, Kim, and Pilgrim all carry some version of this argument.[96] It would not be enough for the rich man to throw his money in a ditch and become poor. Neither would the rich man have escaped judgment if he had never encountered Lazarus or if he had given a paltry handout to Lazarus and continued to live in opulence. The two themes are connected. There is both good news for the poor and resistance to wealth. As Coleman put it, "Luke continues to insist that right response to Jesus and his message always involves the renunciation of personal benefit from wealth for the sake of the poor."[97] The Parable of

93. Metzger, *Consumption and Wealth*, 156.

94. Seccombe, *Possessions and the Poor*, 180–81.

95. Phillips, *Reading Issues*, 155–60.

96. Coleman, "Lukan Lens," 133–38; Hays, *Luke's Wealth Ethics*, 153–58; Kim, *Stewardship and Almsgiving*, 188–91; Pilgrim, *Good News to the Poor*, 59–60, 113–19. See also De La Torre, *Reading the Bible*, 79; Levine and Witherington, *Gospel of Luke*, 454–55.

97. Coleman, "Lukan Lens," 138.

the Rich Man and Lazarus is an excellent example of the interdependence and fusion of Luke's twin themes of liberation.

These two parables—the Parable of the Rich Fool and the Parable of the Rich Man and Lazarus—are among the strongest witnesses to Luke's theme of resistance to wealth. They make it clear that wealth is a danger to followers of Jesus. But they also tie the theme of resistance to wealth together with the complementary theme of good news for the poor. The two are woven together. The strategy of making a clear distinction between themes of renunciation and themes of almsgiving is proved absurd by these parables which present the two as a unity. It is a unity we will also see evidenced in two momentous meetings of Jesus with rich men.

Two Encounters

Much interpretation of wealth and poverty in Luke rests on just two pericopes: Jesus's encounter with the rich ruler (Luke 18:18–30) and Jesus's later encounter with another rich man: Zacchaeus (Luke 19:8–10). If we are to know what Jesus requires of wealthy persons, the answer will be found in these two encounters. In fact, nearly every interpreter pairs these two pericopes in order to answer precisely that question. These are two rich men who are called by Jesus. The second of those calls is successful; the first is not. So, what is the difference between the two?

The Rich Ruler (Luke 18:18–30)

The story is present in all three synoptic gospels (see Mark 10:17–31, Matt 19:16–30). A rich man asks Jesus how he can inherit eternal life. Jesus answers with several commandments from the Decalogue. The man replies that he keeps all of those commandments. Jesus responds, "You lack one thing; go, sell what you own, and give the money to the poor, and you will have treasure in heaven; then come, follow me" (Mark 10:21 NRSV). The rich man is unable to follow Jesus's instruction, and Jesus explains, "How hard it is for those who have wealth to enter the kingdom of God! It is easier for a camel to go through the eye of a needle than for someone who is rich to enter the kingdom of God" (Mark 10:24–25 NRSV). The hearers ask, "Then who can be saved?" and Jesus replies, "For mortals it is impossible, but not for God; for God all things are possible" (Mark 10:27 NRSV). Peter points out that he and his companions have left everything to follow Jesus, and Jesus promises blessings for anyone who has left possession or family to follow him.

Sharon Ringe suggests "the versions of the story in Matthew and Luke differ only in minor details from the original in Mark" and treats the three together.[98] While it is true that all three contain the same basic message, the minor changes in Luke's version are actually quite important, as Schottroff and Stegemann point out.[99] They reframe and intensify the message. Luke introduces Jesus's interlocutor not as a man, as does Mark, nor as a young man, as does Matthew, but as a ruler (ἄρχων). And while Mark and Matthew later describe the man as having many possessions (ἔχων κτήματα πολλά), Luke makes exorbitant wealth a part of the man's character; he *is* extremely rich (ἦν γὰρ πλούσιος σφόδρα). Luke is careful to characterize him as high-ranking and wealthy; these attributes are part of his identity.[100]

Second, Mark has the man leave the scene in sorrow once he realizes the cost of following Jesus; in Luke the rich ruler becomes sad, but he does not exit. He is there to listen as Jesus continues to expound on how difficult it is for rich people to enter God's Empire. Jesus speaks to the ruler when he says, "How hard it is for those who have wealth to enter the kingdom of God!"[101] Furthermore, Luke does not allow the disciples to express surprise at these words, as Mark does. The reason is simple. At this point in Luke's narrative, it is impossible that the disciples would be surprised by this message:

> The fact is that it makes complete sense for Luke to have Jesus address the rich man and to leave the disciples out of it. Why? Because in Luke's Gospel it is no longer possible for the disciples of Jesus to wonder that the wealthy should have difficulty entering the *basileia* or to be startled that such an entrance seems obviously impossible.[102]

Hays makes the case quite succinctly:

98. Ringe, *Jesus*, 60.

99. Schottroff and Stegemann, *Jesus and the Hope of the Poor*, 74.

100. Luke "is explicitly concerned to provide a 'sociological' characterization of this man as a high-ranking and wealthy individual." Schottroff and Stegemann, *Jesus and the Hope of the Poor*, 74–75. See also Kim, *Stewardship and Almsgiving*, 191–92.

101. Kim, *Stewardship and Almsgiving*, 192.

102. Schottroff and Stegemann, *Jesus and the Hope of the Poor*, 75.

By chapter 18, Luke has erected ethical scaffolding sufficient for
providing a context within which to understand the command
of 18.22. Luke has repeatedly demanded downward mobility
(13.30; 14.12–24; 18.14, 17). He has established renunciation of
all as a fundamental requirement of discipleship (14.33), and
starkly dichotomized between service of God and Mammon
(16.13). He instructed Jesus' followers "sell your possessions and
give alms" (12.33); the only substantial difference between that
command and the one given to the Rich Ruler is the insertion
of the word "all" (cf. 14.33). Further, when one appreciates what
a spiritual wonder-drug almsgiving can be, why would Jesus
not prescribe it so vigorously? After all, almsgiving ameliorates
sin and uncleanliness (11.37–44), imitates the generosity of
God (6.35–36), and even garners eschatological reward (12.34;
16.1–13; 17.31–33). Moreover, at this point in the development
of the narrative, it is clear that Jesus could hardly ask the rich
man to do less than to sell his riches and give to the poor.[103]

Put simply, Jesus's command to the Rich Ruler is consistent with the rest
of Luke's wealth ethic. It is stark, but it should not be surprising.

But for all those who want to soften Luke's wealth ethic, want to
minimize the call to renunciation, it is this pericope where they must
make their stand. And the domestication of Luke begins with a question:

But to whom is this demand for the total abandonment of possessions directed? The rich ruler is not being called into the
circle of the Twelve. Is he then being called into a wider circle of
disciples, who must also sell all their possessions to follow Jesus?
If so, is this demand true for all followers of Jesus? Or is this only
an isolated case, in that only for this rich man was it necessary
to break totally with his possessions, his trusted treasure, to gain
the kingdom?[104]

As we know, Kim answers this question and effects a side-step by dis-
tinguishing between two different types of disciples: sedentary disciples
who retain all or most of their possessions, and itinerant disciples who

---

103. Hays, *Luke's Wealth Ethics*, 172. See also Coleman, "Lukan Lens," 141–42. She
largely avoids the controversy of this passage, simply taking for granted that the call
for the rich man to leave all and follow Jesus is consistent with the ethic of the rest of
the gospel.

104. Pilgrim, *Good News to the Poor*, 89. Pilgrim summarizes the question; it is not
his own, nor does he stand against a radical wealth ethic.

make a more radical change.[105] We will return to this argument when we bring the story of Zacchaeus into the conversation.

Seccombe distances himself from the radicality of Jesus's command by consigning it to irrelevance of being "an extreme situation."[106] Very rarely, the cost of discipleship might be leaving family, or possessions, or even one's life. But these instances are very rare, indeed, so rare that they seem to bare no import whatsoever for an ongoing Christian ethic.

> We may conclude that neither Luke 14,25–35 nor 18,18–30 contains any idealization of poverty, nor general demand for renunciation of possessions. . . . Neither of these passages yields anything specific about the Christian's ongoing use of possessions.[107]

Seccombe does acknowledge that "wealth is seen as a terrible obstacle to embracing the Kingdom," but his framing of this story suggests that Christians can only learn anything from it if they are one of the few people who finds themself in the "extreme situation" of having possessions present a distraction to the Kingdom. Hays's warning is apt: "Preventing 18.22 from compelling divestiture for all readers of Luke does not permit one to marginalize it to mythical ignominy."[108] The fact that few—or even none—will be able to meet the ideal does not mean that it has nothing to teach. Seccombe places this difficult text in a locked, opaque box labeled "open only in extreme situations." No. We need this story and its radical demands, though perhaps with the warning "handle with care."

Phillips begins his attack against radicality with a very astute observation. He notes that when Jesus lists the ethical commandments at the beginning of this story, he cleverly leaves out the tenth commandment, the commandment against greed.[109] Phillips is absolutely right when he says that the rich ruler's weakness is his inability to follow the tenth commandment. Phillips's mistake is to think that this in any way blunts the power of Jesus's command or that it somehow limits the command to this person and few others.

Phillips's conclusion follows from the question he asks, namely:

---

105. Kim, *Stewardship and Almsgiving*. So also Levine and Witherington, *Gospel of Luke*, 498.

106. Seccombe, *Possessions and the Poor*, 133.

107. Seccombe, *Possessions and the Poor*, 134.

108. Hays, *Luke's Wealth Ethics*, 173.

109. Phillips, *Reading Issues*, 165.

How much should the receptive reader of the third gospel give away? How much may one possess without being guilty of greed and covetousness? On what scale is the receptive reader to be generous?[110]

By focusing on the "how much" question, Phillips contrives to explain away this encounter altogether. "No other character in the third gospel sells everything and gives the proceeds to the poor," Phillips claims, despite what Hays describes above. By obsessing myopically on the *all*, he attempts to skirt the issue altogether. "This ruler is the only person who is directed to sell everything and this directive is, therefore, uncharacteristic of the third gospel!"[111] Nevermind that the disciples have already given up all in order to follow Jesus (Luke 5:11, 28).[112] And yet, on account of this *all*, Phillips "is reluctant to infer a normative ethic from this negative example."[113] Phillips presents us with a bit of a catch-22: if the command is not to renounce *all*, then it is probably a command to simple almsgiving rather than renunciation; but if the command is to renounce *all*, then it is too unrealistic to be taken seriously. Hays again provides an antidote:

> Recalling the manner in which Levi, Peter, James and John were said to have left πάντα, one need not think that Jesus categorically commands the Ruler to sell each solitary item he owned; it would likely have been acceptable if he kept a house from which to extend hospitality to Jesus and the disciples (as did Levi), and for him to bring along some basic accoutrements for the trip. *Clearly this divestiture is still profound.* The fact that it does not entail the extraction of each solitary possession *does not undercut the radical character of the imperative to renounce all*. Rather, it pays closer attention to how Luke envisions renunciation.[114]

One can try to defang Luke's message either by arguing that it calls for something less than radical action or by arguing that its demand is so radical that it cannot be intended to be followed. Phillips somehow manages to do both, and in doing so he reveals that he simply cannot countenance a radical message, no matter how it is made.

---

110. Phillips, *Reading Issues*, 161.

111. Phillips, *Reading Issues*, 163. The exclamation is Phillips's.

112. Schottroff and Stegemann, *Jesus and the Hope of the Poor*, 75.

113. Phillips, *Reading Issues*, 163.

114. Hays, *Luke's Wealth Ethics*, 174; emphasis added.

Both Hays and Phillips wrestle with what *all* possessions might mean. It is a question we will continue to consider. What is not meant is that every Christian must give up every single thing so that they each die naked in a ditch of dehydration three days after they accept Jesus. In fact, Luke does not seem to fetishize poverty. As we have seen in the first half of this chapter, God works to lift up the poor, not to revel in their suffering. As Stegemann notes, "Luke never commends poverty itself as an exemplary state (for its independence, for example); he commends only the disciples who have voluntarily become poor in their following Jesus."[115] It is important to remember that the ruler is not asked to throw away his possessions, he is asked to give the proceeds to the poor. Metzger writes:

> Jesus' primary rationale for issuing the requirement is neither to teach this man how to rely on God, to expose his love for worldly, material things, nor to elicit his unwavering loyalty? Rather, in keeping with his programmatic sermon in Nazareth at the inception of his ministry (4:18–19), Jesus is seeking first an equitable redistribution of essential resources for the benefit of the poor (v. 22). The rich ruler may participate in God's Kingdom—indeed, with God's assistance some wealthy persons already are (vv. 24, 27)!—but only if he first ceases to be rich.[116]

We will return to this pericope in chapter 5 in order to put it in the context of early Christianity. For now, it is enough to note that Luke makes this shared story a key part of the gospel's radical economic ethic, a radical ethic that Luke explicates further in this pericope's twin, the story of Zacchaeus, to which we now turn.

Zacchaeus (19:1–10)

Nearly everyone pairs the story of the Rich Ruler with the story of Zacchaeus, the rich (πλούσιος) tax farmer (ἀρχιτελώνης). And nearly everyone holds up Zacchaeus as a model for what wealthy Jesus-followers should do with possessions. The questions is how we characterize what Jesus does. Put another way, if the response of the rich ruler represents a failure and the response of Zacchaeus represents a success, what is the difference between the two? What changes from the one story to the other? Is it Jesus's demands, or is it the response of the rich man?

115. Stegemann, *The Gospel and the Poor*, 50.
116. Metzger, *Consumption and Wealth*, 169–70.

Phillips identifies a number of differences between the two peri-copes, and also provides us a succinct introduction to Zacchaeus's story:

> In the earlier story of the rich ruler (18:18–30), Jesus' dialogue partner is a synagogue leader who stands at the center of Jew-ish life. In this story, Jesus' dialogue partner, Zacchaeus, is a toll collector who stands outside of the mainstream of Jewish life. Whereas the onlookers in the previous story are amazed when the ruler is shown to be unrighteous (18:23–25), the crowds assume that Zacchaeus is a sinner (19:7). In the earlier story, Jesus calls the ruler to follow him (18:22), while in this story he asks Zacchaeus to serve as his host (19:5). Whereas the ruler's encounter with Jesus produces sadness (18:23), Zacchaeus's en-counter with Jesus produces joy (19:6).[117]

But Phillips finds no difference in these two stories quite as meaningful as the difference in Jesus and his demands.

> For those interested in issues of wealth and poverty, however, the most important difference between the stories is the amount of their generosity to the poor. The ruler was *commanded* by Jesus to sell *everything* and to give the proceeds to the poor (18:22), while Zacchaeus is praised by Jesus when he *voluntarily* gives *half* of his possessions to the poor.[118]

It is Jesus who has changed. With the rich ruler he demanded full re-nunciation, but with Zacchaeus, he is happy to praise the voluntary dis-possession of half of his wealth.[119] This allows Phillips to dismiss Jesus's previous command to the rich ruler as some kind of aberration. If Jesus does not require complete renunciation from Zacchaeus, then there must have been something unique about the rich ruler, something that pre-vents Jesus's command to him from being universal.

---

117. Phillips, *Reading Issues*, 169–70.

118. Phillips, *Reading Issues*, 170.

119. The use of present tense verbs in v. 8 is hotly debated. "Ἰδοὺ τὰ ἡμίσιά μου τῶν ὑπαρχόντων, κύριε, τοῖς πτωχοῖς δίδωμι, καὶ εἴ τιωός τι ἐσυκοφάντησα ἀποδίδωμι τετραπλοῦν. Look, Lord, I am giving half of my possessions to the poor, and if I de-frauded someone something, I am giving back fourfold" (my translation). Is Zacchae-us defending himself against a spurious charge by pointing out his habitual practice of giving half and repaying fraud four times? Or is Zacchaeus repenting by promising to make a future act of renunciation and almsgiving? Based on Jesus's statement in v. 9, that salvation has come to Zacchaeus house *today*, I take the second. See, for example, Bovon, *Luke 2*, 598–99. For the counter opinion, see Fitzmyer, *Luke X–XXIV*, 1225.

Seccombe, on the other hand, argues explicitly that the difference is in the response of the two men to Jesus, though he comes to the same conclusion that Phillips does:

> The real contrast lies in the differing responses of the two men to Jesus. No effort is made to explain this difference (each is rich; there is nothing prejudicial about the ruler's piety, nor commendatory about Zacchaeus' profession). The stories should, therefore, be treated as paradigms of response. Bound up in their response to Jesus is the manner in which each meets with the offer of the Kingdom. The ruler meets it as demand and departs sorrowful; Zacchaeus meets it as gracious acceptance, and in his joy resolves to give half his possessions to the poor and to make fourfold restitution. The surprising thing is that *no attempt is made to match the sacrifice demanded of the ruler. Renunciation, therefore, is not the issue.* Presumably Zacchaeus remains materially in a comparable situation to where he began, though he has expressed his love and joy in a concrete manner.[120]

Implicit in the emphasized text is that Jesus has a different reaction to the two men. As with Phillips, if Jesus accepts Zacchaeus and his mere half, then there must be something about the encounter with the rich ruler that prevents it from being binding on other Christians.

Kim also pounces on the difference to be found between the accounts of these two encounters:

> First, the Rich Ruler is commanded by Jesus to sell πάντα that he has and to distribute to the poor (18.22). Secondly, Zacchaeus is said to be willing to give τὰ ἡμίσια of his possessions to the poor (19.8). Except for these two occasions, there are no other accounts in the Gospel which refer explicitly to the amount of material possessions that should be given to the poor. Here what concerns us is that Jesus' exhortation toward the Rich Ruler to sell all he has for alms is not fulfilled, while Zacchaeus takes an initiative to give half of his assets to the poor. In view of this contrast, we may suggest that in Luke's view total renunciation for the purpose of almsgiving is not intended, Or, at least, in the light of these two incidents, we may state that no fixed amount or percentage of almsgiving to one's assets is formally introduced. Then it might be suggested that as we see in the accounts of Zacchaeus, the Galilaean women, and the good Samaritan, the amount or percentage of almsgiving to one's possessions is

---

120. Seccombe, *Possessions and the Poor*, 132; emphasis added.

up to individuals who should make a decision on it voluntarily, not in any forced or legalistic way.[121]

While Kim does provide a bit more nuance than does either Phillips or Seccombe, still the story of Zacchaeus effectively nullifies the story of the rich ruler as it pertains to the behavior of later Christians.

I quote so extensively here because the rhetoric is important. All three of these interpreters start by noting the difference in amounts. They then point out Jesus's positive reaction to Zacchaeus's gift of half. They then work rhetorically to marginalize the encounter with the rich ruler. Finally, they use the difference in percentages as a way of dismissing the notion of renunciation altogether. Use of the language of compulsion and freewill is also important here. Renunciation is rhetorically connected with compulsion. The stage is then set to make the faulty claim that voluntary giving must be something other than renunciation. Now the interpreter has created a perfect escape hatch for the reader who wants to avoid the anxiety that comes from Luke's radical message against wealth. If the important thing about Zacchaeus's gift is that it is voluntary, and if a voluntary gift cannot be renunciation (wink), then even the fifty per-cent example of Zacchaeus cannot be understood as being binding on the reader. We can then discount entirely the concept of renunciation in favor of a paradigm of almsgiving in which sacrificial giving is ex-cluded. Seccombe can make the incomprehensible claim that Zacchaeus's economic situation is essentially the same before and after his gift. Kim can slip into the easy language of voluntary giving. The radical gospel is drained of its radicality; the beast is domesticated; the bite is defanged. All we need do now, when we are faced with the more radical passages in Luke, is point to the example of Zacchaeus, and we can not only soften up what we mean by renouncing *all*, we can dispense with the idea of renunciation altogether.[122]

Of course, this reading proceeds from a logical flaw that leads to the conclusion that what Zacchaeus does is not renunciation; it is. First one must acknowledge that giving up half of one's possessions is radical renunciation in and of itself. It is obviously more than the tithe of the Hebrew Bible.

---

121. Kim, *Stewardship and Almsgiving*, 199.

122. Other waffling interpretations include González, *Luke*, 222; Johnson, *Luke*, 285–86; Lieu, *Gospel of Luke*, 147–48.

> Nowhere [in the Hebrew Bible] do we find any suggestion that it might be consistent with the will of God to share one-half of one's possessions with the poor. In fact, in the rabbinic literature there is a limit of one-fifth of one's entire wealth placed on the first sharing and then an equal limit of one-fifth for one's annual income. So here is a radically new standard, a new paradigm for the godly person.[123]

Presumably Christians of means in any time period would find giving away half of all one has to be a radical act, an act that is not adequately explained or contained with the simple moniker of almsgiving.[124]

What is more—and it is remarkable how easily this seems to be overlooked—Zacchaeus does not just give away half of his possessions; he gives away half *and* pays back four-times on anyone he has cheated. Zacchaeus is a chief tax collector. The fact that the people think he is a cheat is revealed when they tell Jesus he is a sinner (Luke 19:7); exploitation is a part of the job.[125] If we assume that only one-eighth of his wealth comes from some sort of dishonest behavior, then Zacchaeus would be giving away absolutely everything. The claim that Zacchaeus gives away *only* half is a willful misreading of the text. Giving away half is a radical act, but Zacchaeus gives more than half, possibly all.[126]

It is important to note again that voluntary dispossession in Luke is not simply about the dangers of wealth; it is always also about care for

---

123. Pilgrim, *Good News to the Poor*, 133. See also Barclay, *Luke*, 278–79; Tiede, *Luke*, 321.

124. This point is well explicated in Schottroff and Stegemann, *Jesus and the Hope of the Poor*, 109.

125. Malina and Rohrbaugh, *Synoptic Gospels*, 387–88; Wright, *Luke for Everyone*, 222–23.

126. Even Hays is disappointing here. While he does categorize Zacchaeus's act as renunciation, he describes what Zacchaeus gives as "substantially less than the πάντα demanded elsewhere." He suggests that the difference between the all of the rich ruler and the half of Zacchaeus is that the ruler is called as an itinerant disciple while Zacchaeus is a local disciple. Hays, *Luke's Wealth Ethics*, 177, 179. Ringe suggests that Zacchaeus gives less than what was required of the rich ruler, but his divestiture is still "extraordinary." Ringe, *Luke*, 232. Metzger makes a slightly different argument about "half" and "all." He argues that the word order of τὰ ἡμίσιά μου τῶν ὑπαρχόντων suggests that Zacchaeus gives up his half of property that is jointly owned, possibly with a spouse or son. Metzger, *Consumption and Wealth*, 177. Tannehill makes the most reasonable argument, that "Zacchaeus recognizes two requirements for his money—care for the poor and fourfold compensation of those defrauded in his previous dealings—and simply divides his wealth between these two requirements." Tannehill, *Luke*, 277. Also Wright, *Luke for Everyone*, 223.

the poor. Metzger points out that the word order of τοῖς πτωχοῖς δίδωμι in Zacchaeus's proclamation in Luke 19:8 places a particular stress on the poor, emphasizing that Zacchaeus's giving is first about caring for the poor. It is about redistributing wealth in a fairer way, to fulfill Jesus's mission of economic justice.[127] Again we see that renunciation of wealth and care for the poor are inseparably linked.

We must also note that Zacchaeus's radical action represents a rejection of the systems of domination that lead to poverty. Crowder explains:

> Zacchaeus's job and title readily associate him with Roman culture and imperialism. Unlike the previously portrayed tax collectors, however, Zacchaeus no longer desires to be connected with ill-gotten economic gain. His desire to pay the poor shows his willingness to cleanse himself of any Roman monetary "dirt."[128]

The story of Zacchaeus is indeed a model for rich Christians of how to deal with their wealth. It is not, however, a drastically different model than the one implied by the negative example of the rich ruler.[129] Zacchaeus is not an example of mere almsgiving. Zacchaeus is an example of radical divestiture. At the very least he gives away half of his possessions. Almost certainly he gives more, and he may in fact give away πάντα in its most extreme definition. As Miguel De La Torre explains:

> The quest for justice brings about salvation and liberation for the oppressed and their oppressors. From marginality, Jesús challenged the rich in the hopes that they would find their own salvation through solidarity with the poor. To commit one's life to Jesús is to commit one's life to those Jesús opted for. Such a commitment to the poor is not ideological (Marxist or Compassionate Conservatism) but an expression of faith. Some did find God's salvation, as in the case of Zacchaeus. For others, the path to Heaven became impossible to achieve, as in the case of the rich young ruler who, while pious and virtuous and even keeping every commandment, still walked away from salvation out of reluctance to share his wealth with the poor.[130]

---

127. Metzger, *Consumption and Wealth*, 176–77.

128. Crowder, "Luke," 179.

129. Coleman, in particular, detects no difference at all. The rich ruler doesn't follow Jesus's call; Zacchaeus does. Coleman, "Lukan Lens," 145.

130. De La Torre, *Politics of Jesús*, loc. 1966–71.

For Luke, this is how a wealthy person passes through the eye of the needle, with a radical divestiture of wealth for the sake of the poor.[131]

Conclusion

In this chapter, we have taken a closer look at the literary and redactional contours of Luke's twin themes of economic liberation. We have seen how the author adapts their sources to construct a narrative in service of a radical economic agenda. The message of good news for the poor and resistance to wealth is both clear and strong.

While Luke's audience likely contained people of means, there can be no doubt that the gospel has a message of good news for the poor. God's preferential favor for the poor is strongly established in the opening chapters and provides the interpretive framework for understanding the nature of God's empire and the message of the rest of the gospel. Despite the tendency of modern interpreters—who rarely identify as poor—to overlook this message, it is how Jesus explicitly defines his good news and mission, and it is confirmed over and over through the course of the gospel.

The theme of good news for the poor is complemented by an overabundance of material warning against wealth and showing solidarity with the poor. Modern interpreters have worked exceedingly hard to defang the radical message of renunciation for the good of the poor, often by leveraging a false dichotomy between renunciation and almsgiving which is then used to cordon off renunciation for some limited time or for some tightly circumscribed group of people. This is a rhetorical exercise that grossly distorts Luke's message, functionally excising a large proportion of the gospel's text. There simply is no legitimate way to ignore the radical implications of Luke's resistance to wealth.

Nor can the rejection of wealth be separated from the obligation of care for the poor. Again and again, Luke binds these two themes together. Wealth is a danger to the person's soul, can enslave it like a rival God. But dispossessing oneself of wealth without a commensurate distribution to the poor ignores God's justice. Luke's gospel suggests the foundations of a sacred economy, an ideal society in which, as the sequel confirms "There was not a needy person among them, for as many as owned lands or houses sold them . . . and it was distributed to each as any had need" (Acts 4:34–35 NRSV). Luke clearly contains a strong message of

---

131. Metzger, *Consumption and Wealth*, 179; Pilgrim, *Good News to the Poor*, 133.

economic liberation (themes A & B), directed both at the poor and at the rich. However, as we have seen in chapter 2, there is also material in Luke that seems to work against that liberative message (C & D). It is to this material that we now turn.

CHAPTER 4

Challenges to Liberation

*Everyone who has will be given more, but from those who
have nothing, even what they have will be taken away.*

—LUKE 19:26 NRSV

HAVING EXPLORED THE DETAILS of Luke's radical economic message of
good news for the poor and resistance to wealth, we now turn our attention to the parts of Luke that seem to challenge that message. This
includes material that seems to accommodate wealth (C), such as the existence of faithful rich people who do not seem to renounce their wealth.
It also includes material that seems to take the side of the rich against the
poor (D), such as the use of the making of exorbitant profit as a metaphor
for faithful discipleship.

I will show that these challenges to liberation are not the obstacles
they may appear to be. Luke's use of irony means that many of the tropes
that seem to endorse the wisdom of power and empire actually serve to
subvert that worldly wisdom. When read through this lens, nearly all
of Luke's economic material preaches the radical message of liberation,
while those few verses which may not do so present little meaningful
challenge to it. Luke presents a relatively consistent message of good
news for the poor and resistance to wealth.

Accommodation to Wealth (C)

Certain parts of Luke suggest that the gospel may be accommodated to wealth and the wealthy. The most troubling of these are found in connection with words against the poor, and will be covered in that section. The verses that remain fall into two main categories: (1) Jesus is described with kingly language, and (2) rich persons appear in the narrative.

At the beginning and at the end of the gospel, Jesus is presented as royal. He will inherit "the throne of is ancestor David" and "reign over the house of Jacob" (Luke 1:32–33 NRSV). He is descended, through Joseph, from the line of King David (Luke 2:4), a line which includes other notables (Luke 3:24–38). He is hailed as a king during his entry into Jerusalem (Luke 19:38).

None of this should be particularly surprising. Part of the power of Jesus's message is that he represents an alternate empire to the empire of Mammon. When Jesus is described as king or emperor, it is always with a subversive irony. As Pyong Soo Seo effectively argues, Luke constructs Jesus's authority in reference and opposition to the emperor's authority. While the emperor achieved victory through military might, Jesus triumphs over his enemies through righteousness, crucifixion, and resurrection. While the emperor brings peace only through violence and coercive power, Jesus brings peace by rejecting violence, forgiving sins, and loving enemies. While the emperor saves the world through the order and moral imperative of empire, Jesus offers true salvation to all, even tax collectors and enemies, through his moral authority, his forgiveness of sins, and his leading to repentance. Luke uses the language of empire in order to subvert it.[1] Jesus is portrayed as king not as a means of establishing his temporal dominance over people, but as a means of putting to lie the imperial ideology that power saves. We need not be concerned that kingly language around Jesus undercuts his radical economic message, because that kingly language serves in fact as an ironic critique of the economic exploitation of empire.

Second, there are several rich persons who appear in the story, and some of them are not excoriated for their wealth. They fall into a few subcategories.

First are patrons of the Jesus movement. Jesus has female patrons, introduced in Luke 8:1–3, who provide for his mission and show up again at the end of the story to attend to his burial (Luke 23:55—24:1).

1. Seo, *Luke's Jesus*, 116–79.

Joseph of Arimathea also appears at the end of the story to provide for Jesus's burial (Luke 23:50–53). These characters are problematic because they seem to function in the Jesus community with their wealth intact, without renouncing all possessions in order to follow Jesus. They are not condemned for holding on to their wealth. However, it is notable that we hear little more about their wealth than that they use it to support Jesus. Rachel Coleman argues that this, along with the itineration of the women, places these characters within the normal pattern of rich persons leaving possessions and following Jesus.[2]

We must not forget "most excellent" Theophilus, Luke's own patron, whom we can fairly guess is of equestrian rank (Luke 1:3).[3] If he is the primary audience for Luke's writings, does his likely rank and attendant wealth present a problem for Luke's radical economic message? Certainly it does. If he is a real, wealthy person in Luke's community, he would bring to lie the notion that no one can follow Jesus without giving up all (Luke 14:33).

Itumeleng Mosala makes the strongest argument that Theophilus reveals Luke's hidden agenda to accommodate Jesus's radical message to the mores of the cultured Greco-Roman world. He argues that a liberationist interpreter must read against the grain of Luke's narrative in order to recapture the more radical message of Jesus.[4] I agree that the dedication to Theophilus reveals something about Luke's social location. It is clear even without this detail that Luke is not a peasant revolutionary; he writes with some of the best Greek in the New Testament, after all. And it is wise to keep this in mind when reading Luke; it is almost certain that behind Luke's message is an even more radical historical Jesus. A hermeneutic of suspicion is in order. However, this should not lead us to

2. Coleman, "Lukan Lens," 116–17, 187–88.

3. Based in part on Luke's use of κράτιστε (most excellent) in Acts, Kim makes a convincing argument that Theophilus is a real patron of equestrian rank. Kim, *Stewardship and Almsgiving*, 37–38. Fitzmyer suggests that κράτιστε may refer to someone of lower standing than an equestrian and that Theophilus may not even be Luke's patron. Fitzmyer, *Luke I–IX*, 299–300. Bovon argues that while Theolphilus is a historical person, it is not necessary to think that he was a high-ranking official. Bovon, *Luke 1*, 23.

4. Mosala, *Biblical Hermeneutics*, 173–89. See also Schottroff and Stegemann, *Jesus and the Hope of the Poor*, 67–69; Burrus, "Luke and Acts," 142. They suggest that Luke is an evangelist to the rich, not to the poor. However, Crowder takes the contrary position that "Luke employs 'most excellent Theolphilus' as a symbol that represents and pays tribute to his entire 'God/gospel-loving' community of believers." Crowder, "Luke," 159.

dismiss the level of radicalism that Luke actually shows. In the particular case of the dedication, there is no reason to assume that Theophilus has passed unchanged through Luke's socio-ethical wringer. If Theolphilus is among the elites of Roman society, which is much disputed, he may still have engaged in some form of renunciation, or Luke may be trying to encourage him to do so in the future.

Among the wealthy persons Jesus meets are two wealthy tax collectors, Levi and Zacchaeus, both of whom make radical acts of renunciation and almsgiving (Luke 5:27–28; 19:8). As we have seen in chapter 3, Levi makes a complete renunciation and becomes one of Jesus's itinerant followers, while Zacchaeus gives up no less than half of his wealth, but likely much more, perhaps all. As López Rodriguez effectively argues, these two figures do not represent an accommodation to wealth; rather they enforce Luke's radical ethic.[5]

Jesus also encounters two well-to-do Pharisees, in Luke 11:37 and Luke 14:1. While Jesus is not ashamed to accept the hospitality of these wealthy figures, this should not be construed as an acceptance or accommodation to their wealth. In both cases, Jesus is antagonistic toward his hosts, and in both cases, Jesus speaks against their wealth or status (Luke 11:39; 14:7–14). These meals function as a jumping-off point for Luke's radical economic message, not as a hinderance to it.

More problematic is the centurion of Luke 7:2–10. He is clearly a man of means, more means that we might expect from a centurion.[6] He has at least one slave, probably more. He has enough surplus resources to build a synagogue for the Jewish community in Capernaum. He is a patron, though a middling one. Jesus does not condemn his wealth, his slaveholding, or his power. He does not suggest an amendment of life. He heals the centurion's slave, and does so at a distance. The centurion is allowed to stand as a positive model of faith, even though he is a slaveholder and does not completely dispossess himself of possessions. Though we should not fail to note that, as Roman centurions go, he is much more faithful to Jesus's economic ethic than are most. He shows reverence for the God of Israel, and he offers patronage to the Jews in Capernaum, even though they are an occupied nation, a detail not included in Matthew's version of this pericope (Matt 8:5–13). This story is primarily about Jews and Gentiles and about creating a parallel to the

---

5. López Rodriguez, *Liberating Mission*, 54.

6. Phillips, *Reading Issues*, 115–17.

story of Elisha and Naaman the Syrian, referenced in Luke 4:27. It is not about wealth. It does, however, relate to one particular type of wealth: slavery. This is clearly a limit on Luke's radical economic ethic; it does not extend to a critique of slavery.[7] The centurion is not a perfect example of Lukan economic ethics, and his story highlights Luke's blindness concerning slavery. He is, however, significantly closer to Lukan ideals than we would expect from a Roman centurion, and he can hardly be said to undermine them.[8]

These possible accommodations to wealth in Luke's gospel do not function as a significant distraction from Luke's radical economic message. Describing Jesus with royal language serves to criticize imperial power, not accommodate to it. Jesus's encounters with wealthy individuals often leads to a criticism of their wealth or to an act of renunciation. In the few instances that wealthy persons pass without criticism, Luke is careful to indicate that the thing they do with their wealth is to patronize God's mission. Moreover, these few stories of patrons, which are at best ambiguous, are far outweighed by the overwhelming thrust of Luke's radical economic message. We should not be fooled into thinking that Luke comes out of a context of poverty, but we should also not overstate the effect that these few references have on Luke's overall message. They create no direct challenge to it, and their tangential challenge to it is relatively insignificant.

7. Smith, "Slavery," 17–18.

8. Most commentators say little about the centurion's wealth, except that his patronage for the Jewish synagogue is laudable. Kim uses this as an example, contra Johnson, of when a person of means does show faith in Jesus. Kim, *Stewardship and Almsgiving*, 20. Phillips makes the strongest argument that this pericope indicates Luke is not talking about the literal poor or the literal wealthy but is rather using wealth as a cipher for other attributes, e.g., disbelief or arrogance. Phillips, *Reading Issues*, 116–17. I am not convinced that this episode, which is not about wealth and in which the centurion's possessions are mentioned only to say that he tends to give them away to others, is enough to significantly blunt the sharp edge of Luke's radical economic ethic. Coleman argues that Jesus's healing of the centurion's slave is completely in line with a radical economic ethic because, in this case, the fact of his being a gentile makes him poor in spite of any material wealth. Coleman, "Lukan Lens," 163–64. So too López Rodriguez, *Liberating Mission*, 38. I don't find this argument very convincing. How can a propertied member of the oppressing class be considered poor or marginalized in any meaningful way? There is some boundary-crossing happening here, but it confuses matters to describe the centurion as poor.

Words against the Poor (D)

There are other parts of Luke that are potentially more problematic. Specifically, there are parts of Luke that seem to speak against the poor. The most significant of these are the Parable of the Shrewd Manager and the Parable of the Pounds. We will find, however, that even these need not present a disqualifying challenge to the radical ethic.

Six Scattered Sayings

Before we address the two most problematic pericopes in the gospel, there are a few scattered sayings that present challenges to the otherwise radical economic message of Luke. The first is Luke 8:18, in which we get the first of two iterations of the troubling apothegm: "to those who have, more will be given; and from those who do not have, even what they seem to have will be taken away." This seems to present an ideal of increasing economic disparity. However, in the context in which Luke places this saying, economics do not seem to be at issue. What is on the table here is understanding, specifically the disciples' ability to understand Jesus's sayings. Those who listen well and understand his sayings will gain ever more understanding, while those who fail to listen and understand Jesus's sayings will become ever more clueless as they hear more from Jesus.[9]

Several more sayings are problematic because of the way they cast disciples as the slaves of absentee landlords. The Parable of the Faithful Manager (Luke 12:42–48) imagines a slave who is in charge of other slaves. If the slave manager mistreats the other slaves, the master will punish him on his return. On the positive side, this suggests that God demands fair treatment for the poorest of the poor and the least of the least. And yet, this master also demands that even those who have unknowingly done wrong be beaten, and the parable ends with an apothegm that cuts both ways: "From everyone to whom much has been given, much will be required, and from the one to whom much has been entrusted, even more will be demanded" (Luke 12:48 NRSV). On the one hand, it suggests that those of means have a greater responsibility for caring for

9. None of our primary interlocutors treat Luke 8:18b economically. All commentators treat it as applying to knowledge or word. Barclay, *Luke*, 121–22; Bovon, *Luke 1*, 315; Fitzmyer, *Luke I–IX*, 718–19; González, *Luke*, 106; Marshall, *Gospel of Luke*, 330; Ringe, *Luke*, 115–16; Tannehill, *Luke*, 143; Tiede, *Luke*, 168–69. Interestingly Luke T. Johnson does not address Luke 8:18b in either his dissertation or commentary.

the poor; on the other hand, it still puts God at the head of a hierarchical system of domination in which certain persons are ordained to exercise authority over others.[10] Justo González pushes back against this image, insisting that God cannot be held responsible for the unjust distribution of resources in the present time. "We live in an unjust world, and to attribute the present order to God is to attribute injustice to God. It may well be that we have some things unjustly, and not as a gift of God."[11]

In another short parable, unique to Luke, the disciples are asked to imagine themselves first as masters and then as slaves (Luke 17:7–10). Jesus suggests that if they were masters, they would not congratulate their slaves for completing their work; they would instead demand more work from their slaves. In like fashion, Jesus says, the disciples should not expect congratulations for their work, but should instead say to themselves: "We are worthless slaves; we have done only what we ought to have done!" (Luke 17:10 NRSV). Again, this parable seems to cut both ways. It seems to put God in the position of slave master, in this case as an ungrateful slave master. Sharon Ringe, in particular, points out how problematic the slave metaphor is for a message of good news for the poor.[12] At the same time, it seems to be critiquing the very system that it

10. Kim sees the faithful steward as a primary example of what rich Christians should do with the money entrusted to them. This is in contrast to most, who see the faithful steward as a model for church leaders. Kim, *Stewardship and Almsgiving*, 145. Our other primary interlocutors have little to say about this pericope. Most commentators are untroubled by God's role as master here. Bovon, *Luke 2*, 237–43; Craddock, *Luke*, 165–66; Fitzmyer, *Luke X–XXIV*, 984–90; Johnson, *Luke*, 204–6; Ringe, *Luke*, 180–81; Tannehill, *Luke*, 211–13. Tiede finds the image troubling but believes it is meant to shock. Tiede, *Luke*, 241–42. Levine and Witherington, though are careful to point out how troubling it is. "The depiction of God as a master who would beat his slaves, and so the violence of Jesus' language, will disturb some readers. It should. By the twenty-first century, we should have developed the sense that violence only begets more violence, and that to describe the divine as violent risks encouraging the faithful of whatever sort to take up arms in conformity." Levine and Witherington, *Gospel of Luke*, 355.

11. González, *Luke*, 163.

12. Ringe, *Luke*, 219. Craddock recognizes the dangers of using the master-slave relationship as a model for discipleship but settles on the idea that no slave is more worthy than any other slave. Craddock, *Luke*, 200–201. Lieu notes that in this and other parables, the social *status quo* is rarely questioned. Here the *status quo* is that a master will have no special regard for a slave who does their assigned work. Lieu, *Gospel of Luke*, 133. Levine and Witherington also note the problematic nature of the metaphor. Witherington argues that it seeks to "inject Christian values into an existing difficult and fallen social structure," but Levine suggests "it generally conforms to rather than challenges the status quo." They also note that while it may be helpful for

uses as model. It is the disciples themselves whom Jesus suggests would be ungrateful masters, were they themselves masters. Jesus, on the other hand, comes as one who serves (Luke 22:27). And, as Crowder points out, asking the disciples to consider themselves as useless slaves is also an act of solidarity with the poor, both for the disciples and for the author.[13] They are to consider their work as no more worthy of praise than is the work of those slaves whom Jesus comes to liberate. Their status as apostles can be no grounds for boasting.[14]

A third parable—found also in Mark, Matthew, and the *Gospel of Thomas*—imagines God as master: the Parable of the Wicked Tenants (Luke 20:9–19). The narrator says explicitly that Jesus tells it against the scribes and chief priests (Luke 20:19), that they are the wicked tenants who harass and kill God's messengers and even God's son. The parable is tricky on account of a curious reversal pointed out by Ringe. The crowd listening to Jesus might well have had sympathy with the rebellious tenants, standing up against the abuses of absentee landlordism.[15] Inversely, the scribes and chief priests would likely have identified with the revenging owner. And yet the religious leaders are forced to identify, against type, with the tenants.[16] Is the parable problematic because it identifies God as an absentee master, the like under which common people suffered every day? Is it, in its Lukan form, an allegory from which we need

---

someone of high status and power to think of themselves as a slave, for someone of low status to do so may be destructive. Levine and Witherington, *Gospel of Luke*, 468–69.

13. Crowder, "Luke," 177.

14. Again, Kim is our only primary interlocutor who gives a full treatment of this text. It fits well into his conception that disciples are slaves of God the master. Kim believes this parable is directed not at the apostles, who have already given up their possessions to follow Jesus, but to rich Christians. Kim, *Stewardship and Almsgiving*, 120–21. Bovon stresses that disciples do their job without expecting special reward or praise. Bovon, *Luke 2*, 497. Fitzmyer similarly notes that disciples have no grounds for boasting. Fitzmyer, *Luke X–XXIV*, 1145–46. So also Tannehill, *Luke*, 256. González thinks it sets an impossible standard that opens disciples to God's grace. González, *Luke*, 203. Johnson makes the surprising point that the poor can find themselves on the wrong side of Jesus's judgment if they are boastful about their favor with God. Johnson, *Luke*, 261. Malina and Rohrbaugh suggest that "we" as slaves are not worthless, but are owed nothing for our service. Malina and Rohrbaugh, *Synoptic Gospels*, 378–79. Tiede, somewhat optimistically, suggests that there is no denigration of the position of slave here since Jesus also comes as one who serves. Tiede, *Luke*, 294–95.

15. So also Malina and Rohrbaugh, *Synoptic Gospels*, 394.

16. Ringe, *Luke*, 244–45.

not try to derive economic lessons?[17] Or is this, as González argues, a parable of liberation, because it suggests resources will be taken away from the current elites and given over to new tenants, that is, to the common people?[18] That it can be reasonably interpreted with González suggests that it need not be a fatal challenge to our overall thesis regarding Luke's radical economic message.

Jesus suggests at one point that his hearers should settle legal disputes before they are brought before a judge. If they don't, Jesus warns, they will be thrown in prison "until you have paid the very last penny" (Luke 12:59 NRSV). This assumes the sort of domination system in which the rich control the levers of justice and are able to extract wealth from their underlings under threat of imprisonment, but it does not assume endorsement of that system. Jesus could simply be warning of the powers of that domination system.[19] Alternatively, he could be using it as an eschatological metaphor.[20] In either case, Luke's Jesus is not endorsing the domination *per se*, but offering a warning against it or using it metaphorically to describe an unrelated topic.

Finally, in Luke 22:36 Jesus reverses his previous instructions that his disciples should travel light without extra provisions: "But now, the one who has a purse must take it, and likewise a bag. And the one who has no sword must sell his cloak and buy one." This would be a greater problem were it not for the following verse in which Jesus explicitly explains that they should do such things in order that he be "counted among the lawless." The reversal is a betrayal of Jesus's values, which is precisely what Jesus intends here.[21] As we find in Luke 22:38, the instructions were

17. Johnson characteristically interprets this passage allegorically about a change in the leadership of Israel to the apostles. Johnson, *Literary Function*, 119–20; Johnson, *Luke*, 308–9. Phillips rejects that this parable has any implications for wealth-poverty ethics. It is purely allegorical. Phillips, *Reading Issues*, 174. Kim makes the uncharacteristic acknowledgement that the slave metaphor might carry with it unsavory baggage. Kim, *Stewardship and Almsgiving*, 127. Barclay revels in the judgment of God against Israel here. Barclay, *Luke*, 290–93. Tannehill reads this allegorically but does not want to identify the master completely with God. Tannehill, *Luke*, 289–91; Bovon, *Luke 3*, 34–46; Craddock, *Luke*, 233–34; Fitzmyer, *Luke X–XXIV*, 1281; Lieu, *Gospel of Luke*, 158–61; Tiede, *Luke*, 339–43.

18. González, *Luke*, 231; Malina and Rohrbaugh, *Synoptic Gospels*, 394.

19. Bovon, *Luke 2*, 258–62; Fitzmyer, *Luke X–XXIV*, 1002; Malina and Rohrbaugh, *Synoptic Gospels*, 281; Ringe, *Luke*, 182–83.

20. Craddock, *Luke*, 167; González, *Luke*, 169; Johnson, *Luke*, 209.

21. For some, notably Phillips, this reversal has the effect of undoing all or most previous warnings against wealth and calls to renunciation. For them, the call to

unnecessary; the disciples had already been violating Jesus's values: they already had two swords.

The content of these six sayings are enough to make a liberation-minded reader uncomfortable, but they are not enough to present a serious challenge to Luke's overarching radical economic message. Themes of slavery are invoked, but they are used to indict the rich and powerful and to unmask the workings of the domination system. While these sayings use the language of economic oppression, their purpose is not to endorse such oppression, but through irony to subvert it. There are thoughtful interpreters who will not let Luke off so easily, though, and they will be addressed in chapter 6.

Parable of the Shrewd Manager: Luke 16:1–13

The parable traditionally known as the Parable of the Unjust Steward is notoriously difficult to interpret. Many preachers and scholars do little more than throw up their hands when forced to explain it.[22] There are two main problems. First, in Luke 16:8a, how could a master possibly praise a manager for cheating him out of his deserved debt payments?[23] Second, how can vv. 9–13 be incorporated into an understanding of the

---

renunciation was an exception, meant only for the twelve and for the seventy. This reversal shows that those calls were not meant to be normative for later disciples. Phillips, *Reading Issues*, 178–80. Phillips and others follow Hans Conzelmann here, who sees this as a break in eras between the time when Jesus kept his disciples safe and the later time when they must see to their own safety. Conzelmann, *The Theology of St. Luke*; Bovon, *Luke 3*, 181–83; Craddock, *Luke*, 259–60; Fitzmyer, *Luke X–XXIV*, 1430; Levine and Witherington, *Gospel of Luke*, 598–99; Johnson, *Luke*, 346–47; Ringe, *Luke*, 264–65. However, as Hays convincingly argues, Luke 22:36 should be considered the exception, a way for Luke to explain how disciples of the renouncing rabbi are found to be with swords at his arrest. As soon as the swords have fulfilled the function of labeling Jesus a brigand, he orders they be rejected (Luke 22:51). Hays, *Luke's Wealth Ethics*, 93–100; Lieu, *Gospel of Luke*, 184; Tannehill, *Luke*, 321–23; Tiede, *Luke*, 387–90. Gonzalez suggests that only in times of "rejection, opposition, and even persecution" can modern disciples be justified in "amass[ing] wealth and resources." González, *Luke*, 250.

22. See, for example, Turrell, "Dishonest Manager," 415–17. Lamborn sidesteps the issue altogether by suggesting that the manager is not unjust, but that he is a victim of the injustice that he is required to manage. Lamborn, "Stewarding Unrighteousness," 4.

23. Seccombe, *Possessions and the Poor*, 162.

parable. Put another way, how can it be that the manager's behavior is praised by both his master and by the Lukan Jesus?

The first issue—how the master can praise the manager—is not what makes the parable problematic for this study. If an absentee landlord fails to extract the full sums of the debts he is owed, that hardly challenges God's liberative message of good news to the poor and warnings against wealth. Much more problematic for us are the verses that follow the parable:

> And I tell you, make friends for yourselves by means of dishonest wealth so that when it is gone, they may welcome you into the eternal homes. Whoever is faithful in a very little is faithful also in much; and whoever is dishonest in a very little is dishonest also in much. If then you have been faithful with the dishonest wealth, who will entrust to you with the true riches? And if you have not been faithful with what belongs to another, who will give you what is your own? (Luke 16:9–12 NRSV)

These words are problematic for us for the same reason that verse 8a is problematic to so many other interpreters: they seem to contradict the lesson of the parable.[24] In 8a, the manager is praised for being irresponsible with his master's possessions. He discounts debts that he should be collecting at full value. He cheats his master of some of the profit that is due him. Yet vv. 9–12 suggest that disciples must be responsible with earthly possessions, with dishonest wealth, if we ever want to be entrusted with true, heavenly riches. They suggest that the model of faith would be a steward who worked hard for his master's betterment, who ruthlessly extracted as much wealth as possible, who maximized the profit his master could make. Isn't that what it means to be faithful with dishonest wealth? Isn't that what it means to make friends with the mammon of unrighteousness?[25]

For some interpreters, vv. 9–12 are the verses that make sense, but one must struggle to explain v. 8: "And his master commended the dishonest manager because he had acted shrewdly; for the children of this age are more shrewd in dealing with their own generation than are the children of light" (NRSV). It seems clear that a faithful servant is one who

---

24. Kim, *Stewardship and Almsgiving*, 155.

25. Udoh, "Unrighteous Slave," 331; Kim, *Stewardship and Almsgiving*, 159; Tiede, *Luke*, 325–26.

works for the profit of his master. How then can this servant be praised by his master for failing at this simple task of stewardship?[26]

For this study, the opposite is true. The steward's failure to maximize his master's profit is no threat to my thesis. However, vv. 9–12 seem to promote a business-as-usual approach to profit making, wealth extraction, and absentee landlordism. It seems to suggest that one cannot enter into heavenly riches unless one has spent their life on earth helping some rich man accumulate dishonest mammon. How can that possibly be squared with the overwhelming thrust of Luke's radical economic message?

The simple answer is that the forgiveness of debts is the model behavior for how to use worldly wealth. The steward's last-minute machinations to secure himself a place in the community after he is fired: these are the very actions that Luke is seeking to promote.[27] While some interpreters think the reduction of debts is just more proof of the steward's corruption, we must conclude that debt reduction is a model for the economics of God's empire.[28] In fact, many interpreters, even those who are skeptical of the manager's mark-downs, still come to the conclusion that the proper use for wealth is to share it or distribute it, that this is paradoxically what is meant by making friends with dishonest mammon.[29]

---

26. Dinkler, "Interior Monologues," 388; Hawkins, "Living by the Word," 21; Schumacher, "Saving Like a Fool," 273; Turrell, "Dishonest Manager," 415.

27. Coleman, "Lukan Lens," 131–32; Hays, *Luke's Wealth Ethics*, 145; Kim, *Stewardship and Almsgiving*, 158; Lehtipuu, "The Rich," 236. Long suggests that the money of this world has a limited shelf-life because the world is passing away, so we should use it while it still has value in order to make friends for God's kingdom. Long, "Making Friends," 54–55. Pilgrim suggests that the manager reduces the debts by giving up his own cut of the profit. Pilgrim, *Good News to the Poor*, 125–29; Schertz, "Shrewd Steward," 19.

28. Crowder makes an interesting alternate interpretation. This parable justifies the oppressed and powerless in manipulating an unjust economic system for their own survival. "There was a 'system' in Luke's day, and there is a 'system' today. It is a system that benefits from keeping the poor poor and the rich rich. It is a system in which some, like the manager, are able to discern how to work within it and survive, while others, like Lazarus, die trying. . . . There is a capitalistic, well-established economic 'system' in place. Women and men of God must learn to use it or be abused by it." Crowder, "Luke," 176–77.

29. Johnson, *Literary Function*, 157; Kim, *Stewardship and Almsgiving*, 150–58. Metzger finds the steward to be completely unlaudable, though his actions still suggest almsgiving for followers of Jesus. Metzger, *Consumption and Wealth*, 125–28; Schumacher, "Saving Like a Fool," 275; Stegemann, *The Gospel and the Poor*, 62; Seccombe, *Possessions and the Poor*, 171–72; Tannehill, *Luke*, 248–49. Levine and Witherington, though, find no example here. The situation is comical, and while everyone in the story

Which still leaves us with the puzzle of 8a. Praise for the shrewdness of the steward may comport with Lukan wealth ethics, but how could it possibly square with the values of a debt-collecting absentee landlord? This is why some interpreters have tried to read 8a with an alternate vocalization. Perhaps Jesus stops speaking after v. 7, and the narrator takes over in v. 8 to say that the Lord Jesus praises the steward for his shrewdness. It is not the master of the parable who does the praising, it is the master of the Gospel: Jesus.[30]

This reading is hopelessly clumsy, though. If the narrator interjects in v. 8, then we have no choice but to conclude that the narrator also speaks vv. 8b–13. But the narrator of Luke never delivers this kind of material. Verses 8b–13 are clearly meant to come from the lips of Jesus, and if they are, then we have no choice but to conclude that 8a also comes from the lips of Jesus. We cannot avoid the rather vexing fact that the master of the parable gives his errant steward uncharacteristic praise.

We are left with three choices. The first is that the master praises the steward even though the actions the master praises are not in his own best interest. Perhaps the master simply has to hand it to the steward for cleverly wriggling his way out of a difficult situation, even if it was at the economic expense of the master.[31] More convincing is the social-science twist on this first interpretation, that the manager backs the master into a corner where he has no choice but to publicly praise the manager. By forgiving portions of the debts of all of the master's debtors (not just the two that are explicitly narrated), the manager builds up a tremendous amount of goodwill among the people. The master cannot reverse the manager's actions; if he does, he will have to deal with a hoard of angry peasants. Neither can he publicly admonish the manager, because the

---

turns out better for the manager's machinations, there is nothing exemplary in him. Levine and Witherington, *Gospel of Luke*, 442.

30. Krüger, "La opción decisiva," 102; Tannehill, *Luke*, 247–48. For Fabian Udoh, the speaker is both the master and Jesus simultaneously. This makes the (L)lord's praise subversive. The steward, who for Udoh is also a slave, acts shamefully and plans to flee from slavery, an even greater shame. If this behavior is praised, that represents a threat to the stability of the slave system. Udoh, "Unrighteous Slave," 327, 335.

31. Johnson, *Literary Function*, 157; Kim, *Stewardship and Almsgiving*, 160. Kim suggests that the master praises the steward for cleverness, but Jesus praises him for almsgiving. Hays, *Luke's Wealth Ethics*, 143; Metzger, *Consumption and Wealth*, 123; Phillips, *Reading Issues*, 154–55. Peterson argues that the master praises the manager because the master is exceedingly gracious, as God is also gracious. Peterson, "Gospel Rascals," 32; Story, "Twin Parables," 110; Tiede, *Luke*, 282–83.

manager's actions have brought honor not only to the manager, but also to his master. The master thus has no choice but to grudgingly praise the manager, to pretend as if it had been his plan all along to reduce those debts, to bite his tongue concerning the loss of profit and accept instead the goodwill and praise of the peasants.[32] In this case, the parable is no threat to our thesis.

Second, perhaps the manager did not cheat his master because his last-minute deals didn't affect the master's profits. Perhaps he reduced usurious interest rates. Perhaps he chose to forgo his own commission. Perhaps he declined to take money that he had been embezzling from the master. If any of these were the case, the master would be free to praise the manager's revisions because they didn't hurt his bottom line.[33] While this reading is possible, it is strange that the author would make no mention of the manager's personal stake in such arrangements. However, in this case as well, there is no threat to our thesis.

A third option comes from John K. Goodrich: perhaps the master praises the manager because the manager's debt reductions actually benefit everyone involved, including the master.[34] Using the writings of Pliny the Younger and manuscript evidence from Roman Egypt, Goodrich shows that voluntary debt remission was a known business practice in the Roman imperial period. When a master reduces his clients' debts, the clients are more likely to pay back the remaining debt and the master's lands remain more productive. For one thing, the benefaction of debt reduction demands reciprocity from the clients. They now owe a debt of honor to the master and will be more disposed to paying off debts in the future. Furthermore, debt reduction helps to keep the clients productive. If their indebtedness keeps them from obtaining the right tools and lands them in prison, then their productivity goes down. If some debt reduction keeps the clients on the land and productive, then the master is likely to be better off economically than if the debts were mercilessly collected. Again, the evidence suggests that Pliny and others actually practiced debt

32. Hays, *Luke's Wealth Ethics*, 143; Levine and Witherington, *Gospel of Luke*, 442; Marulli, "And How Much Do You Owe?," 201; Talbert, *Reading Luke*, 154; Tannehill, *Luke*, 247.

33. Fitzmyer, *Luke X–XXIV*, 1098; Krüger, "La opción decisiva," 104–6; Metzger, *Consumption and Wealth*, 122; Pilgrim, *Good News to the Poor*, 126–27; Talbert, *Reading Luke*, 154.

34. Goodrich, "Voluntary Debt Remission," 547–66.

reduction for similar reasons. It was good for business, at least in the long term, and good for public honor.[35]

This interpretation has the benefit of making sense of every verse in the pericope, of holding vv. 1–9 in conformity with vv. 10–13.[36] The master can rightly praise the manager not only for his ability to wrangle a position for himself after he is fired, but also because his actions benefit the master both in terms of public honor and in terms of economic interest. At the same time, Jesus can use the manager's debt reduction as a model for how his disciples should use wealth, which is inherently unrighteous. An acceptable use of wealth is to lend it without expecting a return (Luke 6:35).

This suggests an alternate economy, the economy of God's empire, which stands in opposition to the economy of Mammon's empire (Luke 16:13).[37] In Mammon's economy, contracts must be enforced ruthlessly, regardless of the social consequences, because the lowly cannot be allowed to take advantage of the wealthy. In God's economy, debt forgiveness serves a salvific function both for the lender and the borrower. It forges stronger relationships, it promotes human dignity, and it is in the end reimbursable in heavenly riches. Daniel Steffen makes precisely this point, building on Goodrich's work, to show how the economic situation in modern Latin America, with countries trapped in crushing debt, could be greatly relieved with an application of the principles of God's economy, i.e., debt reduction, as prescribed by this parable.[38] But the lesson applies equally well in other contexts. Those who live as stewards of God's riches must use them in conformity with the principles of God's economy: "Por esto, los verdaderos mayordomos de Dios no pueden tener la prioridad

35. Goodrich, "Voluntary Debt Remission," 555–63. Boer and Petterson suggest this kind of adjustment to debts is part of the system of economic control and wealth extraction. Their argument will be addressed in chapter 6. Boer and Petterson, *Time of Troubles*, 98.

36. Steffen, "La justicia," 148. In contrast, Levine finds that they just don't match. Luke 16:9–13 is clumsily added on to the end of the parable by Luke in a failed attempt to tame it. Levine and Witherington, *Gospel of Luke*, 443.

37. Many who interpret this parable differently nevertheless agree that Luke sees the use of possessions as a moral battleground where the disciple must choose between God and Mammon, between worship and idolatry. Johnson, *Literary Function*, 158; Pilgrim, *Good News to the Poor*, 129. Wells contrasts the economy of mammon with the economy of manna. Wells, "It's the Economy, Stupid," 59. Hauerwas insists that enslavement to Mammon is not just a matter of attitude; it is the possession, not the attitude, that leads to enslavement. Hauerwas, "Living on Dishonest Wealth," 16.

38. Steffen, "La justicia," 151–55.

de aumentar sus riquezas para si mismos; sino subyugar su uso del dinero a su servicio a Dios."[39] Possessions must be used not for personal enrichment, but for the furtherance of God's liberative mission.

What seemed problematic—Jesus's instruction to make friends by means of dishonest Mammon (Luke 16:9)—has in fact strengthened Luke's radical economic message. Those friendships are made with the poor by means of debt forgiveness. This is not a parable of profit-making, an allegory of acquisition. Instead, it destabilizes the system of wealth extraction with its ironic use of economic language and forces the reader to make a choice. Are you with God, or are you with Mammon (Luke 16:13)? No one has the power to serve both. Despite first appearances, Luke's Parable of the Shrewd Manager is a parable of liberation, consistent with the rest of Luke's radical economic message.

Parable of the Pounds: Luke 19:11–27[40]

Finally, we come to the most problematic pericope in the gospel: the Parable of the Pounds. It takes little digging to notice how this parable might challenge the general liberative message of Luke's gospel. The main character is an absentee lord who expects profits from his capital. This lord appears to be cruel, since his citizens hate him and do not want him to be their ruler, and since he admits that he is harsh and takes things that do not belong to him. When he comes back after taking the kingship, he demands profit from the ten pounds given to ten slaves. Two who have made enormous gains, 1000 percent and 500 percent respectively, find themselves rewarded with governing authority in the new kingdom. One that returns only what was given is chided for not becoming a usurer to make at least some profit from interest. The whole emphasis is on the return of more money, preferably for no work. Then the pound is taken from the third slave and given to the first, and we get a reprise of the apothegm, heard earlier in the gospel, "to all those who have, more will be given; but from those who have nothing, even what they have will be taken away" (Luke 19:26 NRSV). It is spoken expressly in relation to money, and the king comes out looking like a classic robber-baron.

This certainly looks like bad news for the poor and seems to completely counter many of the previous sayings of Jesus in Luke's gospel.

39. Steffen, "La justicia," 152.

40. An early version of this section was presented as King "Perplexing Problem."

How can the same Jesus who warned people against striving for earthly wealth now tell a parable with a protagonist who is completely obsessed with wealth and power, even to the detriment of his own citizens? What is more, how could Jesus actually be that evil king?

The overwhelming majority of commentators have seen the Parable of the Pounds as an eschatological allegory.[41] Johnson summarizes this position, which is not his own, quite succinctly:

> The nobleman is Jesus who "goes away" to become king. He is opposed by the Jews. He entrusts the Church to the disciples. When he returns, he bestows authority on those who were trustworthy. He punishes those who opposed his rule.[42]

None of these interpreters see the use of possessions in this parable as in any way problematic to the overall themes of wealth and poverty in Luke. Since they have allegorized the parable, so too they have allegorized the commodity into some kind of spiritual wealth. David Tiede, in particular, though, leans so heavily into the image of the "severe boss" as an ideal of good business practice that one has a hard time remembering that Jesus is not also asking for monetary profits from his followers.[43] Even Justo González, who elsewhere highlights the privileged position of the poor in Luke, accepts unquestioningly that this is a parable about discipleship in anticipation of Jesus's return, though he does note that this king "can give his servants no more than a paltry pound or mina."[44]

Other interpreters reject the idea that this parable is eschatological, notably Johnson, but still maintain the idea that these slaves represent Christians who have to make a return on the responsibilities Jesus has granted them.[45] Again, no attention is given to the idea that these economic activities might be problematic within Luke's economic framework. They are simply understood allegorically to represent some sort of action of discipleship.

41. For example, Bovon, *Luke 2*, 608–9; Conzelmann, *Theology*, 113; Craddock, *Luke*, 220–23; Fitzmyer, *Luke X–XXIV*, 1228; González, *Luke*, 224; Lieu, *Gospel of Luke*, 148–49; Marshall, *Gospel of Luke*, 700–701; McGaughy, "Fear of Yahweh," 236–37; Schmidt, *Hostility to Wealth*, 106–7; Talbert, *Reading Luke*, 177–78; Tannehill, *Luke*, 279–80; Tiede, *Luke*, 324; Weinert, "Throne Claimant Reconsidered," 506.

42. Johnson, *Luke*, 293.

43. Tiede, *Luke*, 325–26.

44. González, *Luke*, 224.

45. Johnson, "Lukan Kingship Parable," 143, 148–52, 158. See also Wright, *Luke for Everyone*, 226–27.

Elizabeth Dowling helpfully places all of the above interpretations into one category: those who argue "that the third slave has failed while the first two slaves model the appropriate response to their master."[46] Standing against this majority position are those, including Dowling, who believe "that the actions of the third slave are to be commended and that it is the master, the one who has the power, who is the 'villain' in the story."[47] Nearly all of these seek to problematize the use of capital accumulation as a model for the work of the kingdom of God. Most also explore the parable outside the context of Luke.

One of the most influential of these studies is that of Richard Rohrbaugh. Believing that neither Luke's nor Matthew's treatment of the parable represent its original context, he instead tries to dig back to an original parable in an original context.[48] Pointing out that western interpreters have relished the profit-making elements of the parable and seen in it "nothing less than praise for a homespun capitalism on the lips of Jesus," Rohrbaugh suggests that peasants—who, according to Rohrbaugh, made up more than ninety percent of the populace—would have had a drastically different understanding of these words.[49] They lived in a world characterized by the concept of limited good, a world in which all goods were limited and had already been apportioned. To make a gain necessarily meant taking from someone else.[50] He draws on ancient thinkers, including Aristotle, Jerome, and Plutarch, to bring home the point that profit-making was generally considered evil and immoral in the ancient world.[51] Thus, while the standard interpretation may have seemed like good news to the rich, or to modern western interpreters, to ancient peasants it could

---

46. Dowling, *Taking Away the Pound*, 52.

47. Dowling, *Taking Away the Pound*, 52. Studies that explore the idea of the third slave as hero include: Carter, *Matthew and the Margins*, 487–91; Ford, *Parables*, 32–46; Fortuna, "Underclass Eyes," 211–28; Herzog, *Subversive Speech*, 150–68; Kitchen, "Rereading," 227–46; Myers, "Economy of Grace," 39; Rohrbaugh, "Peasant Reading," 32–39. For an argument against Herzog and Rohrbaugh, see Wohlgemut, "Entrusted Money," 103–20. For an intermediate position, that the nobleman-king is a villain even if the third slave is not a hero, see Braun, "Reframing."

48. Rohrbaugh, "Peasant Reading," 33. Rohrbaugh does not try to reconstruct an original text of the parable, but does lay out a basic framework of the supposed original parable.

49. Rohrbaugh, "Peasant Reading," 33.

50. Rohrbaugh, "Peasant Reading," 33.

51. Rohrbaugh, "Peasant Reading," 34–35.

have only been received as a "text of terror."[52] On this account, Rohrbaugh questions whether the parable originated with Jesus at all, or whether it was developed later to protect the position of wealthy persons in Christian communities.[53] As an alternative, he suggests an interpretation based on a third extant version of this parable: that found in the Gospel of the Nazoreans. It is recorded, with commentary, by Eusebius, and Rohrbaugh thinks it should be understood in a chiastic structure.

> But since the Gospel [written] in Hebrew characters which has come into our hands enters the threat not against the man who had hid [the talent], but against him who had lived dissolutely—
> For he [the master] had three servants:
>
> A one who squandered his master's substance with harlots and flute-girls,
>> B one who multiplied the gain,
>>> C and one who hid the talent
>>>> and accordingly . . .
>>> C' one was accepted (with joy),
>> B' another merely rebuked,
> A' and another cast into prison
>
> —I wonder whether in Matthew the threat which is uttered after the word against the man who did nothing may refer not to him, but by epanalepsis to the first who had feasted and drunk with the drunken [Eusebius, *Theophania* 22].[54]

Arranging the parable chiastically, Rohrbaugh sees this version as embracing the third slave, for he returned to the master what was his, but refused to participate in profit-making schemes that would defraud and oppress the people.[55]

Building on Rohrbaugh's work, William Herzog paints a vivid picture of the social and economic realities of masters, retainers, and peasants like the ones described in this parable. According to him, wealthy landowners depended upon intermediaries, like the three (or ten) slaves of this parable, to squeeze wealth out of the peasants and dispossess them of their land while at the same time deflecting displeasure with these

---

52. Rohrbaugh, "Peasant Reading," 33–35.

53. Rohrbaugh, "Peasant Reading," 37.

54. Rohrbaugh, "Peasant Reading," 36.

55. Rohrbaugh, "Peasant Reading," 36–38. This use of chiasm is strongly criticized by Wohlgemut, "Entrusted Money," 113–14.

actions away from the master, who had the most to gain. In the process, these retainers stood to gain a great amount as well.[56] Peasant hearers of this parable would have understood immediately the actions of the master and the first two slaves, and identified it as the sort of exploitation they had grown accustomed to. The actions of the third servant, on the other hand, would have seemed very strange.[57] Nevertheless, he is the hero of the story. By taking the master's money out of circulation, he ensures that it will not be used to exploit others.[58] Furthermore, he blows the whistle on the deceitful practices of the master, and for this he must be silenced. This the master effectively does in his judgment of the third slave,[59] so effectively, in fact, that he has largely been silenced even until today.

Many others have expanded on the insights of Rohrbaugh and Herzog, but the one remaining interpretation that is most significant for the purposes of this study is that of Merrill Kitchen.[60] She uses a socio-narrative analysis to explore how the Parable of the Pounds should be understood in its Lukan context.[61] This begins with the character of Jesus. She states the problem clearly:

> In the wider narrative Jesus is identified as the awaited Messi-anic saviour (Lk 2:10) with a self-proclaimed mission to bring good news to all who are poor, prisoners, handicapped or op-pressed (Lk 4:18–21). If he is a consistent character, his speech will affirm his imputed ethics. It is Jesus who tells the parable of the pounds, so the reader must assume that the ethic depicted in the parable is intentional and careful, directly reflecting the ethical intention of the Lukan Jesus. But scholars give two diver-gent interpretations, so the reader's challenge is to decide which of the two dominant voices in the parable reflects the mind of Jesus, the nobleman-king or the third slave.[62]

Through various proofs, she argues that it is the third slave who most closely represents Jesus. She sees the relationship between the nobleman-king and the third slave as analogous to the relationship between the Devil and Jesus. Jesus and the slave are both offered special power in

---

56. Herzog, *Subversive Speech*, 157–62.

57. Herzog, *Subversive Speech*, 162.

58. Herzog, *Subversive Speech*, 167.

59. Herzog, *Subversive Speech*, 165.

60. Kitchen, "Rereading," 227–46.

61. Kitchen, "Rereading," 228.

62. Kitchen, "Rereading," 232.

return for collaboration, they both refuse, they both confront their opponents, and while the third slave only loses his pound, Jesus loses his life.[63] At the same time, both the nobleman-king and the Devil demand obedience, claim a kingdom, and promise rewards for collaboration.[64] The first two slaves can be compared with Judas in that they are supported by the ruling establishment and receive rewards for collaborating.[65] She does not claim that the parable is an allegory for the story of Jesus and the Devil, only that the character of the third slave shows affinity with the character of Jesus, while the character of the nobleman-king shows affinity with the character of the Devil. There is some patristic warrant from understanding the first two slaves as antagonists in the story. In addition to the Gospel of the Nazoreans, cited by Rohrbaugh, 2 Clement, Irenaeus, and Origen all present interpretations that prefer the third slave to the first two.[66] Kitchen also dismisses the apothegms of judgment spoken against the third slave (Luke 19:21, 26) because they appear on the lips of the story's antagonist: the nobleman-king.[67] Instead, hearers are left to determine which kingdom they will serve: the kingdom of the nobleman-king, Mammon, and the Devil, or the kingdom of the third slave, the poor, and Jesus.

63. Kitchen, "Rereading," 235.

64. Kitchen, "Rereading," 237.

65. Kitchen, "Rereading," 237.

66. Kitchen, "Rereading," 238–39. Kitchen writes and quotes: "Later, Second Clement interprets the protagonist in the parable of the pounds as being the one who guards the entrusted deposit: 'For the Lord says in the Gospel: If you have not kept that which is small, who will give you that which is great? For I tell you that the one who is faithful in the least is faithful also in much. He means then, this: Keep the flesh pure, and the seal spotless, in order that we may receive eternal life' (2 Clement 8:6). At much the same time, Irenaeus described the compliant servants in the parable as consumers and therefore antagonists. For him, the believers who 'guard against sinning' represent the kingdom of God, for 'if you have not been faithful in what is little, who will give you what is great?' (*Against Heresies*, Book I, VI.4; Book II, XXXIV.3). Origen, probably influenced by the Clementine interpretation, also comments: 'Certain persons, then, refusing the labour of thinking, and adopting a superficial view of the letter of the law . . . being disciples of the letter alone, are of the opinion that the fulfilment of the promises of the future are to be looked for in bodily pleasure and luxury; . . . they think they are to be kings and princes, like those earthly monarchs who now exist; chiefly as it appears, on account of that expression in the Gospel: "have thou power over five cities" . . . Such are the views of those who, while believing in Christ, understand the divine Scriptures in a sort of Jewish sense, drawing from them nothing worthy of the divine promises' (*De Pricinpiis*, Book II, XI.2)."

67. Kitchen, "Rereading," 245.

Luke introduces this parable saying that Jesus told it "because he was near Jerusalem, and because they supposed that the kingdom of God was to appear immediately" (Luke 19:11 NRSV). For eschatological interpretations, Jesus tells the parable to explain that the disciples are going to have to wait before the eschaton. For interpretations that embrace the third slave, Jesus tells the parable to warn his disciples that they shouldn't root for him to seize power like any other earthly king. The image of the nobleman-king creates a start contrast between the oppression of worldly empires and the liberation of the alternate empire that Jesus is proclaiming.

Rohrbaugh, Herzog, Kitchen, and many others bring to light the importance of the Parable of the Pounds when considering issues of poverty and wealth in the Gospel of Luke. As Kitchen in particular shows, the traditional interpretation of this parable is simply not consistent with the character of Jesus that we get from the rest of the gospel. And as Rohrbaugh notes, it is all too easy for us to slip into an interpretation in which Jesus overtly preaches the capitalistic acquisition of wealth, an interpretation that has been explicitly made by at least one scholar.[68]

With these issues in mind, how do recent major studies of wealth and poverty in Luke (or Luke-Acts) deal with the Parable of the Pounds? How do they incorporate it into the overarching message about possessions in this text? How do they deal with the apparent inconsistencies we have seen?

Johnson argues that possessions function symbolically in Luke-Acts as a metaphor of acceptance or rejection of the prophet, Jesus. Those who have wealth or are unwilling to share possessions are likely to reject Jesus; those who have nothing or are willing to share are likely to accept Jesus. The use of possessions also acts as a metaphor for transferring authority from Jesus to the Twelve. It is in this symbolic sense that he interprets the Parable of the Pounds, that it explains the enthronement and rejection of Jesus and of the authority of the Twelve.[69] He expands on this in a subsequent article, arguing against the traditional interpretation of the parable as an eschatological allegory.[70] While not taking it eschatologically, he still interprets it as an allegory, symbolizing that Jesus will enter Jerusalem and be enthroned by means of crucifixion. He will then put his faithful disciples in charge of his mission and kingdom, just as the master

---

68. Zodhiates, *Did Jesus Teach Capitalism?* His answer is emphatically "yes."

69. Johnson, *Literary Function*, 168–70.

70. Johnson, "Lukan Kingship Parable," 143.

puts them in charge of cities.[71] In neither of these works, nor in his later commentary on the gospel,[72] does Johnson deal with any of the economic issues, including identifying Jesus with a self-admitted evil, ruthless, absentee landlord. His interpretation of possessions is so symbolic as to ignore the implications of their real use.

Others have done little better. Pilgrim, Metzger, and Coleman fail to treat the parable at all.[73] Hays mentions it only briefly in the context of pre-parousia ethics.[74] Phillips notes the parable but says it has nothing to do with possessions.[75] Seccombe admits that it might have something to do with the use of possessions but does not admit that this might be in any way problematic.[76] Kim has the fullest explication of any. He admits in a footnote that it may at first appear that the third slave has done nothing wrong. However, he concludes, the slave should have ruthlessly pursued profit at any cost simply because that is what his harsh master expected of him.[77] Furthermore, Kim sees this parable as a model for stewardship, and is careful to assert that it should not be over-spiritualized: it really does have to do with possessions.[78] He connects it to the Zacchaeus story, apparently thinking that those who rapaciously pursue wealth will have more to give to the poor,[79] but failing to note that there might be any downside for the poor to this wealth-gathering.

In short, none of these major studies on wealth and poverty in Luke take seriously the questions raised about the Parable of the Pounds by Rohrbaugh, Herzog, Kitchen, and others. Perhaps we should excuse Johnson, Pilgrim, and Seccombe for having written before Rohrbaugh. Nonetheless, the fact remains that there is no extensive study of wealth and poverty in Luke that accounts for the problems that have been raised about this parable—none that even addresses them directly.[80]

71. Johnson, "Lukan Kingship Parable," 158.

72. Johnson, *Luke*, 288–94.

73. Pilgrim, *Good News to the Poor*; Metzger, *Consumption and Wealth*. Metzger's scope is intentionally limited. Coleman, "Lukan Lens."

74. Hays, *Luke's Wealth Ethics*, 164.

75. Phillips, *Reading Issues*, 174.

76. Seccombe, *Possessions and the Poor*, 190–94.

77. Kim, *Stewardship and Almsgiving*, 162–63.

78. Kim, *Stewardship and Almsgiving*, 165.

79. Kim, *Stewardship and Almsgiving*, 165.

80. Although it should be noted that Levine and Witherington give a full and honest review of all of these issues, though without agreeing that the third slave is the hero

And yet, as I have argued throughout this study, the Parable of the Pounds represents the greatest challenge to the radical economic message of Luke. It is the only place in the gospel where God's favor for the poor and warnings against wealth meet any significant challenge. But as Kitchen, following Rohrbaugh and Herzog, has pointed out, when taken within the narrative context of the rest of Luke, it is impossible to argue that the nobleman-king is analogous with Jesus or that the third slave can be analogous with a lazy disciple. Jesus's own actions are much more consistent with those of the third slave than they are with the actions of the nobleman-king, and the nobleman-king's value system seem utterly opposed to the one expounded by Luke's Jesus. Once we accept Kitchen's interpretation of the parable, the last remaining challenge to Luke's radical economic message is removed. Instead of the inconsistent economic message Johnson and others insist upon, we find an economic message that is consistent: consistently radical.

A Newer Accounting

Luke Timothy Johnson set the stage for a generation of economic study on Luke by deducing that Luke's message regarding possessions is inconsistent.[81] However, by systematically addressing each verse that seems to be inconsistent with Luke's radical economic message, we have discovered that there is not nearly the inconsistency we might have first imagined. We see that Luke uses the imagery of power and empire in order to subvert it. We see that Luke crafts ironic parables that highlight the destructiveness of the current order and contrast it with the way of God's Kingdom. Most importantly, we see that many of the supposed loopholes in Luke's radical message can easily be closed.

---

or should be commended. They tend to find all of the characters ambiguous. Levine and Witherington, *Gospel of Luke*, 513–18.

81. Johnson, *Literary Function*, 130.

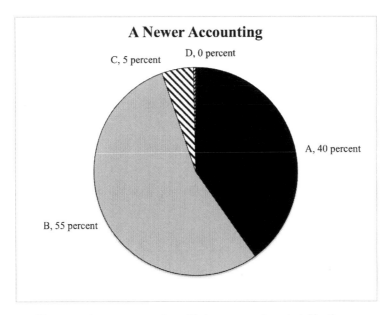

Figure 21. A newer accounting of Lukan economic material by theme

Taking these insights back to the statistical analysis from chapter 2, a much more coherent wealth ethic is revealed. By reclassifying the verses of Luke in light of the findings of this chapter, we see that a full 95 percent of the economic material in Luke can be read in consonance with the radical message of good news for the poor and warnings against wealth. Of the remaining 5 percent, the most problematic verses narrate the existence of a few wealthy people who come into contact with Jesus and are not excoriated for their wealth. They are not offered up as examples of the proper use of possessions, but neither are they condemned. In many of these verses, something other than economic concerns seem to be in the foreground.

This, admittedly, is a best-case scenario for the radical message of Luke. In it, nearly all of Luke presents a message of liberation, while the remaining verses present no meaningful disapproval of that message. Even given the worst-case scenario of chapter 2, Luke reads as strongly radical. Given the insights of this chapter, it is nearly univocal. Our first sub-thesis is upheld: Luke has a radical economic message of good news for the poor and resistance to wealth.

CHAPTER 5

Roman Economic Domination and Luke's Radical Alternative

There is still one thing lacking. Sell all that you own
and distribute the money to the poor, and you will
have treasure in heaven; then come, follow me.

—LUKE 18:22 NRSV

HAVING EVALUATED THE RADICAL economic message of Luke at the redactional and literary level, we move to our second sub-thesis: that Luke
was radical in the context of early Christianity. In this chapter, I will explore Roman economic forms as a preliminary to addressing Luke's economic themes in early Christianity. I will introduce a key methodological
framework: the Friesen-Longenecker economy scale, which provides a
way of understanding the economic structure of Roman society beyond
the oversimplified rich/poor dichotomy. I will also offer a critique and
an improvement of this scale. I will detail the ways that Christian wealth
ethics shifted Roman practice away from benefaction for the welfare of
the city to charity for the benefit of the poor. In particular, I will show
how Luke 22:25–27 provides a surprising critique of the system of patronage and benefaction. Finally, I will show how Jesus's encounter with
the rich ruler and his saying regarding a camel passing through the eye
of a needle represents a deeply radical message in the context of early

Christianity. Scribes tried to soften it; authors like Clement of Alexandria tried to negate it; it was embraced most fully in a work like *De divitiis*, which was deemed heretical. Luke's economic message is so radical that it cannot be allowed to stand in early Christian theology.

Defining Rich and Poor

> In recent years, most sociologists have come to see social stratification as a multidimensional phenomenon; to describe the social level of an individual or group, one must attempt to measure their rank along *each* of the relevant dimensions. For example, one might discover that, in a given society, the following variables affect how an individual is ranked: power (defined as "the capacity for achieving goals in social systems"), occupational prestige, income or wealth, education and knowledge, religious and ritual purity, family and ethnic-group position, and local-community status (evaluation within some subgroup, independent of the larger society but perhaps interacting with it). It would be a rare individual who occupied exactly the same rank, in either his own view or that of others, in terms of all these actors. The generalized status of a person is a composite of his or her ranks in all the relevant dimensions.[1]

When Luke talks about wealth status, he uses simple language. Luke speaks of the rich (πλούσιος) and of the poor (πτωχός). This simplicity of language masks a far more complicated social structure. Up until this point, I have been content to use Luke's binary language while discussing the economic themes in the gospel. However, if we are to put Luke into context in its first-century Roman milieu, greater nuance is required. How can we talk meaningfully about *the* rich and *the* poor in antiquity? What sort of demographic profile might we find to shed light on these categories?

Most scholars of ancient Roman economy caution against binary formulations of rich and poor. Social class and economic status are much more complicated than this-or-that, as Wayne Meeks suggests above. A well-placed slave or freedman, for example, could wield significantly more power than the average freeborn peasant or merchant. Class and station are not as simple as citizen or non-citizen, slave or free, *honestores* or *humiliares*. A complex system of graduated honors is evidenced throughout Roman society—in a legal system that had different sentences based

---

1. Meeks, *First Urban* Christians, 54.

on the relative nobility of the defendant, in the finely-tuned seating arrangements at meals and public games, and in the class-based divisions
of activities at the public baths.[2] Clothing, pottery, grave markers, style of
speech—all of the stuff of life was ground for honor claims.[3] With such a
rich contestation of honor and class in society, it is clear there can be no
neat division between rich and poor that will hold in all contexts.

The classic scholarly debate on how to model social class in ancient
Rome centers more on the presence or absence of a middle class than it
does on the relative positions of rich and poor. On one extreme is Michael
Rostovzeff, who unapologetically applies Marxist categories like "bour-
geoisie" and "proletariat" to the ancient world and sees proto-capitalism
and market economies at work in the distant past.[4] Robert Grant operates
within the same basic paradigm.[5] On the other end of the spectrum is
M. I. Finley, who doesn't even feel comfortable using the word "class"
because it evokes dangerous anachronisms.[6] Along with Finley, Richard
Duncan-Jones, Peter Garnsey and Richard Saller emphasize the vast gulf
between rich and poor and the absence of any meaningful middle class.[7]
Emanuel Mayer, while recognizing that using Marxist class labels might
be anachronistic, is still a major proponent of the thesis that there is a
strong middle class in ancient Roman society. What is more, he wants to
assert that the Roman middle class behaved much like a modern middle
class: they were entrepreneurial, self-starting social climbers.[8] Taking
up middle positions are William Harris and Bruce Longenecker. Longenecker is fairly optimistic about the existence of "middling classes" but
certainly wants to avoid slipping into Rostovzeff's casual use of Marxist
terms.[9] Harris asserts that the Roman economy was neither the proto-

2. Smith, "Slavery," 14; Garnsey, *Social Status*; Bablitz, "Roman Society in the
Courtroom," 317–34; Dunbabin and Slater, "Roman Dining," 438–66; Coleman, "Public Entertainments," 336–57; Fagan, "Socializing at the Baths," 358–73.

3. Lendon, "Roman Honor," 377–403; Connolly, "Rhetorical Education," 101–18;
MacMullen, *Roman Social Relations*; Pina Polo, "Public Speaking in Rome," 287–303.

4. Rostovtzeff, *Social and Economic History*.

5. Grant, *Augustus to Constantine*.

6. Finley, *Ancient Economy*.

7. Duncan-Jones, *Economy of the Roman Empire*; Duncan-Jones, *Money and Government*; Garnsey and Saller, *Roman Empire*.

8. Mayer, *Ancient Middle Classes*.

9. Longenecker, *Remember the Poor*.

capitalism of Rostovzeff nor the primitive economy of Finley, but something between the two.[10]

Given all this complexity and ambiguity, I find the most useful model for approaching a definition of the rich and the poor in ancient Roman society to be that introduced by Stephen Friesen and later developed by Bruce Longenecker. Friesen presented his seven-tiered poverty scale in response to what he perceived as an inattention to poverty in New Testament studies, in particular the New Consensus scholarship of Wayne Meeks (quoted above) and Gerd Theissen.[11] He thought that the emphasis on social status had served to sideline any meaningful engagement with poverty in the biblical world or in economic analysis more generally. In doing so, biblical scholars had neglected an important area of analysis and failed to engage sufficiently with the economic and justice implications of the Pauline corpus, and the New Testament more generally.

> The shift everyone has noticed between [Adolf] Deissmann and the new consensus looks to me like a shift within the discipline from one capitalist orientation to another: from Deissmann's perspective of bourgeois industrial capitalism of the early twentieth century, to the new consensus perspective of bourgeois consumer capitalism in the late twentieth century. At both ends of the century, the dominant interpretations of Paul's assemblies fit comfortably with their respective contemporary, dominant, Western ideologies. As a result, the discipline of Pauline studies in the early twenty-first century appears to have no interest in why people were poor or how the Pauline assemblies dealt with economic injustice. Instead of remembering the poor, we prefer to discuss upwardly mobile individuals and how they coped with the personal challenges of negotiating their ambivalent social status.[12]

The avoidance of poverty that Friesen sees in Pauline studies is reminiscent of the "middle-class bias" that Esler identifies in Lukan studies, the same sort of domestication of the radical that is the impetus for this dissertation.[13]

Friesen suggests a Poverty Scale that avoids the obvious failings of a rich-poor binary and is nuanced enough to make sense in a world of

---

10. Harris, *Rome's Imperial Economy*.

11. Friesen, "Poverty in Pauline Studies," 331–37; Meeks, *First Urban Christians*; Theissen, *Social Setting*.

12. Friesen, "Poverty in Pauline Studies," 336.

13. Esler, *Community and Gospel*, 170.

copious and competing status markers. It stretches from PS1, the wealthiest individuals, such as senators, down to PS7, those existing below the level of subsistence. Friesen is interested in understanding the economic profile of urban centers, not the empire as a whole, and the percentages in table 1 reflect that.

The top three categories represent elites of various levels. PS1 are imperial elites, such as senators and some equites, who are significant enough to maintain a profile across the empire. People who have influence at the provincial level are PS2, like equestrians and regional officials. Finally, PS3 are people who are leaders at the level of a city, like decurions and other local notables. According to Friesen, all three of these categories together represent only 3 percent of the urban population. When seen in the context of the entire empire, they account for only 1.23 percent of the population.[14]

PS1	Imperial elites	Imperial dynasty, Roman senatorial families, a few retainers, local royalty, a few freedpersons	0.04 percent
PS2	Regional and provincial elites	Equestrian families, provincial officials, some retainers, some decurial families, some freedpersons, some retired military officers	1.00 percent
PS3	Municipal elites	Most decurial families, wealthy men and women who do not hold office, some freedpersons, some retainers, some veterans, some merchants	1.76 percent
PS4	Moderate surplus resources	Some merchants, some traders, some freedpersons, some artisans (especially those who employ others), and military veterans	7 percent
PS5	Stable near subsistence level (with reasonable hope of remaining above the minimum level to sustain life)	Many merchants and traders, regular wage earners, artisans, large shop owners, freedpersons, some farm families	22 percent

14. Friesen, "Poverty in Pauline Studies," 340.

PS6	At subsistence level (and often below minimum level to sustain life)	Small farm families, laborers (skilled and unskilled), artisans (esp. those employed by others), wage earners, most merchants and traders, small shop/tavern owners	40 percent
PS7	Below subsistence level	Some farm families, unattached widows, orphans, beggars, disabled, unskilled day laborers, prisoners	28 percent

Table 1. Friesen's 2005 Poverty Scale with percentage of
the urban population in the Roman Empire.[15]

The three lowest categories on the poverty scale (PS5–7) represent people who live near subsistence. Friesen defines subsistence as "the resources needed to procure enough calories in food to maintain the human body," that is between 1500 and 3000 calories per day. Those who cannot regularly maintain this level of sustenance, and whose lives are "usually shortened by chronic malnutrition and disease," are in PS7.[16] Friesen marks them as 28 percent of the urban population. Just above them are the people of PS6, representing 40 percent of the urban population, who could at times fall below subsistence level.[17] In modern parlance, we might say that they experience food insecurity. By contrast, those who can regularly feel safe that they and their families will have enough food to survive are PS5.

Friesen admits difficulty in determining the percentages of the population that were either PS5 or PS4, those who have not reached the wealth and prestige of a town councilor, but who have achieved enough wealth and honor to make some impact in their local communities. Together they represent 29 percent of the urban population. Friesen speculates that PS4 would be 7 percent while PS5 would be 22 percent.

15. Friesen, "Poverty in Pauline Studies," 341, 347. Notably, Friesen's percentages do not add up to 100 percent. Friesen is clear that PS1–3 equals 2.8 percent of the urban population, but never assigns the remaining 0.2 percent to one of the lower categories.

16. Friesen, "Poverty in Pauline Studies," 343.

17. Friesen, "Poverty in Pauline Studies," 343–44.

To get a sense of the difference in wealth between these various categories, Friesen turns to the monumental works of Ekkehard and Wolfgang Stegemann and Richard Duncan-Jones.[18] An annual subsistence wage would be about 250–300 denarii in the country, 600–700 in a city, and 900–1000 in Rome. This is the income we would expect for someone around PS6 or PS5.[19] By contrast, in order to become an equestrian (PS2), a man had to prove a minimum wealth of four hundred thousand sesterces (four hundred million denarii). To become a senator (PS1), the minimum was one million sesterces (one billion denarii). But this was the minimum. A proconsul might have an annual income of one million sesterces, four million times the income of someone at subsistence.[20]

Bruce Longenecker adopts Friesen's model with some changes. First, he prefers to talk about an economic scale rather than a poverty scale and renames Friesen's categories ES1–ES7. More importantly, Longenecker quibbles with Friesen's percentage estimates. Longenecker is a proponent of robust "middling classes" in the ancient empire. In 2009, he publishes a paper arguing for lower percentages at and below subsistence (30 percent ES6 and 25 percent ES7) and higher percentages above subsistence and in the middling class (17 percent ES4 and 25 percent ES5).[21]

Later the same year, Friesen publishes another article, co-authored with Walter Scheidel, an absolute masterwork with an extraordinarily robust analysis of the ancient economy. It uses three independent methodologies crosschecked against each other—one based on consumption, another on income, and a third on GDP—to model income distribution in the second-century empire.[22] Longenecker describes its genesis:

> This article evidenced ground-breaking erudition from start to finish, enabling even further refinement in the discussion of economic distribution. The notable thing about this article, however, was that it was co-authored by Walter Scheidel and Steven Friesen—distinguished scholars who had already published vastly different estimates about the size of the Greco-Roman economic middling groups. Friesen had estimated their number at 7% in 2004, while Scheidel had proposed 20–25% in 2006.

18. Stegemann and Stegemann, *Jesus Movement*; Duncan-Jones, *Economy*.

19. Friesen, "Poverty in Pauline Studies," 344; Stegemann and Stegemann, *Jesus Movement*, 81–85.

20. Friesen, "Poverty in Pauline Studies," 345; Duncan-Jones, *Economy*, 343–44.

21. Longenecker, "Exposing the Economic Middle," 264.

22. Scheidel and Friesen, "The Size of the Economy," 62–63.

> Then at the meeting of the Society of Biblical Literature in 2007, Scheidel participated alongside Friesen in a discussion of the Roman economy and became interested in Friesen's attempts to attribute levels to the overall imperial economy. A partnership transpired, and in the process, Scheidel adjusted his estimate for the middling groups significantly downwards.[23]

The new Scheidel-Friesen study showed that Longenecker's estimates were impossibly optimistic regarding ES4, and he adjusted his figures in his 2010 monograph, shifting 2 percent of the urban population from ES4 to ES5 while leaving the rest of his figures in place.[24]

Scheidel and Friesen's 2009 paper had two important differences from Friesen's earlier work. It did not use the seven-tier poverty scale, instead opting for an infinitely graduated scale but publishing the figures in sixteen tiers. Also, rather than measuring the urban population, it measured the entire imperial population and economy. Scheidel and Friesen provided two estimates of income distribution: an "optimistic" model that showed the most egalitarian income distribution imaginable and a "pessimistic" model that showed the least egalitarian distribution possible. To get his 2010 numbers, Longenecker took the most optimistic Scheidel-Friesen estimate for ES4, then made it more optimistic in an attempt to account for a supposed greater concentration of middling classes in the cities.

I will attempt something more complicated: to reverse-engineer the Friesen-Longenecker seven-tiered scale using the Scheidel-Friesen dataset. The Scheidel-Friesen analysis can hardly be challenged in terms of methodology, but the presentation of data in sixteen tiers—though any number of tiers would theoretically be possible—is overly complex and cumbersome. The economy scale is much to be preferred for usability in understanding the relative economic location of characters within the biblical narrative.[25]

---

23. Longenecker, *Remember the Poor*, 47.

24. Longenecker, *Remember the Poor*, 53.

25. Scheidel and Friesen do, however, present a Gini coefficient for the ancient Roman economy, which facilitates comparison of wealth inequality with modern and historical economies. Rome's Gini coefficient of 0.42–40.44 makes it slightly less unequal than the United States at 0.45, but far worse than, for example, the United Kingdom (32.4), Canada (32.1), Germany (27.0), or Finland (21.5). Scheidel and Friesen, "Size of the Economy," 86; CIA, "Country Comparison."

	Friesen 2004 Urban Percentages	Longenecker 2009 Urban Percentages	Longenecker 2010 Urban Percentages	Scheidel-Friesen Pessimistic Empire percent	Scheidel-Friesen Optimistic Empire percent
ES1	0.04			0.018	0.015
ES2	1	3	3	0.14	0.13
ES3	1.76			1.5	1.1
ES4	7	17	15	6	12
ES5	22	25	27	10	22
ES6	40	30	30	60	55
ES7	28	25	25	22	10

Table 2. Comparative population percentages using
the Friesen-Longenecker Economy Scale.[26]

Pushing the Scheidel-Friesen data into the Friesen-Longenecker economy scale reveals a society populated mostly by people living at or below subsistence level.[27] Between 65 and 82 percent of the population was ES6 or ES7, constantly worrying about where basic subsistence was coming from and sometimes not achieving it. Another 16 to 24 percent of people were in ES4 or ES5, able to comfortably meet their basic needs, but not

26. Friesen, "Poverty in Pauline Studies," 347; Longenecker, *Remember the Poor*, 53; Scheidel and Friesen, "Size of the Economy," 83–85. Scheidel and Friesen do not present their data in a way perfectly suited to converting to the Friesen-Longenecker economy scale. My methodology is as follows. The elite categories are roughly defined in footnote 85 as ES1=Level 75 and above, ES2=Level 24–74, and ES3=Level 6–23. ES4 is explicitly stated on p. 84 as ranging from 6 to 12 percent of population. On p. 83, ES7 is defined as Level 0–0.49 and ES6 as Level 0.50–50.74. ES5 can then be calculated as the remaining percentage. ES5 ends up including Level 0.75–70.99 and about half of Level 1, or Level 0.75–71.5. ES4 includes Levels 2 through 5 and about half of Level 1, or Level 1.5–5.

27. It shows 65–82 percent of the population living in what we would now call food insecurity, compared with 11.8 percent in the modern United States. ERS, "Food Security in the U.S."

wealthy or powerful enough to be a significant influence on city politics. Which leaves us with ES1–3, roughly the ancient version of the "1 percent," in this case between 1.15 percent and 1.66 percent. The truly rich senators and equites or ES1 and ES2 accounted for less two tenths of one percent.

Given this economic scale, how can we define rich and poor? Literary sources are not particularly consistent in how they use the terms. Elite writers tend to ignore the most impoverished (ES6 & ES7) altogether. People in categories ES5, ES4, or even ES3 could routinely be described as poor, especially if they had sunk there from a greater fortune.[28] Even someone like Pliny the Younger, who is clearly ES1, might be thought of as relatively poor when compared with the mega-rich, like Paulinus of Nola or Symmachus of Rome. On the other hand, someone in ES4 might well be thought of as rich by someone in ES6 or ES7.

Longenecker suggests that Jesus would have come from ES5 or ES6, and that his audience would be mostly ES6 and ES7. He further suggests that Paul directed most of his writing to ES5 and that urban Pauline communities would have ranged from ES4 to ES6 (or ES7). Thus, in the Pauline context, he is comfortable speaking of "the poor" as ES6 and ES7 (which still accounts for about 50 percent of the population). It's the relatively well-to-do in ES4 and ES5 whom Paul enjoins to care for the poor.[29]

How do we define rich and poor in a Lukan context? Luke presents characters from every strata of the economic scale. Augustus and Tiberius are at the top of ES1. Pilate and Herod are ES2. The rich young man and Jairus are likely ES3. Zacchaeus might be a good candidate for ES4, along with Jesus's female patrons (Luke 8:1–3). Many of the disciples come from ES5, and many of the people Jesus talks with are ES6 or ES7. Is it safe to assume that Luke's community looks similar to Paul's urban communities, topping out at ES4? Or does the mere presence of "most excellent" Theophilus suggest an equite patron at ES1 or ES2?

It is completely safe to put ES7 (about a quarter of the population) in the category of "the poor" in Luke. Jesus's teachings and parables about peasant tenant farmers suggest that ES6 can safely be considered "the poor" as well. The rich are more complicated. Obviously ES1–3 can be called "the rich" in a Lukan context, even though elite Romans would have considered ES3 fortunes laughable. However, even people in ES4 and ES5 are called upon in Luke to renounce wealth, as Peter notes in

---

28. Humfress, "Poverty and Roman Law," 188; González, *Faith and Wealth*, 17–18.

29. Longenecker, *Remember the Poor*, 279–80.

the story of the rich ruler (Luke 18:28). Even they have the potential to become slaves to mammon (Luke 16:13).

The Friesen-Longenecker model provides some helpful nuance for discussing rich and poor in the Roman world. It certainly is not as simple as the binary: the rich vs. the poor. There is a broad scale not only of wealth but also of honor and prestige in Roman society. Nevertheless, if we are forced to define the terms for a Lukan context, the poor are ES7 and sometimes ES6, while the rich are ES1–3, sometimes ES4, and occasionally ES5.

This leads to a couple of important conclusions. First, no matter whose numbers one uses or where one places Luke's community in the urban-rural continuum, the people Luke refers to as "poor" represent a majority of the population: no less that 55 percent and as much as 82 percent. While we consider them marginal, they are still the majority, suggesting that despite the author's social location, it is ill-advised to consider Luke without considering the perspectives of the poor. Second, Luke seems to have a fairly generous definition of "rich," including not only those whom the rich would consider rich, but those whom the poor would consider rich. While harsh condemnations of the rich seem to be directed more toward the 1–3 percent of ES1–3, even those of the more middling classes are asked to consider their relationship with Mammon and divest for the sake of the poor. Luke's economic message applies in some way to all sectors of society.

From Benefaction to Care for the Poor

The Christian gospels, and most especially Luke, promote the practice of giving money and possessions for the benefit of others. There was already a longstanding tradition of giving from aristocrats in the Greco-Roman world. What was different was where that giving was directed and how it was understood. Affluent Romans would give for the benefit of their fellow citizens with food, public entertainments, and public buildings, and they would be honored as benefactors for it. The innovation of the Christian message—and particularly the message of Luke—was to redirect that giving for the benefit of the poor.[30]

30. Brown, *Through the Eye*, 53–90; Finley, *Ancient Economy*, 38–39; Garnsey and Saller, *Roman Empire*, 101; Longenecker, *Remember the Poor*, 268; Rhee, *Loving the Poor*, 19. In contrast, Osborne suggests that the shift from giving to citizens to giving to the poor had more to do with urbanization than with Christianization. Osborne, "Roman Poverty in Context," 10–11.

As Peter Brown, Helen Rhee, Justo González, and others have argued, charitable giving in pagan Rome was not directed at the poor, who were thought to be lazy and unworthy of aid, but at fellow citizens. The benefactor was living into the role of *amicus civicus*—friend of the city—by giving money to sponsor public buildings, games, and feasts. Such benefactors were then accorded honor for their gifts. Offices at the municipal, provincial, or imperial levels often came with the implied expectation of benefaction.[31]

These sorts of benefactions were political and competitive. Emperors who found their popularity or power slipping might spend extravagantly on buildings or games. Provincial governors might do the same. On a much smaller scale, local social climbers might make a benefaction for their city in a play to be elevated to the level of decurion. Even trade guilds and *collegia* might band together to make some kind of benefaction, and proudly claim credit in the engraved dedication.[32]

Benefaction wasn't just a way of impressing your peers or those under you; it was also a way of currying favor with your social betters. Cities would compete to build the grandest shrines to the imperial cult or throw the most lavish games in the emperor's honor. Herod built entire cities in honor to the emperor. Such benefactions and honors, as Clifford Ando points out, had a kind of reciprocal function. The benefactor was able to gain favor with his patron, particularly the emperor. The emperor or patron was able to claim the show of honor as legitimization of his rule. At all levels, benefaction was bound up in an elaborate dance of identity and honor.[33]

Of course, the money for all of these honor-building projects came from squeezing the lower classes through taxes and rents. The Roman landowner could use the crudest forms of pressure, or the emperor could use the brute force of the army, to extract wealth from the laborers of society.[34] They could then turn around and use part of that wealth in ways that would make everyone praise them for their generosity.[35]

31. Brown, *Through the Eye*, 53–71; Rhee, *Loving the Poor*, 21; González, *Faith and Wealth*, 37; Veyne, *Bread and Circuses*, 10–11, 19; Garnsey and Saller, *Roman Empire*, 101; Finley, *Ancient Economy*, 38; Jones, *Roman Economy*, 14; MacMullen, *Social Relations*, 61.

32. Brown, *Through the Eye*, 114–16; Duncan-Jones, *Economy*, 32; Rhee, *Loving the Poor*, 13–17; Veyne, *Bread and Circuses*, 246–47; González, *Faith and Wealth*, 37.

33. Ando, *Imperial Ideology*; González, *Faith and Wealth*, 49.

34. Goodman, *Roman World*, loc. 2051–131.

35. Rhee, *Loving the Poor*, 18.

This dynamic is highlighted in a surprising way in Luke 22:25. In all three synoptics, Jesus addresses his disciples at the last supper with similar words, contrasting the hierarchy and leadership style of the world with that which he requires of his disciples. Mark reads, "οἴδατε ὅτι οἱ δοκοῦντες ἄρχειν τῶν ἐθνῶν κατακυριεύουσιν αὐτῶν καὶ οἱ μεγάλοι αὐτῶν κατεξουσιάζουσιν αὐτῶν, You all know that those who are supposed to rule the gentiles dominate them, and their great ones exercise authority over them" (Mark 10:42; my translation).[36] Matthew reads almost identically: "οἴδατε ὅτι οἱ ἄρχοντες τῶν ἐθνῶν κατακυριεύουσιν αὐτῶν καὶ οἱ μεγάλοι αὐτῶν κατεξουσιάζουσιν αὐτῶν" (Matt 20:25). Both emphasize the power that the strong exert over the weak.

Luke heavily redacts this verse to very interesting ends. "Οἱ βασιλεῖς τῶν ἐθνῶν κυριεύουσιν αὐτῶν καὶ οἱ ἐξουσιάζοντες αὐτῶν εὐεργέται καλοῦνται, the kings/emperors of the gentiles lord it over them, and those who have power over them are called (call themselves) benefactors" (Luke 22:25; my translation). Luke has changed nearly every word. The first phrase is given more political bite with the substitution of king/emperor for the more generic ruler of Mark and Matthew.

Much more striking, though, is Luke's redaction of the second phrase. In Mark and Matthew, the second phrase is a kind of Hebraic parallelism; it is little more than a repeat of the first phrase. Luke breaks that pattern and makes an altogether new point. For the fairly mundane subject in Mark and Matthew, "great ones" (μεγάλοι), Luke substitutes a word that emphasizes an oppressive power over another (ἐξουσιάζοντες). These are not commendable or notable people, they are people who exert a merciless and domineering power. But Luke's change to the last two words is even more profound. Those who exert power over them *are called (call themselves) benefactors*. Not only do they exert their power more baldly, they expect to be thanked for it. They expect to be honored as benefactors.

This is a stab directly at the heart of Roman aristocratic ideology. Mark and Matthew simply suggest that Jesus-followers are expected to exercise a different kind of leadership than do the elites in the broader culture, a kind of servant leadership. Luke makes the same point but at the same time takes a swipe at the very system of benefaction by which honor and virtue are measured. You know those generous men who lavish gifts upon the city, who build public works and pay for feasts and

36. There exists a rare variant in the second phrase, "their kings/emperors (βασιλεῖς) exercise authority over them."

games? Do not be fooled into thinking that their self-aggrandizing gestures make them somehow noble. Their spending is little more than a means of exerting power and deflecting criticism.

Luke's heavy redaction extends through Jesus's subsequent instructions. Mark emphasizes the *will* to *become* great:

> Οὐχ οὕτως δε ἐστιν ἐν ὑμῖν, ἀλλ' ὃς ἂν θέλῃ μέγας γενέσθαι ἐν ὑμῖν ἔσται ὑμῶν διάκονος, καὶ ὃς ἂν θέλῃ ἐν ὑμῖν εἶναι πρῶτος ἔσται πάντων δοῦλος. This will not be with you. Whoever might will to become great among you will be your servant, and whoever might will to be first will be a slave of all. (Mark 10:43–44; my translation)

Matthew is nearly identical. The saying seems to address people who are not currently powerful or wealthy but who wish to become so. It seems to assume that no one has yet established themself as prominent in the group. But for those who desire to become prominent, the path must be through service, even to the point of slavery.

Luke reads very differently. It seems to address people who have already established themselves as prominent:

> Ὑμεῖς δὲ οὐχ οὕτως, ἀλλ' ὁ μείζων ἐν ὑμῖν γινέσθω ὡς ὁ νεώτερος (μικρότερος) καὶ ὁ ἡγούμενος ὡς ὁ διακονῶν. But not with you. The greatest among you will become as the youngest (least), and the one who leads as one who serves. (Luke 22:26; my translation)

Luke suggests that those with power should be, behave, or appear the same as those who are without power, the great like the least, the leader like the servant. Missing from Luke is Mark's suggestion that leaders should become slaves to all.

Both Mark and Matthew continue with Jesus citing himself as an example: "For the Son of Man came not to be served but to serve, and to give his life a ransom for many" (Mark 10:45 NRSV; cf. Matt 20:28). Luke takes the time to emphasize the point:

> Τίς γὰρ μείζων, ὁ ἀνακείμενος ἢ ὁ διακονῶν; οὐχὶ ὁ ἀνακείμενος; ἐγὼ δὲ ἐν μέσῳ ὑμῶν εἰμι ὡς ὁ διακονῶν. For which is greater, the one reclining at the table or the one serving? It's the one reclining, isn't it? But I am in your midst as one serving. (Luke 22:27; my translation)

According to all three evangelists, Jesus identifies himself as a servant. But Luke makes the power dynamics far more explicit. The one being served is actually greater, he doesn't just appear to be greater, and yet Jesus still takes the position of servitude and expects his disciples to do the same. This is a much fuller rejection of the patronage and benefaction systems.

Understanding how Luke's audience would have received this redaction depends on just how we conceive of their demographics. As we have noted repeatedly before, it is one of the great puzzles of Luke that, among the gospels, it is simultaneously the most radical about wealth and the most familiar with the wealthy.

It seems clear that most of Luke's mostly Gentile audience, regardless of class, would have found the message revolutionary, paradigm-shifting. Wherever they might find themselves on the socio-economic scale, no one could miss the way that this subverts they entire system of honor and shame, the primary framework for understanding one's place in society.

It is fair to assume that among Luke's audience there are some marginal figures, those from the ranks of ES6 and ES7. How might they understand this reversal? They could well appreciate Luke pointing out the hypocrisy of the benefactions of the wealthy, upending their claims to honor. It is not only the power imbalance that is being indicted, but also the cultural narrative that confers legitimacy to it.

But what about the relatively wealthy who must have been part of Luke's audience, those in ES4, but especially those in ES3 and higher? They might well find this message shaming. Luke is indicting their supposed generosity as little more than a tool for self-promotion. However, if they were to make the shift from public benefaction to care for the poor, perhaps they could feel a certain sense of superiority; they were following Jesus's imperative to give to the poor while their pagan peers were still showing off their wealth with self-aggrandizing public monuments and spectacles. In any case, it must be acknowledged that Luke's redaction here presents a much greater resistance to patronage and benefaction than does Mark or Matthew's treatment of the same material.

Nearly all scholars agree that in the republic and early principate the concept of giving to the poor was utterly unknown and that the concept of charity for the poor arose out of the Judeo-Christian tradition. There are two notable exceptions. Longenecker argues that there was giving to the poor in pre-Christian Rome but admits that most of it probably reached only ES4 and ES5, not ES6 or ES7. Patrons or friends might often give to those whose status had recently fallen, to help them regain their stature and honor.[37] In fact, it is quite clear that rich persons who had fallen on hard times were considered more pitiable than the destitute.[38] Robin Osborne doesn't identify the shift from civil benefaction to charity for the poor with Christianization, but with urbanization. As the city of Rome grew, so did the ranks of the urban poor. Eventually they became numerous enough that something had to be done to deal with them, and Roman giving began to shift from benefaction to charity.[39]

According to Brown, Rhee and others, Christianity introduces a very different concept of giving. Whereas Romans considered wealth honorable and the liberal sharing with "friends" evidenced that honor, Christians, following Jesus, thought that wealth was a problem. In particular, wealth made it harder for a rich person to "pass through the eye of the needle" (Luke 18:25 NRSV) and enter the heavenly realm.[40]

According to Brown, Grant, and others, charity to the poor was likely important from the beginning of the Christian movement, even before there were Christians with any sizable fortunes. In the early, more apocalyptic phase of the Jesus movement, the dead were thought to wait in a state of rest for the end of things and the sorting out of each person's final destiny (which might not include eternity either in paradise or torment). Later, martyrs and great saints were thought to skip the waiting altogether and go on to the heavenly realm immediately.[41]

As apocalypticism faded, and as Greek philosophical notions of the immortality of the soul gained currency in Christian theology, the idea of a purging or purgatory, after death but before heaven, began to grow. The purely bad were going straight to hell. The purely good were going straight to heaven. But the not-altogether-good had to be purged of sin before they could enter paradise.[42]

The wealthy, whose wealth could well be counted as sin, had to find a way to shorten their time in purgatory, and that way was the prayers of the poor. The rich could give money for the benefit of the poor, and in return, the poor—both living and dead—would petition God to shorten their time in purgatory. The rich could ransom their soul with their wealth.

---

37. Longenecker, *Remember the Poor*, 60–107.

38. Rhee, *Loving the Poor*, 21–23.

39. Osborne, "Roman Poverty in Context," 4–11.

40. Brown, *Through the Eye*, 53–90. Rhee notes the particular role of Luke in this ideology. Rhee, *Loving the Poor*, 35.

41. Brown, *Ransom of the Soul*, 1–24.

42. Brown, *Ransom of the Soul*, 1–24.

They could store up treasures in heaven by selling their possessions and giving alms (Luke 12:33). Giving to the poor was a kind of sacramental act by which persons of means could encounter and gain the favor of God.[43]

As the empire became more Christian, this new model of charity began to overtake the old model of benefaction. However, rich and powerful Christians soon found ways to accommodate their wealth to the new order. As Rhee says,

> What we see mainly developing in the second and third centuries is that, while the theology of the pious poor is still current (in the recognition of God's favor on them and of the efficacy of their intercession), the theology of the wicked rich is increasingly toned down, perhaps for practical reasons.[44]

Someone like Ambrose of Milan could find work in the administration of the church, where he could wield quite as much power and wealth as his peers in civil authority.[45] In fact, the leadership of the church increasingly came from the elite of society, where many exchanged their government responsibilities for consecrations as bishop or abbot.

The emphasis, particularly under Augustine, moved away from renunciation of wealth and toward regular almsgiving for the benefit of the church, through which the poor were served. He still believed that the wealthy should give to the poor, but not in a way that disrupted Roman society. As González summarizes:

> He could preach and teach that those who loaned money ought not to demand payment or collect interest, but when the poor rebelled and destroyed the extortionate letters of credit by which the rich held them in bondage he thought it a great crime. He could affirm that apart from the outward dress of their wealth the poor and the rich are equal; yet when "land-owners of honorable birth and gentlemanly breeding" were harshly treated he could call on the support of the state to restore an order in which the poor were treated with equal harshness. By "divine law" all things belong to the just, Augustine would say. And he would add that those who misuse or abuse things are not their true owners. But by human law, which is an extension of the divine, all things belong to those to whom the existing order confers

43. Anderson, *Charity*, 8; Brown, *Ransom of the Soul*, 25–33; Rhee, *Loving the Poor*, 65.

44. Rhee, *Loving the Poor*, 58–59.

45. Brown, *Through the Eye*, 120–47.

them. If the result is that some are poor and some are rich, that is God's doing and not for us to question.[46]

In another turn, a third model of giving emerged in the late western empire: giving not to the actual poor, but to the holy poor—that is, monks—who could pray for the souls of the rich even more efficiently than could beggars.[47] The more radical model of renunciation and care for the poor metamorphosed into a new kind of benefaction, now not for the city, but for the church. Benefactors started to become rivals with bishops for power in the church. Christian leaders, benefactors and bishops alike, were being drawn largely from the upper classes of society.

What is left in the late fourth century and moving into the middle ages is a system of giving that is still about conferring honor and benefit on the giver. The wealthy can give their regular alms for the benefit of the church, which is governed by similarly upper-class people, while cloaking these donations as generosities for the benefit of the poor. Renunciation is not required, and both honor and heavenly treasure are accrued in return for payments made. A mega-rich person like Paulinus of Nola can even get credit for total renunciation while maintaining control over nearly all of his massive fortune and directing his wealth not towards the poor but towards the enrichment and beautification of a money-making shrine over which he maintains control.[48]

Luke represents a first look (or perhaps a second look, after Paul) of what happens when Christian communities begin to include people of higher class than the people who followed the earthly Jesus. While Jesus's message may have been directed most at "the poor," Luke must also address "the rich" and how they are to relate to Jesus's radical message. Luke undermines the Roman honor system, praising the servant over the served and pushing people of means, at all levels, to move toward renunciation and care for the poor. Even after Christianity becomes more aristocratic, becomes the religion of the empire, and as wealth begins to find a more comfortable place in the church, there still stands in the late imperial church ideals of care for the poor and of the dangerousness or sinfulness of wealth. Over time, the edge is worn off Luke's radical message, though it cannot be completely destroyed. Renunciation and care for the poor must still be addressed, at least rhetorically if not always practically.

46. González, *Faith and Wealth*, 221.
47. Brown, *Ransom of the Soul*, 196.
48. Brown, *Through the Eye*, 208–40.

Through the Eye of the Needle

As we have seen, one of the strains of economic thought in Luke is a resistance to possessions, a call to renunciation (theme B). Among the clearest calls to renunciation in the gospel is Jesus's interaction with the rich ruler and the teaching and dialog that follow (Luke 18:24–30). This pericope is also a locus for later debate over whether Luke does actually idealize renunciation or whether something less radical is suggested. The camel through the eye of a needle (Luke 18:25) becomes a shorthand for both the theme of renunciation and the debate over whether it is legitimate.[49]

In fact, the debate begins even at the level of the manuscripts themselves. In five key verses—18:24–25 and 18:28–30—we can see the theological wrangling of copyists and editors. Just how radical will they allow Luke's Jesus to be?

After Jesus has commanded the rich man to sell everything and give the money to the poor (in order to gain treasure in heaven), and after the man responds with sorrow on account of his many possessions, Jesus begins to explain himself, saying, "How difficult it is for those who have wealth to enter into God's Empire" (Luke 18:24; my translation). Many manuscripts include the detail that Jesus became sad before saying this.[50] However, this textual variation seems insignificant when compared with the highly volatile text of Luke 18:25. The base text of NA 28 reads:

> Εὐκοπώτερον γάρ ἐστιν κάμηλον διὰ τρήματος βελόνης εἰσελθεῖν ἢ πλούσιον εἰς τὴν βασιλείαν τοῦ θεοῦ εἰσελθεῖν. For it is easier for a camel to enter through the eye of a needle than for a rich person to enter into God's Empire. (Luke 18:25; my translation)

While the second half of this verse is stable, the first half certainly is not. Certain later manuscripts substitute κάμιλον for κάμηλον here, a ship's rope rather than a camel.[51] While it still may be difficult to get a rope through the eye of a needle, it would certainly be easier than getting a camel through one. The manuscripts offer us three different words for "eye": τρήματος perforation, aperture, orifice; τρυπήματος that which is

---

49. As evidenced by the title of Brown's book: *Through the Eye of the Needle*.

50. The words περίλυπον γενόμενον (becoming sad) are included in square brackets in the NA 28 text, though they are excluded from several modern translations, including the NRSV.

51. Specifically: S *f*13 579vid 1424. The same variant is found in *f*13 and 579 at Mark 10:25 and in 579 and 1424 at Matt 19:24.

bored, a hole; and τρυμαλιᾶς a hole.[52] The difference in shading in these words is not entirely clear, but the existence of these variants shows that the text is being worked. There are also multiple options offered for "needle": βελόνης, ῥαφίδος, and βελόνης μαλιᾶς ῥαφίδος.[53] Again, the difference between βελόνης and ῥαφίδος is not entirely clear—both mean needle—but the fact that there is a variant indicates that there is tension in this text. The verb of this phrase also contains variants: both εἰσελθεῖν enter into and διελθεῖν pass through. Luke 18:25a contains only eight words, and four of them show significant variants. What is more, the variants occur in several different configurations. Reuben Swanson lists sixteen different attested readings of this one phrase.[54] Clearly, the scribes cannot keep their hands off of it.

Scribal discomfort with renunciation can be seen in variants that come just verses later in Luke 18:28. NA 28 gives what I would call the later reading of Peter's words: "ἰδοὺ ἡμεῖς ἀφέντες τὰ ἴδια ἠκολουθήσαμέν σοι. Look, we left our homes (the things that are ours) to follow you." However, most manuscripts have the disciples leaving everything (πάντα) or everything they own (πάντα τὰ ἴδια) in order to follow Jesus. Most telling is the treatment in Codex Sinaiticus (ℵ). The original document has the disciples leaving πάντα, but a later hand has corrected it to read τὰ ἴδια instead. The more radical message of total divestiture seems to make some scribes uncomfortable.

And we can detect the same discomfort in patristic writings. For example, Cyril of Alexandria is among those who imagines a ship's rope, rather than a camel, passing through the eye of a needle, and he notes that it would in fact be easier to get the rope through.[55] Hillary of Poitiers makes a metaphor of the needle. The needle is the preaching of the gospel, and a Jew like the rich man cannot pass through because he is puffed up by pride in the law. A Gentile, however, in weakness and unburdened by the law, can pass through.[56] Ambrose of Milan shifts the discussion from the possession of wealth to one's attitude toward wealth. If one is not

---

52. *LSJ*, s.v. "τρῆμα, τρύπημα, τρυμαλιά." There is also one misspelling attested: τριμαλιᾶς. Interestingly, the NA 28 chooses a different of these three words for each evangelist.

53. The last of these, from the ninth-century Codex Koridethi (E) is likely some kind of copying error from a text that carried references to the variants.

54. Swanson, *NT Manuscripts: Luke*, 313.

55. Oden, *ACCS*, s.v. Luke 18:24–30, Matt 19:23–24.

56. Oden, *ACCS*, s.v. Matt 19:23–24.

arrogant about one's riches, they can pass through.[57] All three endeavor, to some degree, to bring this radical verse to heel.

There are numerous excellent studies on wealth and poverty in early Christianity, notably those of Peter Brown, Susan Hollman, Helen Rhee, Justo González, and Gary Anderson.[58] They document the struggle amongst early Christian groups over how to understand poverty and wealth. Some authors pushed hard for a radical reading of the gospel. Others sought to soften its impact.

Rather than retracing the broad arc of these studies, I will focus on just two ancient sources. Both are expositions on the story of the rich ruler. Clement of Alexandria works hard to domesticate the story, while the Pelagian *De divitiis* revels in its radicality. These two writings, one orthodox and the other heterodox, demonstrate the range of early Christian reaction to this *crux interpretum* in Luke. Clement will use every available tool to subvert the call for rejection of wealth. *De divitiis* will resist even the slightest softening of its revolutionary implications, and for its trouble, will be declared heretical.

Clement of Alexandria: *Quis dives salvetur?*

One of our key interlocutors, Thomas Phillips, marshals evidence from early Christian writings to defend his reading of wealth and poverty in Luke-Acts. He finds in Clement of Alexandria a kindred spirit.[59] *Quis dives salvetur?, Who Is the Rich Man That Shall Be Saved?*, promotes the idea that it is one's *attitude* toward wealth that is important, not one's *possession* of wealth. Phillips argues that this makes his own reading of Luke-Acts plausible.[60] In fact, it does. Clement demonstrates the same kind of blunting of Luke's radical economic message that we have seen from Phillips and others. By shifting from possession to attitude, Clement effectively escapes the imperative of the gospel altogether.

---

57. Oden, *ACCS*, s.v. Luke 18:24–30.

58. Brown, *Through the Eye*; Brown, *Ransom of the Soul*; Brown, *Power and Persuasion*; Holman, *The Hungry Are Dying*; Holman, *God Knows There's Need*; Rhee, *Loving the Poor*; González, *Faith and Wealth*; Anderson, *Charity*.

59. Phillips, *Reading Issues*, 260–66; Clement of Alexandria, *Quis div.* Unless otherwise specified, translations are Butterworth.

60. Phillips, *Reading Issues*, 266.

Clement represents "the first attempt at a systematic discussion of the relationship between faith and wealth."[61] While he draws upon a number of New Testament texts, *Quis dives* is essentially a response to the story of the rich young ruler, found in Mark 10:17–31, Matt 19:16–30, and Luke 18:18–30; it is an apology for the rich man. Throughout the essay, we can see evidence of Clement's resistance to the radical economic message of the Gospel of Luke.

Clement opens the work with his pastoral concern for rich persons in the church and his fear that they will hear Jesus's saying regarding the camel passing through the eye of a needle, "despair of themselves, thinking that they are not destined to obtain life," and abandon the Christian venture altogether, since they have no hope of heaven.[62] He aims to rescue them from their despair and show "that the inheritance of the kingdom of heaven is not completely cut off from them."[63] He wants to incorporate the wealthy into the church, with some amendment of life, but with their wealth mostly intact.

Toward the beginning of his argument, Clement quotes the passage in full, stating explicitly that he is quoting the Gospel of Mark.[64] As we have shown above, Mark's version of the story is not as stark as is Luke's, which works to Clement's benefit. However, Clement does not seem to quote Mark faithfully. His version contains several variations, some of which are not attested in any known manuscript of Mark. Scholars tend to take Clement at his word that the synoptics tell basically the same story and he is simply using Mark for convenience.[65]

There are linguistic variations throughout the quotation, but I will only treat here those that represent a significant change in the meaning of the text. The first comes in Mark 10:21 (see Luke 18:22; Matt 19:21), where he inserts a phrase not found in Mark. Clement's version reads, "Looking, Jesus loved him and said, 'You lack one thing. *If you would be perfect*, sell what you have and give to the poor.'"[66] Not only does Clement

---

61. González, *Faith and Wealth*, 112. See also Hoek, "Widening," 69.

62. Clement, *Quis div.*, 2; my translation.

63. Clement, *Quis div.*, 3; my translation. See also González, *Faith and Wealth*, 112; Phillips, *Reading Issues*, 261; Rhee, *Loving the Poor*, 78.

64. Clement, *Quis div.*, 4, for quotation. Clement, *Quis div.*, 5, for explanation.

65. Hoek, "Widening," 71; Rhee, *Loving the Poor*, 78. Curiously, González states without explanation that Clement is following the Matthean version. González, *Faith and Wealth*, 112.

66. Clement, *Quis div.*, 4; my translation. Clement adds the italicized text, εἰ θέλεις

lack the "sell *all* your possessions" found in Luke, but he inserts the quali-
fier, "if you would be perfect," from Matthew. This variant is not found in
any known copy of Mark, only in Matthew. It seems that Clement inserts
it here as a means of de-radicalizing the message. In Matthew, the phrase
comes in response to the rich man's question, "What am I still missing?"
(Matt 19:20 CEB). Jesus responds, "If you would be complete . . ." Inserted
into Mark without the context of Matthew, the phrase changes meaning.
It no longer responds to the rich man's sense that he is still missing something. Instead it undermines the power of Jesus's instruction, making it
optional, extra credit. The implication is, *only* if you want to be *perfect*
should you consider selling possessions for the benefit of the poor. In fact,
Clement will come back to this inserted phrase in his exegesis and use it as
a means of dematerializing Jesus's instruction, as we will see.[67]

Clement does another interesting piece of editing in Mark 10:23–24.
In Mark, Jesus makes a statement, waits for a reaction, and then repeats
the statement. The first statement reads, "How hard it is for those who
have wealth to enter the kingdom of God!" (Mark 10:23 NRSV). After
a reaction of shock, Jesus repeats, "Children, how hard it is to enter the
kingdom of God!" (Mark 10:24 NRSV). This repetition occurs only in
Mark. There is a variant to this second statement, found in several manuscripts: "Children, how hard it is *for those who trust in their wealth* (τους
πεποιθοτας επι τοις χρημασιν) to enter God's Empire!" (Mark 10:24; my
translation). In this variant, focus has been shifted from the possession
of wealth to trust in wealth. It is about attitude, not possession. This is
also the reading that Clement follows, shifting the focus away from possession and toward attitude. Though it is found in only some versions of
Mark and never in Matthew or Luke, this is the statement that Clement
seizes upon. In fact, he focuses on the second statement in its variant
form to the exclusion of the first statement, "How hard it is for those who
have wealth . . ." For Clement, there will be nothing about possession of
wealth that imperils one's spiritual life, only trust in wealth, which can be
avoided without resorting to dispossessing oneself.

As noted above, scribes cannot seem to keep their hands off of the
camel verse (Mark 10:25; Matt 19:24; Luke 18:25), and neither can Clement. He presents a unique edition: "εὐκόλως διὰ τῆς τρυμαλιᾶς τῆς βελόνης

τέλειος εἶναι. Hoek, "Widening," 71.

67. Clement, *Quis div.*, 10.

κάμηλος εἰσελεύσεται ἢ πλούσιος εἰς τὴν βασιλείαν τοῦ θεοῦ."[68] Clement opts for the camel rather than the ship's rope, at least. There is a shift in word order bringing the image of the needle's eye before the image of the camel. Most notable, though, is Clement's twist on "easier." There is surprisingly little variation in the manuscript tradition; across Mark, Matthew, and Luke, all but a handful of sources read εὐκοπώτερόν, which simply means "easier."[69] Only Clement provides the non-comparative adjective εὐκόλως, which usually has a more specific meaning of being "easily satisfied, contented with one's food."[70] What exactly Clement intends with this odd word choice is not entirely clear, but it may contribute to his shift from possession to attitude.[71]

Finally, Clement makes another major edit to Mark in the end of the pericope. In terms of words, it is a subtle change, but the change in meaning is significant. Mark 10:30 makes clear that those who give up earthly possessions for Jesus or for the gospel will receive back a hundredfold in similar earthly possessions, plus eternal life. Clement does something different. Those who give up earthly possessions will receive back a hundredfold, with no elucidation of what kind that hundredfold will be. Instead, before going on to the promise of eternal life, Clement changes the meaning of the list by placing a few new words on the lips of Jesus, "νῦν ἐν τῷ καιρῷ τούτῳ ἁγιοὺς καὶ χρήματα καὶ οἰκίας καὶ ἀδελφοὺς ἔχειν μετὰ διωγμῶν εἰς ποῦ; *To what end is it* that in this present time

---

68. Clement, *Quis div.*, 4. Compare to the NA 28 base text of Mark 10:25: "εὐκοπώτερον γάρ ἐστιν κάμηλον διὰ τρήματος βελόνης εἰσελθεῖν ἢ πλούσιον εἰς τὴν βασιλείαν τοῦ θεοῦ." Codex Alexandrinus (A): "ευκοπωτερον δε εστι καμηλον δια τρυμαλιας ραφιλος εισελθειν· η πλουσιον εις την βασιλειαν του θεου εισελθει." Codex Sinaiticus (א): "ευκοπωτερον εστιν καμηλος ραφιδος εισελθειν η πλουσιον εις την βασιλιαν του θεου εισελθιν." Codex Vaticanus (B): "ευκοπωτερο εστιν καμηλος δια της ραφιδος διελθειν η πλουσιον εις την βασιλεια του θεου εισελθειν." Family 13 (ƒ13): "ευκοπωτερον εστιν καμιλον δια τρυπηματος βελονης διελθειν η πλουσιον εις την βασιλειαν του θεου εισελθειν." There are numerous other permutations across all three gospels.

69. The exceptions, including Codex Bezae (D), read ταχιον and also reverse the order of verses 24 and 25.

70. *LSJ*, s.v. "εὔκολος."

71. Clement also contains a unique version of Mark 10:27. The base texts reads "παρὰ ἀνθρώποις ἀδύνατον, ἀλλ᾽ οὐ παρὰ θεῷ πάντα γὰρ δανατὰ παρὰ τῷ θεῷ, for mortals it is impossible, but not for God; for God all things are possible." Clement reads more simply, "ὅ τι παρὰ ἀνθρῶποις ἀδύνατον, παρὰ θεῷ δυνατὸν, that which is impossible for humans is possible for God." Clement's version here is closer to Luke than to Mark: "τὰ ἀδύνατα παρὰ ἀνθρώποις δυνατὰ παρὰ τῷ θεῷ ἐστιν, What is impossible for humans is possible for God" (Luke 18:27).

we have lands and riches and houses and brothers with persecutions?"[72] This phrase has some relation to Mark 10:30—it lists some of the same possessions—but the meaning has been transformed. Whereas Mark makes clear, by promising actual, earthly replacements, that disciples should give up actual, earthly possessions, Clement muddies the waters by asking a philosophical question about the nature of ownership. The reader's mind is diverted from the physical to the spiritual, facilitating the spiritual reading that Clement is about to make.

Clement makes subtle changes to the biblical text, but these subtle changes are very important. He claims that Mark, Matthew, and Luke all carry basically the same message, and that he is simply quoting the Markan version for convenience's sake.[73] What he actually does is much more cunning. He picks and chooses the words from each gospel that are most advantageous for his argument. He inserts material from one gospel into a different context in another. He even introduces new words that change the meaning of what otherwise looks like familiar material. Clement has already rewritten the scripture before he has even begun to lay out his exegesis.

As he turns toward exegesis, Clement states his method: "As we are clearly aware that the Saviour teaches His people nothing in a merely human way, but everything by a divine and mystical wisdom, we must not understand His words literally."[74] He has already stripped the text of most of its literal meaning. Now he insists that his readers give up any sense of literalism that is left. It is in that mode that he continues.

Coming to the saying of Jesus, "If you would become perfect," which he has cleverly inserted out of context into the Markan text, Clement moves the focus from possession to attitude. The fact that the man is not yet perfect indicates both that works of the law cannot lead to perfection and that the rich man is insincere in his intention. "For he did not truly wish for life, as he said, but aimed solely at a reputation for good intentions." Clement also provides his own definition for the one thing lacking: "the one thing, that which is Mine, the good, that which is already above law, which law does not give, which law does not contain, which is

---

72. Clement, *Quis div.*, 4.

73. Clement, *Quis div.*, 5.

74. Clement, *Quis div.*, 5; Hoek, "Widening," 72; Rhee, *Loving the Poor*, 78.

peculiar to those who live."[75] All this draws away from Jesus's demand for an amendment of life and pulls toward an ethic of attitude.[76]

This is all the more clear as Clement addresses the actual command to give all. What does it mean to sell what one possesses?

> It is not what some hastily take it to be, a command to fling away the substance that belongs to him and to part with his riches, but to banish from the soul its opinions about riches, its attachment to them, its excessive desire, its morbid excitement over them, its anxious cares, the thorns of our earthly existence which choke the seed of the true life.[77]

But that interpretation only holds in the new version of this story that Clement has created. Without his clever editing, this shift in focus would not be possible.

And the reason behind Clement's interpretation is quickly revealed. Clement simply cannot imagine a theology as radical as Luke's, in which possessions are left behind for the sake of the gospel and in which the poor are blessed by God.

> For it is no great or enviable thing to be simply without riches, apart from the purpose of obtaining life. Why, if this were so, those men who have nothing at all, but are destitute and beg for their daily bread, who lie among the roads in abject poverty, would, though ignorant of God and God's righteousness be most blessed and beloved of God and the only possessors of eternal life, by the sole fact of their being utterly without ways and means of livelihood and in want of the smallest necessities. Nor again is it a new thing to renounce wealth and give it freely to the poor, or to one's fatherland, which many have done before the Saviour's coming, some to obtain leisure for letters and for dead wisdom, others for empty fame and vainglory—such men as Anaxagoras, Democritus and Crates.[78]

Clement reveals a few things here. The first is that he understands anything less than elite wealth as basically equivalent to total impoverishment. For someone from ES1 or ES2 to fall to ES3 would be tragic. To fall to ES4 would be like total destitution. For him there is no effective

---

75. Clement, *Quis div.*, 10.

76. González, *Faith and Wealth*, 113; Rhee, *Loving the Poor*, 78.

77. Clement, *Quis div.*, 11; Phillips, *Reading Issues*, 262–63.

78. Clement, *Quis div.*, 11.

difference between ES4 and ES7. All of it is poverty. All of it is unthinkable as a state of being, wholly without honor.

Second, Clement seems to think of the renunciation of wealth as complete folly, never more praiseworthy than a publicity stunt. This is indicated by the examples he gives, ancient Greek philosophers known for giving up wealth in the pursuit of their studies.

Most importantly, Clement cannot conceive of the possibility that God would favor the poor. He understands poverty, defined broadly, as completely detestable. He makes the point later, when referring to the beatitudes. He is careful to reject Luke's version and accept only Matthew's spiritualized rendering.

> Therefore Matthew added to "Blessed are the poor": how? "in spirit." And again, "Blessed are they that hunger and thirst after God's righteousness." Those then who are poor in the opposite [material] sense are miserable, being destitute of God, more destitute still of human possessions, and unacquainted with God's righteousness.[79]

For Clement, it is not possible that the poor could have God's favor. Nor can Clement conceive of the idea that God would wish to lift the poor out of the most crushing poverty, to lift the poor up while bringing the rich down. Since anything less than ES3 seems like utter destitution, a rise in status from ES7 to ES6 simply does not register for Clement. It is not conceivable that poverty could be eliminated if one thinks that 98 percent of the population lives in poverty.

Clement can imagine a person who is both rich and also caught in the sway of greed. He can imagine a person who is rich and yet free from greed.[80] He can imagine a person who has become poor, but still desires wealth and thus is controlled by greed.[81] What he cannot imagine is someone who has little but is not plagued with desire. Only in the presence of overflowing abundance can someone be free from avarice.

> It is possible for a man, after having unburdened himself of his property, to be none the less continually absorbed and occupied in the desire and longing for it. He has given up the use of wealth, but now being in difficulties and at the same time yearning after what he threw away, he endures a double annoyance,

79. Clement, *Quis div.*, 17; Hoek, "Widening," 73.

80. Clement, *Quis div.*, 13.

81. Clement, *Quis div.*, 12.

the absence of means of support and the presence of regret. For when a man lacks the necessities of life he cannot possibly fail to be broken in spirit and to neglect the higher things, as he strives to procure these necessities by any means and from any source. And how much more useful is the opposite condition, when by possessing a sufficiency a man is himself in no distress about money-making and also helps those he ought? For what sharing would be left among men, if nobody had anything?[82]

It is clear here that Clement can only imagine a life free of worry in a person who is so wealthy that they need not work, that is ES1–2, possibly ES3. Clement employs the familiar hyperbole of suggesting that renunciation of wealth necessarily means utter destitution, ES7 status.

He continues his argument by suggesting that if Jesus were calling for renunciation here, it would contradict his other teachings. For example, how could one make friends for oneself with the mammon of unrighteousness if one did not retain mammon? How could one provide for the needy if one was not free from want?[83]

And Clement puts forward examples of wealthy men who have remained wealthy while still holding favor with Jesus. "The Lord Himself is a guest with Zacchaeus and Levi and Matthew, wealthy men and tax-gatherers, and He does not bid them give up their riches."[84] He seems to conveniently forget that all three of these characters do in fact renounce their wealth as a result of their encounter with Jesus. In fact, the point of each of their stories is that these men are able to find salvation in Jesus as a result of their renunciation of wealth.

Further example of Clement's incomprehension of renunciation is found in his treatment of Peter's words, "We have left everything and followed you" (Matt 19:27 NRSV; see Luke 18:28). Peter cannot be referring to material possessions because he is already poor by Clement's standards.

> If by "all" he means his own possessions, he is bragging of having forsaken four obols or so, as the saying goes, and he would be unconsciously declaring the kingdom of heaven a suitable equivalent to these. But if, as we are just now saying, it is by flinging away the old possessions of the mind and diseases of the soul

82. Clement, *Quis div.*, 12–13; Hoek, "Widening," 73; Phillips, *Reading Issues*, 264.

83. Clement, *Quis div.*, 13; González, *Faith and Wealth*, 113; Rhee, *Loving the Poor*, 78.

84. Clement, *Quis div.*, 13.

that they are following in the track of their teacher, Peter's words would at once apply to those who are to be enrolled in heaven.[85]

Since God's Empire cannot be bought for the net worth of an ES5 fisherman—an amount Clement compares to a few pennies—then both Peter and Jesus must be referring to an attitude rather than to actual possessions. And here we see Clement resisting Luke's more material reading of the same passage: "We have left our homes and followed you" (Luke 18:28 NRSV).

We could continue with more analysis of Clement's exegesis and theology, but the point is sufficiently made. Clement does want his rich people to offer aid to the poor. However, he does not want them to do so in a way that would change their economic status. They should devote their customary beneficent spending to the poor, but they should not consider giving to an extent that would reduce their economic or social standing. They should refrain from lavish living, but they should not renounce their wealth. To do so would be to renounce the means of being free from desire. Throughout his argument, Clement clearly resists Luke's more radical version of the gospel.

This is not to say that Clement demands nothing of rich Christians. He encourages freeing oneself of greed, refraining from opulence, and giving both to the poor and to the church. He insists that all persons must free themselves from attachment to wealth.[86] This is not nothing. It simply falls far short of the radical message of divestiture found in Jesus's encounter with the rich man.[87]

And this suits Phillips just fine. Without acknowledging the ways that Clement avoids and resists Luke, without noting his careful editing of the biblical text, without admitting that Clement presents an apology for the wealthy, Phillips uses Clement's assertion that one's attitude toward wealth is more important than possession as a justification for his similar reading of Luke-Acts. Clement's position "demonstrates that some persons within the Greco-Roman world did espouse ideas similar to this idea, an idea around which the reader [Phillips] created a consistent reading of the third gospel and Acts."[88] Phillips is careful to say that Clement's position does not prove his own reading, but he also fails to

85. Clement, *Quis div.*, 21.

86. González, *Faith and Wealth*, 116; Rhee, *Loving the Poor*, 80.

87. Hoek, "Widening," 75.

88. Phillips, *Reading Issues*, 266.

acknowledge the degree to which he relies on cover provided by Clement's creative rewriting of scripture. Clement is able to argue that the story of the rich man is really about attitude concerning wealth because he changes the text. Without Clement's edits, Mark's text says little or nothing about attitude. Luke's text is still more radical.

Careful reading of Clement's *Quis dives salvatur* has shown that in his effort to shift from an ethic of possession to an ethic of attitude, Clement has distorted the biblical text. The story of Jesus's encounter with the rich man has not only been interpreted in a way that deradicalizes it, it has also been edited to better fit that deradicalized meaning. The early efforts of interpreters like Clement make it all the easier for latter-day exegetes to present deradicalized readings of the economic material in Luke-Acts. Both in the third century and in the twenty-first, such interpretive efforts rob Luke of its power.

De divitiis, a Pelagian Writing on Wealth

To find an ancient interpreter who, in contrast to Clement, embraces the radical economic message of Luke, we turn to an early fifth-century (408–14 CE) Pelagian treatise called *On Riches* or *De divitiis*.[89] *De divitiis* is not a direct response to Clement, of course, but it does cover much of the same ground. It argues against a number of interpretations that seek to blunt the radical economic message of the gospel, including interpretations that argue for an ethic of attitude, as Clement does. It dismisses "an entire inherited conglomerate of notions that had made wealth seem tolerable in the Christian communities."[90] The main argument of *De divitiis* is simply that Jesus's words in favor of the poor and against wealth are not meant to be allegorized, they are meant to be interpreted plainly. In defending this thesis, the author draws heavily on the Gospel of Luke.

The treatise begins by identifying its opponents as those who argue that wealth need not be a hindrance to faith:

> I would marvel that some men's minds are held captive and are possessed by their love and craving for earthly things to such an extent that they come to think that worldly wealth is a hindrance to no one, if I did not remember that all human beings

89. Citations from *De divitiis* are taken from the volume edited and translated by B. R. Rees. See Brown, *Through the Eye*, 308–21.

90. Brown, *Through the Eye*, 311.

suffer from the vice of thinking that what they love is better than anything else and of identifying deep down in their minds as the greatest good what they espouse with such love that they become totally incapable of being separated from it.[91]

The author identifies three vices that are capable of producing such self-deception—gluttony, avarice, and lust—but concludes that the most powerful of these is avarice. People can overcome slavery to gluttony and lust, but it is very difficult to overcome slavery to greed.[92]

What wonder then if its worshippers continue to defend it quite shamelessly, when its power is so great that sometimes even those who have begun to denounce it remain to some extent under its sway![93]

In an apparent allusion to Luke 16:13, *De divitiis* suggests that avarice, the attitude, is produced by riches and that riches are not so much possessed by a person; instead the person is possessed by the riches.[94]

Right away we can see that *De divitiis* is setting itself against interpretations, like Clement's, that suggest that one can divest oneself of greed without divesting oneself of wealth. For *De divitiis*, the two are inseparable. An ethic of attitude is not tenable, because whether one is striving to gain wealth, or whether one simply holds on to the wealth they have, they are still in thrall to greed.

But perhaps you will say, "It is one thing to want to become rich, another to want to remain rich." What is the difference between wanting to become rich and wanting to remain rich? I suppose it is that the man who wants to become rich is not yet rich, whereas the man who wants to remain rich is rich already. Are we then to understand that the man who wants to become rich is culpable but that the man who is known to be rich already is not culpable, seeing that the sin consists only in coveting riches and not in possessing them? If that is so, then those who desire to be rich must make haste to be even sooner what they desire to be, because according to this interpretation they will be liable to punishment only so long as they are not what they desire to become: But as soon as they have begun to be what they desire to be, they begin to want no longer to become rich but to want

91. *De div.*, 1.1.
92. *De div.*, 1.2–3.
93. *De div.*, 1.3.
94. *De div.*, 2.

to remain so, and since they have begun no longer to want to become rich but to remain so, they are exempt from the apostle's judgement, by which, according to some, those who want to become rich are held to be guilty only so long as they are not. And if assent is given to this interpretation, all who are taking away another's possessions have, as I have mentioned earlier, to hurry up in order to arrive at the sum total of their own riches in the sure knowledge that they will be culpable only so long as they have not become what they wish to become.[95]

Wealth cannot be morally neutral, as Clement suggests. Wealth is a source of sin not only in its acquisition, but also in its possession. This is true even if one inherits their wealth, because all wealth derives from some kind of oppression of the other.[96]

De divitiis grounds its argument in Jesus's saying, found only in Luke, that no one can be his disciple unless they give up all of their possessions (Luke 14:33), quoting it over and over in the course of the treatise. It relies specifically on Luke, and on the Lukan insistence that one give up "all" possessions (Luke 14:26; see Matt 19:21; Mark 10:21).[97] Whereas Clement tries to avoid Luke, *De divitiis* embraces Luke's radical message, coming back to it again and again.

At the same time, it resists the sort of economic dualism found in Clement and others. For Clement, one is either rich or poor, either wealthy or destitute. To give all seems ridiculous, because it would result in destitution. As we imagined above, everything below ES3 or ES4 would seem to be ES7. But for *De divitiis*, there are not two, but three categories. There are

> the rich, the poor, and those who have enough; for every man must be accounted to be either rich or poor or self-sufficient. To be rich, so far as my meagre understanding is able to determine, is to have more than is necessary; to be poor is not to have enough; and to have enough, the mean between these two extremes, is to possess no more than is absolutely necessary.[98]

95. *De div.*, 4.3.

96. *De div.*, 7.3; Brown, *Through the Eye*, 314–15.

97. *De div.*, 5.3.

98. *De div.*, 5.1. Brown points out that this is a novel use of *sufficientia*. Using the term was often a means of allowing "a generous fudge factor in what counted as 'sufficient' possessions. In the *De divitiis*, however, *sufficientia* was a polemical slogan. It traced with unforgiving clarity, an economic poverty line below which the poor had been dragged by the very existence of the rich." Brown, *Through the Eye*, 315–16.

The gospel is not calling all to poverty, it envisions a world in which all have enough. *De divitiis* takes seriously the idea that God not only brings down the rich, but also lifts up the lowly. All are brought into a comfortable middle, likely ES5, possibly including ES4. The tiny minority in ES1–3 are brought down so that the majority languishing in ES7 and ES6 can be lifted up.

> Does it seem just to you then that one man should have an abundance of riches over and above his needs, while another does not have enough even to supply his daily wants? That one man should relax in the enjoyment of his wealth, while another wastes away in poverty? That one man should be full to bursting-point with expensive and sumptuous banquets far in excess of nature's habitual requirements, while another has not even enough cheap food to satisfy him. That one man should possess a vast number of splendid houses adorned with costly marble statues in keeping with the instincts of his vanity and pride, while another has not even a tiny hovel to call his own and to protect him from the cold or the heat? That one man should maintain countless possessions and enormous expanses of land, while another cannot enjoy the possession even of a small portion of turf on which to sit down? That one man should be rich in gold, silver, precious stones and all kinds of material possessions, while another is harassed by hunger, thirst, nakedness and all kinds of poverty?[99]

As *De divitiis* moves into its biblical exegesis, it marks out its methodological framework. Clement insists that one must not read wealth and poverty literally, but *De divitiis* rejects this entirely: "Let there be an end to false allegory."[100] Referring again to Luke, it insists that, as the biblical text clearly says, it is possessions that must be given up, not one's attitude toward possessions, if one is to be a disciple of Jesus (Luke 14:33).[101]

It also rejects the vocational and temporal arguments found in Kim and others. Jesus's words are not only for a few apostles. They are not only for a time of persecution. "In fact, the light of plain reasoning will establish that such an interpretation is incorrect."[102] When the rich man encounters Jesus, Jesus had already called the twelve, and yet he still

---

99. *De div.*, 8.1.

100. *De div.*, 10.1.

101. *De div.*, 10.3.

102. *De div.*, 10.4.

commands this man and all disciples to give up possessions. Ananias and Sapphira were not apostles either, but were held to the same standard (Acts 5:1–11).[103] Furthermore, the disciples did not give their possessions away because they lived in a particular time of persecution, but because it was a part of Christ's command that all divest.[104] These words are a key part of the gospel, not some secondary message that can be thrown away as no longer applicable.

De divitiis addresses the common argument of those who would domesticate Luke's message: the presence in the text of faithful rich people like Joseph of Ariamthea and Zacchaeus. It argues, somewhat unconvincingly, that Joseph could very well have divested himself after coming to Jesus. "If you think that Joseph was rich after becoming a believer in Christ, because the scripture calls him 'rich', then Matthew will remain a tax-gatherer, because he was called 'the tax-gatherer' after he became an apostle."[105] More convincing is his treatment of Zacchaeus, whom we are plainly told, voluntarily gave up his wealth upon encountering Jesus.

> Having welcomed the Lord not only into his house but also into his faithful heart, he said of his own accord and without prompting or teaching of any kind: Behold I give half of my goods to the poor, and if I have defrauded anyone of anything, I restore it fourfold [Luke 19:8]. By this we understand that, after reasoning with himself, he laid out half of his wealth in compensation for fraud and distributed the remaining half to the poor, so that he might share in that state of blessedness which was promised to paupers in return for their sufferings.[106]

As we have repeatedly pointed out above, Zacchaeus cannot be relied upon as an example of a rich person who remained faithful to Jesus without giving up possessions. Zacchaeus gives up his possessions—more than half and likely all—in response to his encounter with Jesus.

De divitiis also addresses Clement's argument that it is impossible to follow Jesus's commands if one gives away all one's possessions, because then there would be nothing left to give. How can one make friends with the mammon of unrighteousness if one has no mammon left to use?

---

103. *De div.*, 10.5–6.

104. *De div.*, 11.1–4.

105. *De div.*, 11.6.

106. *De div.*, 11.7.

> For they say, 'If all men are willing to distribute their possessions
> and to keep nothing at all for themselves, where would we then
> find works of godliness and compassion to perform, when the
> supply of objects to which to direct them have been exhausted?'
> Or, 'How are the poor to be sustained, where are guests to be
> entertained, from what source are the hungry to be fed, the
> naked covered and the thirsty given drink, if worldly wealth is
> lacking?' Great indeed is their love of compassion and godliness,
> if they care more for the poor than for God! And I would that
> they really cared for the poor and not rather for riches, which
> they try to defend on the pretext of helping the poor and under
> the pretense of being obliged to practise godliness, not realizing
> that some are in need because others have more than they need.
> Get rid of the rich man, and you will not be able to find a poor
> one. Let no man have more than he really needs, and everyone
> will have as much as they need, since the few who are rich are
> the reason for the many who are poor.[107]

Again we see *De divitiis*'s refusal to buy into the argument that if there
are no rich people, everyone will be destitute. Giving up wealth does not
mean destitution, it means sufficiency. It means enough. And the reason
that the rich cannot trust in 'enough' is because they do not heed the
counsel of Jesus not to worry about what they will eat or drink (Matt
6:31–33; cf. Luke 12:22). The rich trust in their wealth rather than in
God.[108] They are slaves not to God, but to Mammon (Luke 16:13).

Citing the Lukan version of the Beatitudes, *De divitiis* clearly argues
that God both blesses the poor and reprimands the rich. We saw above
how Clement negated Luke's Beatitudes with the more spiritualized version in Matthew. Here, *De divitiis* favors the Lukan version.

> But if we are to believe that the man who gives always attains the
> highest blessedness and yet he will not always be able to give un-
> less he remains rich, why does God so often criticise the rich and
> eulogize the poor, since the latter, being able to attain to a higher
> state of blessedness, are more worthy to be praised? 'But it is the
> *evil* rich that he blames,' you will say. Did you then read: Woe to
> you *evil* that are rich! (cf. Luke 6:24)? Or what need was there
> to add the label 'rich' at all, if he were not passing his judgement
> of condemnation upon them because of their riches? If he was
> rebuking the evil of men specifically, he would simply have said,

107. *De div.*, 12.1.
108. *De div.*, 13.1—15.1.

'Woe to you that are evil!' And if he is criticising not the rich in general but only the evil that are rich, he ought to have praised the rich that are good, if there are any such men to be found anywhere. And if you want his words, 'Woe to you that are rich!' to refer only to the evil rich, then he ought to say also of the good that are rich, 'Blessed are the rich'. He says quite clearly that there are men who are blessed but they are the poor (cf. Luke 6:20); if he had said, 'Blessed are the rich', then he would have been seen to be reducing to an even lower state the very class of men whom he pronounces blessed for being the opposite.

At this point I believe you will say, 'He praises the *good* poor'. Why then did he add the label 'poor', if he knew that no special mark of goodness was attached to poverty? For just as he would never have named riches in his statement of censure if he had not seen that they were worthy of censure, so too he would never have named poverty in his commendation of blessedness if he had felt that it was no aid to the attainment of goodness. I suppose that, in fact, the Word of God had left out from his utterance words which, if added, would have led to the censure of the evil and commendation of the good! Omitting the names of those attributes which, in some men's judgement, can neither hinder nor help, he would have said, 'Woe to you that are murderers or adulterers or greedy for plunder or idolaters or slaves to any other kind of vice or sin!' Why does he leave out all other sins and misdeeds and name only riches as an object of censure, as one who knows that they are frequently the cause of all our faults? Again, why does he omit the names of all the other virtues in praising the beatitudes and name only poverty, if he did not know that it is the source of all our virtues? And if he is not specifically addressing his censure to riches and his commendation to poverty by extolling it, he ought somewhere to have praised the rich and censured the poor. Since, however, he both censures the rich in general and commends the poor in general, he plainly and clearly demonstrated that, by the authority of his judgement, he both condemned the greed for riches and extolled the name of poverty.[109]

Here we clearly see *De divitiis* arguing our thesis, that God has good news for the poor and warnings against wealth, and we see it being argued explicitly on the grounds of Luke. It argues against spiritualizing rich and poor or creating an allegorical interpretation. It argues for a simple, direct reading of the text, in opposition to other contemporary interpreters

109. *De div.*, 16.1–2; emphasis in Rees' translation.

who seek to rob it of its power. Importantly, it does not take into account only the position of the rich. It also takes seriously the position of the poor. Where Clement sees only pitiable wretches, *De divitiis* sees those blessed by God.[110]

De divitiis continues to resist deradicalizing interpretations as it moves on to the ever-central saying about a camel passing through the eye of a needle (Luke 18:25). We saw Clement working diligently to widen the eye of the needle so that the rich could more easily fit through. *De divitiis* points out the foolishness of such attempts.

> What need have we to debate any further a passage whose meaning is absolutely clear—unless it is necessary to remind rich men to recognize that they will be able to possess the glory of heaven only if they find a needle large enough for a camel to pass through its eye, and a camel so small that it can go through the very narrow entrance provided by such a needle? Or if this proves to be something which is quite impossible, how will it ever be possible to accomplish something which is by definition still more impossible? Only, perhaps, if the rich man makes a proper distribution of his wealth so as either to become poor or to leave himself with just enough to live on, and then strives to enter where a man of substance cannot.[111]

The rich cannot pass through unless they cease being exorbitantly rich. They cannot pass through unless they cease being camels. *De divitiis* even mentions and derides what we saw above in the manuscripts of Luke 18:25: the attempt to soften this passage by substituting κάμιλον for κάμηλον, a ship's cable rather than a camel.

> What an intolerable excess of ingenuity a man is forced to employ by his love of riches if he has to betake himself to names for ship's ropes in order to avoid being compelled to diminish his abundant supply of worldly resources![112]

De divitiis fights at every turn the attempt to defang the radical, but very plain, message of the gospel. It will not let the reader accept an allegorical interpretation that casts the camel saying as having to do with Jews and

---

110. However, Brown argues that "*De divitiis* was less moved than was Jerome by pathos for the poor. What counted most for him was the stark contrast between poverty and worldly power." Brown, *Through the Eye*, 319.

111. *De div.*, 18.1.

112. *De div.*, 18.2.

Gentiles.[113] Neither will it accept the argument that the saying is negated by what follows in Luke 18:27, "What is impossible for humans is possible for God."[114] It takes this to read that while humans think that one can't be saved "without an abundance of riches," salvation "is made much more possible with God in his wisdom," because "a humble and holy poverty gives him much greater pleasure than the proud and sinful ostentation of riches."[115] *De divitiis* will allow no loopholes in its interpretation of this dominical saying. It is hard. It is radical. It is meant to be so.[116]

In fact, at this point *De divitiis* undertakes an extended argument against reading wealth in the gospels allegorically. The standard practice in biblical interpretation at the time, it argues, is to read the Hebrew Bible allegorically while reading the New Testament more literally. However, when it comes to the issue of wealth, interpreters seem to reverse the process, reading the New Testament sayings allegorically while using the less radical sayings in the Hebrew Bible literally as a means of negating the radicalism of the New Testament.

> They want the riches of Abraham and David and Solomon and the rest to be understood literally; but when they read something about contempt of riches in the gospel, they exert themselves to adulterate its meaning by employing a metaphorical treatment.[117]

If there are rich people in the Hebrew Bible who still find favor with God, it must be that God does not reject actual wealth; if God rejects wealth in the New Testament, it must not be talking about actual wealth. Interpreters do this, *De divitiis* argues, in order to domesticate the gospel. They want it to conform to their own lifestyle, "not to live as they have been commanded to do but to adapt the commandments to the manner in which they live."[118] Metaphorical readings are used here, contrary to regular practice, for the express purpose of exempting the rich from New Testament ethics. It happens only here, *De divitiis* says, only in relation to wealth.[119]

---

113. *De div.*, 18.7–8.
114. *De div.*, 18.3.
115. *De div.*, 18.5.
116. Brown, *Through the Eye*, 319–20.
117. *De div.*, 18.11.
118. *De div.*, 18.11.
119. *De div.*, 18.11.

Conclusion

Why spend so much time with a marginal, heretical text like *De divitiis*? What can it contribute to an understanding of Lukan wealth ethics? Surely if it is not orthodox then it must be a fringe reading.

And yet that is precisely the point. *De divitiis* has a plain reading of the Gospel of Luke. There is no need to embellish Luke in order to derive a message of good news for the poor and resistance to wealth. One need only refrain from allegorizing it. One need only take it at its word. And that is what *De divitiis* does; it takes the radical economic message of Luke at its word. And for that reason it is deemed unorthodox. In its simple reading of Jesus's sayings, it is perceived as heretical. Luke's message is too radical to be orthodox.

There are certainly other early Christian writers who take the radical message of Luke more seriously than does Clement. And yet, it is arguments like Clement's that win the day. The church becomes dependent on wealthy patrons. If the church wants to keep those wealthy patrons, then it must devise a means of deradicalizing the radical economic message. It must find a way of legitimizing wealth, so long as some of that wealth is directed toward the church.

This deradicalized wealth ethic is not wholly without merit. One can certainly argue that it is better for wealthy Christians to give some of their wealth for the benefit of the poor than to keep it all to themselves, though many question whether such charity serves as a screen for obscuring the root causes of poverty.[120] And it is certainly possible to find biblical warrant for such an ethic. But it is not the wealth ethic of Luke. Luke insists that wealth be resisted, not accommodated. Luke insists that the poor are of utmost concern to God. Luke is radical. And as is demonstrated at least in part by this study of the treatment of Luke in *Quis dives salvatur* and in *De divitiis*, Luke is too radical to be orthodox. It must be mellowed. It must be tamed. It must be brought into greater conformity with the realities of the social world. It is utopian. But rather than being maintained as a utopian ideal that offers sharp critique to the real world, it must be marginalized. It must be explained away, lest the wealthy and powerful, on which the church depends, be driven away.

---

120. De La Torre, *Politics of Jesús*, loc. 798–800.

CHAPTER 6

Lukan Accommodation to Roman Economic Domination

So you also, when you have done all that you were
ordered to do, say, "We are worthless slaves; we
have done only what we ought to have done."

—LUKE 17:10 NRSV

A RECENT WORK ON economy in early Christianity demands our attention: *Time of Troubles* by Roland Boer and Christina Petterson. Like the criticism of Itumeleng Mosala and Craig Nessan, it argues that biblical writings, including Luke, do not so much represent a resistance to economic exploitation, but rather are part of the system that legitimizes and props up systems of economic exploitation. Luke blunts the more radical message of Jesus. In fact, Boer and Petterson's critique may be even more thoroughgoing. Both Mosala and Nessan suggest that the biblical texts can be liberated and used for the work of liberation:

> The Bible is the product, the record, the site, and the weapon of class, cultural, gender, and racial struggles. And a biblical hermeneutics of liberation that does not take this fact seriously can only falter in its project to emancipate the poor and the exploited of the world. Once more, the simple truth rings out that

the poor and exploited must liberate the Bible so that the Bible may liberate them.[1]

Boer and Petterson are not so optimistic. While Boer thinks that a kernel of resistance remains even in texts that have done the work of legitimizing expropriation, Petterson argues any perceived resistance is simply a part of the system of domination.[2] In either case, their understanding of the function of texts like Luke within the domination systems of the Greco-Roman world represent a significant obstacle to my thesis that Luke has a radically liberative message. Furthermore, it is an obstacle that is quite different from the critiques of my other major interlocutors. Those writers tend to argue that, thankfully, Luke is not so radical as it seems. By contrast, like Mosala and Nessan, Boer and Petterson argue that Luke is not as radical as it should be. For this reason, and on account of the major contribution that their new economic framework is likely to make to biblical studies, it seems appropriate to spend a chapter addressing it here.

A New Economic Framework

Only a relatively small part of *Time of Troubles* is dedicated to understanding the place of the New Testament text within the economic systems of the Roman Empire. Its major contribution is to offer a new framework for understanding those systems in general: no minor task. A basic understanding of Boer and Petterson's framework is necessary for understanding their critiques of the gospel message.

Boer and Petterson begin their work boldly, not shying away from its paradigm-shifting implications:

> This work proposes nothing less than a new model for understanding the economy of the Greco-Roman era, in which Christianity arose. We do so on two foundations: empirical information, for what it is; and a theoretical model drawn from both *Régulation* economic theory and the work of G. E. M. de Ste. Croix.[3]

---

1. Mosala, *Biblical Hermeneutics*, 193. See also Nessan, "Luke and Liberation Theology," 137.

2. Boer and Petterson, *Time of Troubles*, 186–89.

3. Boer and Petterson, *Time of Troubles*, xi.

Having clearly stated their intent, they proceed to give a very tidy summary and outline of their construction:

> In this light, we propose that the Greco-Roman economy had four key building blocks, or what we call institutional forms: subsistence survival agriculture; the reproduction of space entailed in the relations of *polis* and *chōra*; the permutations of tenure; and the slave relation. These building blocks came together in different constellations in which one institutional form dominated the others. These constellations we call regimes, which signal economic patterns with some staying power over time and place. Three such regimes can be identified: the slave regime; the colonial regime, dominated by *polis-chōra*; and the land regime, in which tenure comes to the fore, so much so that it leads eventually to the colonate. Only when we consider the regimes as a whole can we speak of the overarching category of mode of production. In other words, the economy had three articulated layers beginning with the most specific and moving to a more general framework: institutional forms, regimes, and mode of production. Our attention is primarily focused on the first two layers, for these provide detail on the nuts and bolts of the whole system.[4]

All this detail is contained on the first page of this monograph. Clearly, Boer and Petterson intend a system of understanding that is quite different from those usually used to interpret the economic world around early Christianity. We will return shortly to the detail of this system.

Boer and Petterson actively resist the application of neoclassical economic theory to the ancient world arguing that it distorts our view of the ancient in ways that are often imperceptible to us moderns who are soaked in Smithian norms. They call this phenomenon "economics imperialism," that is, the imposition of *homo economicus* as a universal in all times and places in a way that individualizes, desocializes, and dehistorizes human behavior.

> Thus, the individual—as rational, self-interested, and determined by utility—becomes the focus of analysis; the "market" becomes an entity unto itself with its own dynamics and without any social basis; and this "market" is regarded as without history since it exists whenever any individual exchanges something with another individual.[5]

4. Boer and Petterson, *Time of Troubles*, xi.
5. Boer and Petterson, *Time of Troubles*, 3–4.

This is the construction which they are hoping to replace using Marxist analysis, along with the help of *Régulation* theory and Ste. Croix.

In place of the equilibrium of neoclassical economics, Boer and Petterson suggest a model of disequilibrium. From Ste. Croix they adopt the concept of a class society, in which "a particular (usually small) class controls the conditions or means of production and is thereby able to appropriate a surplus at the expense of other classes which do not control or own the means of production."[6] This imbalance necessarily creates class struggle. All that is needed for class struggle is the fact of economic exploitation. However, this class struggle is often accompanied with visible forms of resistance.[7]

In the period we are studying, economic exploitation was maintained primarily through the ownership of land and through the ownership of other persons through slavery and other forms of unfree labor. With massive estates worked by armies of slaves and other bonded workers, the ancient elite were freed from the burdens of labor to produce what we have come to know as Greco-Roman culture. "Slaves directly supported the existence of a uniformly brutal ruling class who produced all the art, literature, science, and philosophy of the classical world."[8] The tool of debt was used to maintain the necessary dependence of workers to the aristocracy. Slaves and peasants alike were bound to the wealthy through this land ownership and debt.

However, as Ste. Croix pointed out, there were forms of resistance to the economic exploitation of *latifundia*, namely "the common practice of *anachōrēsis* or *secessio*, an 'exodus' by tenant farmers who would collectively refuse to work and even depart until a grievance had been remedied."[9] This might include a legal appeal to an (absentee) landlord or to imperial officials.

> Other age-old practices included not harvesting crops that were to be requisitioned, melting away when labor service was required, hiding small surpluses put aside for a bad season, or absconding entirely and resettling in a more remote area.[10]

6. Boer and Petterson, *Time of Troubles*, 25.

7. Boer and Petterson, *Time of Troubles*, 25–26.

8. Boer and Petterson, *Time of Troubles*, 28.

9. Boer and Petterson, *Time of Troubles*, 32.

10. Boer and Petterson, *Time of Troubles*, 32.

All of Roman culture and economy was built on the engine of agricultural labor. For every one specialist in society—whether tradesperson or elite—it took ten agricultural workers to support them. There simply could be no culture without the power of agricultural labor to fuel it. Besides this, there was cultural bias toward wealth gained by land ownership. Land was the honorable way to produce wealth. Because of their cultural and economic importance, agricultural workers could actually effect some change through these sorts of resistance. While slave revolts were relatively rare, resistance by tenants, peasants, and freedmen were more common, and they could be effective.[11]

Boer and Petterson make an additional claim, separate from Ste. Croix, that becomes very important for their argument going forward. They suggest that one key form of resistance to elite domination is subsistence farming. Peasants who own their own land and produce for themselves are a threat to the system. They do not produce rents for the elite (ES1–3). They may still have obligations to the empire, but they are not part of the engine of wealth generation in the same way that tenants and slaves are. Power must be brought to bear to keep this independent production from happening on a large scale.[12]

And this is where our authors turn to *Régulation* theory. Boer and Petterson cite four key insights of *Régulation* theory for understanding the social-economic world of ancient Rome. First, "economic activity is inescapably social." One cannot separate out the economic as a separate realm in which cultural norms are independent of economic forces. Second, "contradiction and therefore crisis is the norm." Societal imbalances routinely generate resistance. Third, "temporary stability is the exception and needs to be analyzed." If everything in society seems peaceful and in order, that should spark questions about what is giving it that appearance. And fourth, "stability is enabled by institutional, behavioral, and ideological practices." Powers are brought to bear to maintain a sense of equilibrium in the system.[13] These four key insights contrast greatly with the key assumptions of economics imperialism, namely:

> (1) the rational nature of the fictional *Homooeconomicus*; (2) equilibrium as the norm, based on interactions between rational individuals, and crisis as an anomaly caused by external

---

11. Boer and Petterson, *Time of Troubles*, 32–33.

12. Boer and Petterson, *Time of Troubles*, 32–35.

13. Boer and Petterson, *Time of Troubles*, 41.

irrational factors and "interference"; (3) the independence of a
network of markets in which such actions take place. Indeed, a
fictional *Homooeconomicus* released into the messy reality of life
would not survive for a single day.[14]

The most important contribution of *Régulation* theory is that socio-
economic systems do not stay in balance on their own. Power must be
exerted in order to keep them in balance, in order to keep the oppressed
from escaping or destroying the means of their oppression.

Régulation theory provides some language to talk about these forces.
A regime is "the mechanisms by which a specific economic constellation
is able for a time to manage . . . crises so that the regime may reproduce
itself."[15] In a particular time and place, the whole system that maintains
some sense of stability is called a regime.

Within that regime, there are institutional forms. They are "codifi-
cations of the fundamental social relations that underpin economics."[16]
These different institutional forms interact with each other in various
configurations, usually with one dominating over the others in any given
regime. Boar and Petterson name four institutional forms at work in the
Roman world: subsistence survival, which was under constant threat;
polis-chōra, the relationship between a city and the countryside around
it that supplies it and makes it possible; tenure, the gobbling up of land
by large owners who thus have control over their tenants; and the slave-
relation, in which a person's labor is not their own.

Finally, a mode of *régulation* is "an emergent ensemble of norms,
institutions, organizational forms, social networks and patterns of conduct that can temporarily stabilize an accumulation regime despite the
conflictual and antagonistic character,"[17] or an "active process of adjust-
ing disequilibriums on a day-to-day basis."[18] It is the means by which
order—or the appearance of order—is maintained in a system inclined to
disorder. Many cultural forms can be and are brought to bear to maintain
order, to keep the society regulated. The most important for Boer and

---

14. Boer and Petterson, *Time of Troubles*, 41.

15. Boer and Petterson, *Time of Troubles*, 44.

16. Boer and Petterson, *Time of Troubles*, 44.

17. Boer and Petterson, *Time of Troubles*, 44–45, quoted from Jessop and Sum, *Beyond Regulation*, 42.

18. Boer and Petterson, *Time of Troubles*, 45, quoted from Boyer and Saillard, "*Ré-gulation* Theory," 41.

Petterson's study, as for ours, is religion. They argue that "Christianity functioned as a highly effective and supple mode of *régulation*."[19]

And here is the crux of the problem. If Christianity functions as a mode of *régulation*, as a means of maintaining the legitimizing the status quo of economic exploitation, then how can it possibly function as a force for liberation? More specifically, for my study, how does the Gospel of Luke function within this paradigm? Is it a text of liberation, as I have claimed? Or is it a text of *régulation*, simply a deceptive means of perpetuating economics imperialism?

Roman *Régulation*

Boer and Petterson argue that three institutional forms—*polis-chōra*, tenure, and the slave relation—were at work in the Greco-Roman world to regulate society and mitigate against the chief form of resistance to this *régulation*: subsistence-survival production. If peasants are producing agricultural products for themselves on land that they themselves own, then wealth is not being extracted from their labor for the benefit of the elite (ES1–3). The *polis-chōra* relation, the institution of tenant farming, and slavery effectively held peasant labor within the system of economic exploitation.

Key to understanding Roman economics is understanding the relationship between *polis* and *chōra*, that is, between city and countryside. Most economic production was done in the countryside, and the surpluses produced there were necessary for the functioning of the city. But while the smaller but more elite *polis* generated the literature and culture of the society, the much larger but lower-class *chōra* remains largely silent to history. Elite writings romanticized the country lifestyle. Honorable wealth was thought to come from agricultural production, but in practice, the owning class was of the city. The *chōra* existed in order to make the *polis* possible. While lip service was given to the superiority of the rural life, power or prestige were to be found most profoundly in the cities. Furthermore, the planting of new cities served as a means of expanding the reach of economics imperialism. Wherever a *polis* was placed, to bring amenities and culture, the surrounding *chōra* could be more easily exploited, its surplus diverted into the hands of the powerful.[20]

---

19. Boer and Petterson, *Time of Troubles*, 45.
20. Boer and Petterson, *Time of Troubles*, 77–82.

This was inescapably a colonizing economic form in which the *poleis* marked the imposition of new and disruptive economic practices. For those in the *chōra*, the *poleis* were alien impositions by a foreign power and culture, sucking vital produce from the land. In short, the exploiting ruling classes in colonial spaces (including Judea and the backwater of Galilee) were largely of the *polis*, and they did their best to exploit and despise those upon whom their brittle "culture" depended.[21]

Theoretically the *polis* and the *chōra* benefit each other, but in practice the *chōra* is exploited for the benefit of the *polis*.

Another form for maintaining the system of economics imperialism is the practice of tenant farming. Again, in theory, tenure is beneficial to all parties concerned. The landlords get some of the produce of the land while the tenants get security. But in practice, the relationship is unequal. Tenancy is a means of control, binding the tenant to a particular piece of land without the ability ever to realize the profit of their labor or achieve self-sufficiency. The larger the estate, the greater the profit for the landlord. The more precarious the situation of the tenant, the more power for the landlord. Wherever possible, peasants were pushed into situations of tenure, preferably under terms that allowed the landlord to eject them at any time.[22]

One important means of enforcing tenancy was through instruments of debt. Debt, according to Boer and Petterson, had three main functions. The first was to compel labor. So long as a producer was indebted, their labor was in service of someone else. Loans could be made at such high rates that they resulted in default, seizure of land, and even slavery. However, debts could also be adjusted. A lender might offer just enough debt relief to allow their debtor to remain solvent, so that they were not tempted to abscond, but remained plugged into the system. Second, debt offered lenders a reliable source of income. So long as debtors were working to pay off their debts, lenders could rely on their production, without having to resort to any more coercive means of wealth extraction. Third, debt reinforced economic hierarchy. Debtors would always be beholden to lenders. Lenders would always get richer. Debtors would always be held in service.[23]

21. Boer and Petterson, *Time of Troubles*, 85.

22. Boer and Petterson, *Time of Troubles*, 91–98.

23. Boer and Petterson, *Time of Troubles*, 98–100.

Finally, slavery not only functioned as a means of *régulation* on the Roman economic system, it was the institution around which markets formed. Slaves were not one commodity among many that were traded in ancient markets; slavery produced the very concept of private property that could be traded in something like a market. Slaves were for sale everywhere, in every market. The act of abstraction that allowed humans to understand other humans as exchangeable objects was the key factor in the invention of private property. Slaves were not seen as beings in and of themselves, they were objects, things. As things, rather than humans, they were extensions of the master's person and will. The abstraction of a person into a thing, Boer and Petterson argue, is the intellectual move that leads not only to the concept of private property, but to the abstract thinking required for philosophic pursuits.[24] "In short, philosophy as we know it could not have arisen without slavery, since both entail a significant process of abstract thought."[25]

These three institutional forms—*polis-chōra*, tenure, and slavery—correspond to three regimes of *régulation*: the colonial regime, the land regime, and the slave regime, respectively. All three were at work in various times and at various places in the Roman world; they could exist side by side. But all three were attempts to deal with the primary form of resistance: subsistence-survival production.[26]

> We argue that subsistence survival was the persistent form of resistance inside the other three regimes, a ghost that refused to disappear. Indeed, we propose that since it was the institutional form that was primarily allocative, the slave, colonial, and land regimes may be understood as efforts to deal with and negate the constitutive resistance of subsistence survival. . . . Even though common use of the term might suggest the opposite—that resistance is a response or reaction—resistance is primary with respect to power. The real driving force of history is precisely this constitutive resistance to which extractive economic forces and oppressive political powers must constantly adapt and attempt new modes of containment. In other words the dominant and driving reality is precisely this resistance, which can never be contained and harnessed by the powers that be—hence the efforts by the latter at ever-new ways of attempting to do so. The slave regime, colonial regime, and the land regime may thereby

24. Boer and Petterson, *Time of Troubles*, 109–26.

25. Boer and Petterson, *Time of Troubles*, 123.

26. Boer and Petterson, *Time of Troubles*, 130–50.

be seen as efforts to overcome and control the resistance of subsistence survival.[27]

Thus we have the outlines of Boer and Petterson's economic model of the New Testament. Peasants are constantly moved to resist the conditions that exploit them. Systems, or regimes, are developed to restrain that resistance, though they are never perfectly or ultimately successful. Each new form of institutional restraint produces new forms of resistance which in turn give rise to new institutional restraints, in a dialectic. For Boer and Petterson, these systems are best understood in the New Testament period as relating to the *polis-chōra* relationship, the slave relation, and later, land tenancy. Having sketched out their theoretical and historical framework, we can now turn to the ways Boer and Petterson understand Christianity, including the Gospel of Luke, as functioning not as a source of liberation, but as a form of *régulation*, keeping the system of economic exploitation functioning smoothly.

The New Testament, Luke, and *Régulation*

Boer and Petterson argue that Christianity acts as a mode of *régulation* through all three of the regimes they identify: the colonate, slavery, and land tenure. However, as relates to this study of the Gospel of Luke, it is the first two that are most relevant, along with their accompanying institutional forms: *polis-chōra* and the slave relation.

The *polis-chōra* dichotomy is central to Boer and Pettersons claims about how Christianity functioned as a mode of *régulation*. Along with many other scholars, they assume that Jesus's ministry took place primarily in the countryside, among peasants. However, after the death of Jesus, the Jesus Movement very quickly shifted from being a rural movement to be an urban movement. Paul and the gospel writers represent not the *chōra* perspective of Jesus, but the *polis* perspective of the elite.[28]

This is a very common conclusion, famously made by Wayne Meeks in *The First Urban Christians*. Jesus's ministry was among the peasants of the *chōra*, but Pauline (and later) Christianity was an urban movement, focusing on the *polis* and losing touch with the *chōra*. Paul and the gospel writers show a degree of literacy not possible in the countryside.

27. Boer and Petterson, *Time of Troubles*, 131–32.
28. Boer and Petterson, *Time of Troubles*, 154.

And here is where Boer and Petterson begin to diverge from the position of their favored scholar, Ste. Croix. Ste. Croix argued that Jesus was of the countryside and that his sayings represented a peasant resistance to the forces of economic oppression. Boer and Petterson summarize the position:

> For Jesus, property was an evil and a huge hurdle to entering the Kingdom of God. By contrast, Jesus values simplicity (or, in our terms, subsistence survival) over luxury and rejects the power that comes with wealth. Everything about Jesus stands against the deeply-held values of the Greco-Roman ruling class, almost uniquely in the literature of the ancient world. Many biblical scholars, theologians, and even some Marxists would agree. So problematic are the records of Jesus's words that the early Christians "had to play down those ideas of Jesus which were hostile to the ownership of any large quantity of property."
>
> The question remains, why did Christianity so quickly become part of the early Roman urban setting? While Ste. Croix does not pose this question, it is, as mentioned earlier, contained within his observation that within a generation the transfer of Christian ideas from the *chōra* to the *polis* had taken place.[29]

Boer and Petterson agree wholeheartedly with the conclusion that Christian ideas quickly shifted from the countryside to the city. Where they disagree with Ste. Croix is where the words of Jesus and the writings of the New Testament fit into that transformation. Ste Croix finds the words of Jesus recorded in the gospels to be a source of that original *chōra* perspective. Boer and Petterson, however, do not consider the gospels to be good witnesses to the message of Jesus. They "assume that the Gospels are second-generation texts, generated from the *polis* perspective," that are essentially unfamiliar with the *chōra* and the concerns of peasants.[30] They conclude that the parables do not "represent actual rural life," but rather "the representation of rural life as it is imagined by someone not of peasant provenance." For them, "the perspective of the parables has more affinities with the *polis* than with the *chōra*."[31]

Boer and Petterson have correctly identified the most problematic material in the gospel. As we saw in chapters 2 and 4, it is the parables that

---

29. Boer and Petterson, *Time of Troubles*, 156–57, quoting De Ste. Croix, *Class Struggle*, 426–27.

30. Boer and Petterson, *Time of Troubles*, 157.

31. Boer and Petterson, *Time of Troubles*, 165.

most imperil Luke's radical economic message. Boer and Petterson also note that it is especially the parables of slavery that seem to empower the forces of economic oppression. If they are looking for signs that the gospel functions as a mode of *régulation*, they are looking in the right place. In a moment, we will explore their treatment of these parables more fully.

But first let us examine the distinction between *polis* and *chōra*. For Boer and Petterson, it seems in large part to function as a distinction between social classes. Peasants are from the *chōra*; owners are from the *polis*. The sophistication of the writing of someone like Luke indicates that they are from the *polis* rather than from the *chōra*. The *chōra* perspective is missing in the parables because it fails to convincingly depict the point of view of peasants. One wonders why they do not describe this difference in terms of economic class, but the category they do use is that of a rural-urban divide.

As mentioned before, Boer and Petterson argue that by the second generation of Christianity it had been nearly completely transformed from a *chōra* movement into a *polis* movement. There is good reason, though, to question this formulation. A recent study by Thomas Robinson marshals compelling evidence to show that the commonly accepted "urban thesis"—this contention that Christianity quickly transformed itself into an urban phenomenon—is unlikely, if not impossible.[32]

In *Who Were the First Christians? Dismantling the Urban Thesis*, Robinson admits that it is almost universally accepted that early Christianity was an urban movement. Ramsey MacMullen, Derek Baker, W. H. C. Frend, Wayne Meeks, Robert Wilken, Rodney Stark, Henry Chadwick, Peter Brown, Henri Marrou, Robin Lane Fox, Paula Fredriksen—and, we may add, Boer and Petterson—all state some version of this urban thesis.[33] "The thesis of a largely urban Christianity sweeps on with hardly a voice of dissent."[34]

---

32. Robinson, *Who Were the First Christians?*

33. Robinson, *Who Were the First Christians?*, 14–17. References include: Meeks, *First Urban Christians*, 32–34, 73; MacMullen, *The Second Church*, 101–2; MacMullen, *Christianizing the Roman Empire*, 83, 103; Frend, *Town and Country*; Frend, "Town and Countryside," 34, 35, 37; Frend, "Failure of Persecutions," 268; Baker, *The Church*, xv; Meeks and Wilken, *Jews and Christians*, 1; Stark, *Rise of Christianity*, 57; Stark, *Cities of God*; Chadwick et al., *Role of the Christian Bishop*, 1; Brown, *Rise of Western Christendom*, 69; Daniélou and Marrou, *Christian Centuries*, 1:296; Fox, *Pagans and Christians*, 46; Jones, *The Greek City*, 298; Fredriksen, "Christians in the Roman Empire," 587.

34. Robinson, *Who Were the First Christians?*, 18.

However, this consensus view, Robinson argues, suffers from a basic failure of math and an overly rigid separation of *polis* and *chōra*. First, it is almost impossible for Christianity to have been a nearly entirely urban movement given the overwhelming rural nature of the ancient world. Second, city and countryside were not so clearly divided as we moderns would expect; many people routinely passed back and forth.

In a time in which only one-tenth of people lived in cities, pre-Constantinian Christianity would either have to be vanishingly small or in no small part rural in character.

> If Christians were largely urban and if the empire was largely rural, even with remarkable success in the urban areas, Christianity could have represented at best only a small proportion of the overall population of the empire by the time of Constantine— much smaller than the 10% that is often maintained. Indeed, if the empire was 10% urban (as many of those quoted above would have maintained) and Christians, at 10% of the empire, were themselves largely urban, Christians would have made up the entire population of all urban areas by the year 300 C.E. Even with a higher rate of urbanization (20%), Christians (at 10% of the population of the empire) would have made up half the population of all cities of the empire. Given that Christians would have been far more numerous in the eastern part of the empire, Eastern cities would have been swamped with Christians even in a fairly urbanized empire. If, on the other hand, Christians constituted only 10% of the urban population (or even double that) and if the adherents of Christianity throughout the empire were primarily urban, then Christians would have made up only 1% to 4% of the population of the empire in the year 300, a scenario equally problematic and one that would require a radical rethinking of the Christian presence (and success or lack thereof) in the empire. Strangely, the mathematical impossibilities facing most of the reconstructions offered seem to have escaped notice even by those who are generally meticulous in their scholarship. The problem with using numbers in this way is that no one would propose them if the blunt reality of the situation were spelled out. Yet some such highly unlikely scenario is required by the assumptions that are commonly accepted in the urban thesis.[35]

Even if the Christian movement grew disproportionally in the urban context, it is still highly unlikely that it was ever a majority-*polis* phenomenon.

35. Robinson, *Who Were the First Christians?*, 18–19.

The modern world is less than half rural, the European Union 25 percent, and the United States only 18 percent.[36] The ancient Roman world was 90 percent rural.[37] In our world, even a movement that is disproportionally rural will—unless it is exceptionally small—likely find a significant percentage of its support from cities. In the ancient world, the opposite is true. Even if early Christianity was disproportionally urban, it would—unless it was exceptionally small—likely have found a significant percentage of its support from the countryside.

> If Christianity had even a most minimal success in the countryside, gaining but a small percentage of the rural inhabitants, the number of rural Christians easily could have equaled—or indeed surpassed—that of urban Christians in the early period, simply by reason of the fact that the overall rural population was so much more numerous than the urban.[38]

First- and second-century sources describe Christianity growing not only in cities, but also in villages and the countryside, and there is no reason not to believe that there were significant numbers of rural Christians.[39]

Furthermore, the separation between *polis* and *chōra* may not have been nearly as complete as Boer and Petterson imply. As Robinson notes, numerous scholars have written in the past few decades, warning against erecting strong barriers between cities and villages on the one hand and the countryside on the other.[40] Considerable numbers of agricultural workers lived in cities and villages and travelled out to work in the fields each day.[41] Cities were also a location for services for those who lived in the countryside, including religious services. Even the elite—whom Boer and Petterson most associate with the *polis*—likely spent considerable time on their country estates, some becoming involved in the details of management.[42]

36. The World Bank, "Rural Population."

37. The only three modern countries with at least 85 percent rural population are Liechtenstein 86 percent, Papua New Guinea 87 percent, and Burundi 87 percent.

38. Robinson, *Who Were the First Christians?*, 19.

39. Robinson, *Who Were the First Christians?*, 147–48.

40. Robinson, *Who Were the First Christians?*, 65–67. Among others, Robinson cites: Wallace-Hadrill, "Introduction," 1; Rohrbaugh, "The Preindustrial City," 115–19; Scheidel, "Demography," 77; Fox, *Pagans and Christians*, 40–46; North, "Religion and Rusticity," 144–45.

41. Robinson, *Who Were the First Christians?*, 75.

42. Robinson, *Who Were the First Christians?*, 65–67.

> The oft-repeated notion of a stark dichotomy in the Greco-Roman world between rural and urban areas—whether cultural, religious, or linguistic—may be misleading. The line between rural and urban was ambiguous at best. City and country were interwoven in ways that prevent neat definition, and the urban and rural worlds were never mutually isolated enclaves where members of one rarely entered the other. . . . Only at the extremes might one speak of two worlds. For most, the urban and the rural flowed together or ebbed to and fro, making sharp boundaries arbitrary and misleading.[43]

The point need not be belabored. All that is necessary here is to acknowledge that it is very unlikely that early Christianity was almost exclusively urban and that the urban-rural divide was so profound that Christians after the first generation were alienated from and unaware of the details of rural life. Even if the churches of Paul and the evangelists were much more urban than the crowds that Jesus attracted, they would still have touched the countryside in meaningful ways and could easily have had more members in the *chōra* than in the *polis*.

This is not to say that Boer and Petterson have no point at all. As we have noted above, Luke is written by someone with some facility with Greek. It was not written by a peasant farmer. The author likely spent more time in the *polis* than did the average agricultural worker. The author certainly lived higher up the economic scale than a peasant, agricultural slave, or day laborer. The only point necessary here is that an urban-rural dichotomy—which presumes that Jesus came from the *chōra* and did not understand the *polis* while Paul and the gospel writers came from the *polis* and did not understand the *chōra*—is not the most illuminating way to define the difference between Jesus and the early Christian movements.

However, Boer and Petterson's related claim, that the parables found in the gospels reflect the perspective of the owner-class rather than the perspective of the peasant class, is still worthy of examination. They use as their example the Markan version of the Parable of the Wicked Tenants (12:1–12; Matt 21:33–46; Luke 20:9–19). This parable, they argue, is clearly written from the perspective of the land-owning class, not from the perspective of the tenant or peasant classes.[44]

---

43. Robinson, *Who Were the First Christians?*, 65, 90.
44. Boer and Petterson, *Time of Troubles*, 165.

Their chosen opponent for this argument is Luise Schottroff.[45] She makes a case not dissimilar to the one that I made in chapter 4 regarding the Parable of the Pounds, that God should not be associated allegorically with the landowner or slave-master characters in parables. Boer and Petterson derisively describe the approach:

> A rule of thumb is that any parable which depicts God as a slave-owner, landowner, or cranky king is seen by Schottroff not as an analogy, but as an antithetical parable, which intends to present the listeners with the difference between God's kingdom and the current situation.[46]

They think she has a circular argument. Any parable she finds problematic she defines as antithetical, because it is not consistent with what we already know about Jesus. However, any one of these parables is only inconsistent with what we know about Jesus if we have already excluded the other problematic parables from the set of things that tell us about Jesus.

Schottroff does, in fact, give an antithetical reading to Boer and Petterson's example parable, the parable of the Wicked Tenants. She writes:

> In this parable we hear how indebtedness turns those burdened with it into violent people filled with hatred. There is no reason to interpret the sending of the slaves allegorically (sending of prophets by God) or the son christologically. Even that he is the father's "beloved" son can be explained within the imagery of the story: he is the only son and heir. The reference to Isaiah 5 in v. 1, however, suggests an interpretation of the vineyard as Israel. Nevertheless, the matter-of-fact interpretation of the vineyard owner as God, which rules in the interpretive tradition with only a few exceptions, must be fundamentally called into question if we take the social-historical analysis of the text seriously. The owner of the vineyard acts like an opponent of God; he does the opposite of what the God of the Torah and the Lord's Prayer desires and does.[47]

So, shall we read with Schottroff and say that this parable, like the Parable of the Pounds, represents something antithetical to God's Empire, something that stands here as a negative example?

---

45. Schottroff, *Parables of Jesus.*

46. Boer and Petterson, *Time of Troubles*, 166.

47. Schottroff, *Parables of Jesus*, loc. 262–67.

No, at least not when interpreting it within the context of the Lukan narrative. It is true that I have categorized the verses in this parable as C and D. There is no good news for the poor here. There is no resistance to wealth. Luke's version is not quite as problematic as Mark's version, the version used by Schottroff, Boer, and Petterson. Still, if it were standing on its own or in a different context, it would be problematic for my thesis. On the surface, it is told from an owner perspective. The protagonist is an absentee landlord, though not nearly as dastardly a landlord as we find in some of the other parables. However, within the context of the gospel, the problem fades. In Mark, in Luke, in Matthew, we are told the same thing: this parable is told by Jesus against his opponents in the religious elite (Matt 21:45; Mark 12:12; Luke 20:19). The narrator makes it quite clear that we are supposed to read this parable Christologically, despite what Schottroff claims.

But even if we choose not to read it Christologically, it would not be as problematic as Boer and Petterson suggest. The main thing the owner does wrong is be an owner and an absentee. So far as we can tell, he does not mistreat or abuse his tenants. We are not told that he demands excessive profits from them. His opponents in the story are not slaves. If we want to indict the master of this parable, it should be, as Mitzi J. Smith suggests, for the callous way he sends slave after slave to their death, treating both them and his son as expendable.[48] On the other hand, the tenants of the parable clearly do things that are evil. They assault and kill messengers. Relatively high-class tenants assaulting a servile messenger is not an act of peasant revolt. Of all of the parables that cast God as a landowner, this is one of the least problematic. When we heed the evangelists' instruction to interpret it Christologically, we see that the people being indicted by it are not peasant farmers, they are elites: chief priests, scribes. This parable presents no challenge to the proposition the God is on the side of the poor. It may even strengthen it.

We can accept Boer and Petterson's point that trying to read the Parable of the Wicked Tenants from below from the perspective of the tenants is problematic.[49] We can accept their point that this parable is told from an upper-class perspective. But we cannot accept their conclusion:

---

48. Smith, "Slavery," 16.

49. Though a reading from below from the perspective of slaves is more fruitful. Smith, "Slavery," 16.

> Our argument is rather that class conflict is already represented
> from the viewpoint of a certain class, namely, that of the ruling
> class or the landlords—a perspective from which the peasants
> and workers are presented and from which resistance in the
> parables is depicted as wicked rebellion.[50]

One might make this point, but it certainly does not follow from the
Parable of the Wicked Tenants. This parable is not a classic example of
class struggle. It does not show peasants resisting unfair economic conditions. In the parable, those who resist are tenants of a luxury crop; there
is no particular reason to believe that they are not relatively high-class
themselves. What is more, the actual targets of the parable—the religious
authorities—are certainly high-class, probably ES3–4. The parable does
not depict lower-class resistance to high-class owners, it depicts high-
class resistance to God, and the slaves they are abusing are the prophets
who declare God's preferential concern for the poor. There may be room
to argue that the parables represent a high-class perspective rather than
a peasant perspective, but this is not the parable to prove it. Without it,
Boer and Petterson leave their *polis-chōra* thesis ill defended.

Their argument is more convincing as it shifts from tenancy to the
slave-relation and the troubling practice of identifying God as a slave-own-
er and disciples as slaves. As we noted in chapter 4, the slavery parables are
precisely the places the present the most challenge to my thesis, especially
when God is portrayed as a particularly cruel or capricious master, and
most especially in the Parable of the Pounds. Boer and Petterson argue
that the parables serve as a form of *régulation* that is not simply captive to
the institution of slavery, it actively promotes that institution.

Drawing heavily on the work of Ulrike Roth, they argue that early
Christianity—in particular Pauline Christianity—was dependent on the
labor of slaves.[51] The case study is the Letter to Philemon, in which, Roth
argues, Paul reveals that he is a co-owner of the slave Onesimus. Paul's
relationship as κοινωνός with Philemon is a kind of business association,
an association that includes joint ownership of Onesimus.[52] Paul cleverly
accepts Onesimus as a brother in the Christian community while

---

50. Boer and Petterson, *Time of Troubles*, 167.

51. Roth, "Paul," 102–30; Boer and Petterson, *Time of Troubles*, 170–73. Smith
notes that African American biblical interpretation has focused more attention on
Paul than on the gospels when criticizing biblical acceptance of slavery but warns that
Jesus's parables of slavery are also problematic. Smith, "Slavery," 11–12.

52. Roth, "Paul," 108–21.

simultaneously benefiting from his slave labor by employing an apocalyptic argument that symbolically does away with slavery while functionally retaining it.

> The window opened in Philemon shows Paul's theology in action on a particular case (and identifiable individual): Onesimus, once converted, remains a slave under the rules of the "old" world (including his ownership by a fellow Christian, and by the apostle himself), whilst becoming an equal under the rules of the new world. There exists, however, no ultimate contradiction in Paul's thought because of the apostle's apocalyptic stance which transcends the "old" world: whilst in the latter there is Jew and Greek, slave and free, man and woman, it is through the act of active disregard (but not dismissal!) of such statuses and roles that Paul attempts to establish their fundamental unimportance. In Paul's theological construction, active *dismissal* of the worldly statuses and roles of slave and free would, in turn, function to (re)establish their importance. In practice, then, Onesimus' slave status *has to remain* unquestioned by Paul, *thereby* postulating its ultimate insignificance—through the creation of parallel universes.[53]

The practical outcome is that slavery becomes the engine for early Christian missionary work, work that could not be accomplished without slavery.

> We should now add that it is impossible to imagine someone like Paul or Peter or Philip engaging in missionary activity for a whole religion without the aid of slaves, both in secular and religious functions: the Christian "oikos" could not have been built without the utilisation of slave labour by those in charge of its construction and maintenance—just as Paul's theology would have collapsed without the theoretical underpinning provided by the peculiar institution [slavery]. In thus creating a Christian design for mastery—real and conceptual—Paul is likely to have set the agenda for his successors for centuries to come, turning the history of the early Church into the (ongoing) history of slavery.[54]

Boer and Petterson agree and suggest that Paul uses the metaphor of slavery to God as a means of resolving the theological tension between the practice of slavery and supposed freedom in Christ.

---

53. Roth, "Paul," 126.
54. Roth, "Paul," 130.

In this light, we propose that Paul's use of metaphorical slavery is a desperate and brilliant attempt at attempting [sic] to resolve the actual contradiction at an ideological level. It consists quite simply in making everyone slaves, figuratively speaking, while maintaining, supporting, and benefiting from the fundamental inequality of this economic structure in daily life: as Roth says, "Paul has his cake and eats it too."[55]

I do not concede that Philemon reveals Paul's general acceptance of slavery or his co-ownership of Onesimus. It is quite possible to read Philemon as Paul's (near) insistence on the manumission of Onesimus.[56] However, the idea that early Christianity relied on the labor of slaves seems nearly incontrovertible. Slavery was a nearly unquestioned part of Roman society. No doubt wealthy Christians owned slaves, and no doubt the labor of those slaves contributed to the mission of the church.[57] Neither Paul nor Jesus are recorded making a thoroughgoing rebuke of slavery. Therefore Boer and Petterson's claim that the parables of slavery constitute a form of economic *régulation* must still be addressed.

Numerous parables depict God as a slaveholder and disciples as slaves of God. Boer and Petterson concede that there can be both positive and negative connotations to the idea of slavery to God. In Luke 16:13, God and Mammon are proposed as rival slaveholders, but placing God in opposition to Mammon is of little comfort to Boer and Petterson. "What is crucial in this designation is not the positive or the negative valence, but the characterization of the Christian as a slave, one way or another."[58] The parables of slavery to God enforce the idea that good slaves are obedient while bad slaves are disobedient, and slaves are always rewarded or punished based on their obedience. The job of any slave is to be obedient, and the metaphor of slavery to God reinforces rather than resists the reality of slavery to human masters.[59]

---

55. Boer and Petterson, *Time of Troubles*, 174.

56. See, for example, Sanders, "Equality and a Request," 109–14; Horsley, "Paul and Slavery," 195; Lewis, "Philemon," 443. Smith, though, notes that Onesimus has no agency in the situation, being sent back against his will to Philemon. Smith, "Slavery," 12.

57. Though there is evidence that some early Christian communities did practice manumission of slaves. Horsley, "Paul and Slavery," 190–94.

58. Boer and Petterson, *Time of Troubles*, 176.

59. Boer and Petterson, *Time of Troubles*, 176–77.

Boer and Petterson name several Lukan parables in support of this thesis, without providing extensive exegesis. The Parable of the Unfaithful Slave (Luke 12:41–48) is named as promoting slavery, though there is no mention that what the slave is expected to do is treat the other slaves in their care with compassion and fairness. The Parable of the Lost Sheep (Luke 15:1–7), the Parable of the Lost Coin (Luke 15:8–10), and the Parable of the Prodigal Son (Luke 15:11–32) are of particular interest to Boer and Petterson because they define people as possessions. Interestingly, while they mention the Parable of the Talents (Matt 25:14–30), they exclude any reference to the most troubling parable of all, and the only one that I read antithetically: the Parable of the Pounds (Luke 19:11–27).

Of the Lukan texts referenced by Boer and Petterson, the most troubling is Luke 17:7–10. They use it as a sort of definition of the slave ethos.[60]

> Who among you would say to your slave who has just come in from plowing or tending sheep in the field, "Come here at once and take your place at the table?" Would you not rather say to him, "Prepare supper for me, put on your apron and serve me while I eat and drink; later you may eat and drink"? Do you thank the slave for doing what was commanded? So you also, when you have done all that you were ordered to do, say, "We are worthless slaves; we have done only what we ought to have done!" (Luke 17:7–10 NRSV)

As noted in chapter 4, this parable, along with the other parables of slavery, seems to cut both ways. It certainly encourages listeners to identify themselves as groveling slaves. At the same time, it seems to be critiquing the system of slavery that it uses as metaphor. Jesus's own disciples are identified as the ones who would be cruel masters, if they were indeed masters, while Jesus himself comes as one who serves (Luke 22:27). And encouraging the disciples to think of themselves as slaves can be a kind of solidarity with the poor, a recognition that their status as apostles does not make them more worthy than those who find themselves in slavery.[61]

Boer and Petterson come to the conclusion that "the Gospels propagate the slave ethos."[62] These few parables are seen to be the core of the economic message of all three synoptic gospels, and their message is

---

60. Boer and Petterson, *Time of Troubles*, 178.

61. Crowder, "Luke," 177.

62. Boer and Petterson, *Time of Troubles*, 177.

thought to override any possible messages of economic liberation that might be found elsewhere in the gospels.

> The Gospels are not really advocating an alternative society, but remain within the parameters of the *status quo*. The odd rich person—who sells off property, gives it to the poor, and joins Jesus—does not change the dynamics of slaves and slave-owners. Instead, he contributes towards the endurance of the slave-relation.[63]

Boer and Petterson are right that these parables are problematic. They treat slavery as an accepted fact of life. They can and have been used to defend the practice of slavery. As Smith argues, "Luke's characterizations of slaves are not meant to subvert stereotypes of slaves and masters"[64] In Boer and Petterson's language, these parables can be used as a form of *régulation*.

However, Boer and Petterson overstate the case. They put these slavery parables in the balance against "various sayings about camels and eyes of needles, as well as the parable of the rich fool," and they simply state that it is the message of *régulation* that prevails. They have placed the correct things on each side of the scale, but they have misread the balance. As we have already seen, the overwhelming amount of economic material in Luke openly resists the economic *status quo* of the Roman world (chapters 2 and 5), and the relatively small amount of C & D material in the gospel is largely mitigated when it is analyzed closely (chapter 4).

Could the Gospel of Luke be more radical? Yes. Would its radical message be stronger if it included a clear rejection of slavery? Absolutely. Does its failure to do so negate the rest of its clearly radical economic message? Certainly not! The gospel is not a perfect, unblemished message of resistance, but it is still a message of resistance. Parts of it can be used as forms of *régulation*, but that does not mean that it ceases to function as a form of liberation. Reformational messages are always limited by their social context, and they can always be co-opted by the powers of the *status quo*. The relatively radical message of the authentic Paul is domesticated by the deutero-Pauline epistles. The relatively radical message of Luke is domesticated by later interpreters. And we must admit that the message of Luke may well be a domestication of an even more radical

---

63. Boer and Petterson, *Time of Troubles*, 178.
64. Smith, "Slavery," 18.

message of Jesus. But this does not mean we should ignore the degree to which Luke is in fact a radical message of economic liberation.

Conclusion

Boer and Petterson's groundbreaking *Time of Troubles* is an important contribution to the study of economic issues within the world of the New Testament. It is a much-needed corrective to the neoclassical economic approaches that have tended to dominate the field. Its application of the work of Ste. Croix and *Régulation* Theory provides a valuable tool for understanding the systems of exploitation at work in the ancient world. Even their claim that Christianity can and did function as a mode of *régulation* is well-taken.

However, I am not willing to concede that the gospel message is overwhelmingly and inescapably a mode of *régulation*. The Gospel of Luke, in particular, contains a strong message of economic liberation. If that message has been co-opted by the powers of economic oppression— and it most certainly has—the solution is not to abandon the gospel or to deny its radical content. Rather, the radical economic message of the gospel must be reclaimed.

We are now two-thirds through the argument. We have analyzed the economic message of Luke in its literary context and looked in-depth at its message of good news for the poor, its resistance to wealth, and its accommodation to wealth (chapters 2–4). We have also examined the message of Luke within the context of the Greco-Roman world of early Christianity and seen both the ways that Luke resisted economic oppression and the ways that it failed to resist (chapters 5–6).

Now it is time to leave the ancient world behind. Luke has a radical economic message, and it was radical in its own time. But Luke also has a radical economic message today. How does Luke's radical message illuminate and indict the economic practices of our modern world? How might we reclaim a Lukan economic ethic for today? These are the questions of the next two chapters.

CHAPTER 7

Modern Mammonism

No household slave is able to serve two masters,
for they will either hate one and love the other, or
they will be devoted to one and despise the other.
You cannot serve God and Mammon.

—LUKE 16:13

WE NOW MOVE FROM the ancient world to the modern, and to the third part of my thesis. We have surveyed the contours of Luke's radical economic message within its literary context. We have seen how Luke represents a radical message within the worlds of Greco-Roman culture and early Christianity. Now we will see how Luke carries a radical message for today. In particular, in this chapter we will explore the ideals of capitalist economy and how they contrast with the ideals suggested by Luke.

Nearly two millennia separate Luke from our time. As we know from chapters 5 and 6, there is a profound difference between the ancient economy and modern capitalism. Trying to find capitalism in the ancient world tends to distort our understanding of the ancient world. Likewise, there is a risk of distortion when we try to apply the principles of an ancient economy to the modern world.

In this and the next chapter I will attempt responsibly to bridge this gap. The key for this chapter is Luke 16:13, which suggests understanding the Market as a kind of god, a god that can be compared and contrasted to the God of Luke. How can we understand the modern economy by translating it into the conceptual framework of the ancient? In the next chapter, we will attempt to translate the economic ethics of Luke into a form that makes sense within a modern conceptual framework.

The Market as God

The saint of neoclassical economics, Milton Friedman, in defense of positive economic theory, argued that an economic theory does not have to have realistic assumptions in order for it to be used effectively as a predictive theory. Specifically, economic actors do not actually need to go through the calculations necessary for them to determine the best way of maximizing their utility in order for economic theory to be right. Clearly, most economic actors do not spend time formally calculating utility before they make an economic choice. However, we can still treat economic actors like the mythical *homo economicus* because they behave *as if* they were doing the calculations. An expert billiard player does not go through complex calculations before taking their shot. However, a physicist could still use complex calculations to predict the billiard player's actions because the billiard player shoots *as if* they had done the calculations.[1] The same is true for the actor in the economic marketplace.

> It is only a short step from these examples to the economic hypothesis that under a wide range of circumstances individual firms behave *as if* they were seeking rationally to maximize their expected returns (generally if misleadingly called "profits") and had full knowledge of the data needed to succeed in this attempt; *as if*, that is, they knew the relevant cost and demand functions, calculated marginal cost and marginal revenue from all actions open to them, and pushed each line of action to the point at which the relevant marginal cost and marginal revenue were equal.[2]

The assumptions of the theory do not have to be realistic in order for the theory to have predictive or explanatory power.

In this chapter I am suggesting a theory that, though it may not have realistic assumptions, does have explanatory value. That theory: in

---

1. Friedman, *Essays in Positive Economics*, 12–13.
2. Friedman, *Essays in Positive Economics*, 13.

modern capitalistic society, the Market behaves *as if* it were a god. For example, the Market has providence (an invisible hand). Oracles (financial analysts) can read the will of the Market and tell us whether or not it approves of recent political events. The Market has creed and commandments, a set of rules that must be followed in order for humans to secure the benefits of the Market. There is orthodoxy that must be followed by governments, businesses, financial professionals, investors, and consumers, if the blessing of the Market is to be maintained.

The interpretation of Market as god is hardly new. One of the more popular versions of it appeared in *The Atlantic* shortly before the turn of the twenty-first century. Advised by a friend who told him that if he wanted to know about the real world he should read the business pages, Harvey Cox discovered that rather than finding a foreign world, he found the familiar language of theology. He found

> a grand narrative about the inner meaning of human history, why things had gone wrong, and how to put them right. Theologians call these myths of origin, legends of the fall, and doctrines of sin and redemption. But here they were again, and in only thin disguise.[3]

The new god, The Market, exercises the omnipotence of being able to define the reality of every thing as a commodity, the omnipresence of being able to control meaning in every sphere of human life, and the omniscience to provide wisdom and ultimate truth.

> Current thinking already assigns to The Market a comprehensive wisdom that in the past only the gods have known. The Market, we are taught, is able to determine what human needs are, what copper and capital should cost, how much barbers and CEOs should be paid, and how much jet planes, running shoes, and hysterectomies should sell for. But how do we know The Market's will? In days of old, seers entered a trance state and then informed anxious seekers what kind of mood the gods were in, and whether this was an auspicious time to begin a journey, get married, or start a war. The prophets of Israel repaired to the desert and then returned to announce whether Yahweh was feeling benevolent or wrathful. Today The Market's fickle will is clarified by daily reports from Wall Street and other sensory organs of finance. Thus we can learn on a day-to-day basis that The Market is "apprehensive," "relieved," "nervous,"

---

3. Cox, "The Market as God," para. 2.

or even at times "jubilant." On the basis of this revelation awed
adepts make critical decisions about whether to buy or sell. Like
one of the devouring gods of old, The Market—aptly embodied
in a bull or a bear—must be fed and kept happy under all circumstances. True, at times its appetite may seem excessive—a
$35 billion bailout here, a $50 billion one there—but the alternative to assuaging its hunger is too terrible to contemplate. The
diviners and seers of The Market's moods are the high priests of
its mysteries. To act against their admonitions is to risk excommunication and possibly damnation.[4]

Cox, along with other theologians, uses the language of theology in order
to bring meaning to the complex world of capitalist finance.[5]

But it is not only thinkers coming from the theological perspective
who compare the Market to God; so do thinkers coming from the economic perspective.[6] One of the more thoroughgoing of these is a reflec-
tion on the 2008 financial crisis by Larry Elliot and Dan Atkinson, *The
Gods that Failed: How Blind Faith in Markets Has Cost Us Our Future*. In
it, they compare market forces to the twelve Greek gods of Mount Olympus. They suggest that a new pantheon has arisen to sway human events,
a group of governing spirits they refer to as "the New Olympians."[7] They
identify these "twelve gods of the modern Mount Olympus, the ruling
ideas served by the overpaid heroes of the City and Wall Street" as glo-
balization, communication, liberalization, privatization, competition, fi-
nancialization, speculation, recklessness, greed, arrogance, oligarchy, and
excess.[8] Governments, financial professionals, and investors trusted in the
providence of these gods, obeyed their commandments and creeds. And
for a while, they led to prosperity, at least for some. Ultimately, though,
they led to a worldwide financial crisis and a global recession.

> The gods promised us paradise if only we would obey and
> pamper their hero-servants and allow their strange titans and
> monsters to flourish. We did as they asked, and have placidly

4. Cox, "Market as God," para. 17–19.

5. Other such readings include: Blosser, "Can God or the Market Set People Free?";
Bell, *Economy of Desire*; Hinkelammert, *Ideological Weapons of Death*.

6. For example: Brodine, "When the Market God Isn't Worshiped"; Foley, *Adam's
Fallacy*; Frank, *One Market under God*; George and Sabelli, *Faith and Credit*; Kolivakis,
"Sacrifices to Market Gods?"; Krugman, "The Market Speaks"; Oslington, "God and
the Market."

7. Elliott and Atkinson, *The Gods That Failed*, 12.

8. Elliott and Atkinson, *The Gods That Failed*, 14–17. Quoted phrase from page 14.

swallowed the prescriptions of the lavishly rewarded bankers, central bankers, hedge fund managers, and private equity tycoons, while turning a blind eye to the rampaging of the exotic derivatives, the offshore trusts, and the toxic financial instruments. Had they delivered, there would, at least, be a debate to be held as to whether the price was too high, in terms of the loss of democratic control and widening social inequality. But they have not. Chronic financial instability and the prospect of, at the best, years of sluggish economic activity as we pay off borrowings of a debt-burdened society are the fruits of their guidance. These gods have failed. It is time to live without them.[9]

The basic tenant of capitalist ideology, as first espoused by the great prophet Adam Smith, is that society benefits most when the individuals within that society make choices based on their own, narrow, economic self-interests. In the most famous line, Smith asserts that this self-interested economic actor

intends only his own gain; and he is in this, as in many other cases, led by an invisible hand to promote an end which was no part of his intention. Nor is it always the worse for the society that it was not part of it. By pursuing his own interest, he frequently promotes that of the society more effectually than when he really intends to promote it.[10]

If human self-interest is allowed to run free in the economic sphere, markets naturally develop, and those markets naturally guide economic action in a way that is more beneficial to society than if people were trying to act out of charity.[11] Unregulated markets are the best way to promote human flourishing. In this sense, the Market becomes a kind of providential god.

Both theologians and economists find meaning in the metaphor of the Market as god. One does not have to prove that Adam Smith's Invisible Hand has a real, spiritual existence. One does not need to show that economic actors consciously employ themselves in the worship of Mammon. It is enough to see that insight is gained when we consider that the economic functions *as if* the Market were a god.

However, for me to describe how I understand the doctrines of Mammonist theology and then compare them unfavorably to the

9. Elliott and Atkinson, *The Gods That Failed*, 271–72.

10. Smith, *Wealth of Nations*, 335.

11. Foley, *Adam's Fallacy*, 43–44.

economic doctrines of Luke would be a straw man argument. What is needed is a theological defender of the Market, someone who can cast market capitalism in as generous a light as possible, from the perspective of Christian ethics. One of capitalism's more eloquent Christian defenders is Michael Novak.

Michael Novak and the Spirit of Democratic Capitalism

In his 1982 classic, *The Spirit of Democratic Capitalism*, Novak argues that democratic capitalism creates greater good for the poor than any other economic system. His basic argument is that capitalism creates economic growth, and economic growth materially benefits all persons, including the poor; it is the "a rising tide lifts all boats" argument. In addition, capitalism promotes virtues like freedom and liberty, which are destroyed by the only alternate viable economic system: socialism. Avarice and greed may be seen to be contrary to the biblical message, but through the power of capitalism they are transformed, by the principle of unintended consequences, into generators of welfare for all.

Novak spends much of the book praising capitalism on more pragmatic than theological grounds. Reading along with the pragmatism of Adam Smith, the quest for positive outcomes rather than positive principles, Novak asks which economic system is the best for achieving the positive outcomes of "the abolition of famine, the raising up of the poor, and the banishment of material suffering from all humankind."[12] His answer:

> The paradox consisted in attaining a highly moral outcome by placing less stress on moral purposes. Toward the desired moral outcome, the exercise of rational self-interest on the part of every citizen is, in the real world of historical examples, a far more successful means than the exercise of other motivations.[13]

The virtues of market capitalism, summarized as self-interest, may not seem moral on their own, but they are nevertheless the best means for advancing moral ends.

One key to capitalism's near mystical ability to generate wellbeing is its ability to drive economic growth. With an ever-expanding population, the world can only overcome poverty with continuous economic

---

12. Novak, *Spirit of Democratic Capitalism*, 79.
13. Novak, *Spirit of Democratic Capitalism*, 79.

growth, the kind of growth that capitalism alone has proven to accomplish.[14] Capitalism does not make the rich richer and the poor poorer, as many market critics contend; it advances the wealth and wellbeing of all in society.[15] What is more, capitalism has the effect of decreasing the disparity between rich and poor, of making things more equitable.[16]

Even more important for Novak is the idea that democratic capitalism promotes freedom and pluralism while staving off coercion and tyranny. It may seem tempting to try to organize an economy around a positive set of morals, but every attempt to do so ends in tyranny.[17] Whether it comes from the aristocratic classes, from the ecclesial community, or from the socialist state, the attempt to impose moral behavior on all citizens curtails freedom and introduces inefficiency. Democratic capitalism allows individuals to decide for themselves which choices are moral and reins in the forces that are most likely to dominate society.

Novak seems to be able to imagine only four alternatives to democratic capitalism: traditional production, which lacks the power to generate wealth; feudalism, which enslaves people to aristocrats who are neither willing nor able to provide for the welfare of their serfs; totalitarian socialism in the mold of Stalin or Mao; and theocracy (properly hierarchy), which is simply one of the other three but with an additional pretension of righteousness. None of these are acceptable to him, and so democratic capitalism must be society's choice, putting its trust in peddlers rather than peasants, princes, politicians, or priests.

> Democratic capitalism is neither the Kingdom of God nor without sin. Yet all other known systems of political economy are worse. Such hope as we have for alleviating poverty and for removing oppressive tyranny—perhaps our last, best hope—lies in this much despised system. A never-ending stream of immigrants and refugees seeks out this system. Peoples who imitate this system in faraway places seem to do better than peoples who don't.[18]

The theological case then begins as a negative one. What democratic capitalism is not is the Kingdom of God, because it is impossible for the

---

14. Novak, *Spirit of Democratic Capitalism*, 264.

15. Novak, *Spirit of Democratic Capitalism*, 109.

16. Novak, *Spirit of Democratic Capitalism*, 126.

17. Novak, *Spirit of Democratic Capitalism*, 67–68.

18. Novak, *Spirit of Democratic Capitalism*, 28.

Kingdom of God to be manifest in our current reality. It is impossible for the ideals of Christian love and charity to be lived out in a way that changes systems or affects society. Living by biblical values is simply too hard for most people, and no system of economy can be expected to function on its principles.[19] Human sin must be counted upon, and democratic capitalism has the power, through unintended consequences, to transform human sin into the driver of virtuous ends.[20]

When Novak settles down to construct a positive theology for democratic capitalism, he identifies six relevant doctrines: Trinity, Incarnation, competition, Original Sin, separation of realms, and *caritas*.[21] Through these he seeks to give capitalism not only a religious justification, but also a philosophical framework for operation.

Novak invokes Trinity in defense of pluralism. God is revealed not in the Aristotelian *nous* (mind) but in the community and plurality of the Trinity. He cites Jesus's (largely Johannine) self-identity as "Son, one with the Father, and one as well with the Holy Spirit of love whom the Father would send."[22] While appropriately conscious of the potential vulgarity, he finds an analogy of the Trinity in the workings of "a political economy differentiated and yet one."[23] Economic sphere, political sphere, and moral sphere form a unity in plurality. Furthermore, this trinity creates the conditions by which individuals can interact in community with each other: another analogy of the three-in-one God. Families, civil fraternities, labor unions, religious groups, corporations, and other associations allow for the expression of community far better than the usual dichotomy of person and state. Matthew 16:24—"forsake all and follow me"—is cited as a call for each person to give themselves over completely to the human community, something that is apparently best done in the context of democratic capitalism.

In one of his more puzzling arguments, Novak concludes that the Incarnation of Jesus Christ proves that the Kingdom of God is *not* near. Rather than being a harbinger of God's saving action in the world, Jesus is proof that all humans must suffer without hope that God will spare us.

19. Novak, *Spirit of Democratic Capitalism*, 351–52.

20. Novak, *Spirit of Democratic Capitalism*, 82.

21. Novak, *Spirit of Democratic Capitalism*, 337–58.

22. Novak, *Spirit of Democratic Capitalism*, 337.

23. Novak, *Spirit of Democratic Capitalism*, 339.

> The point of Incarnation is to respect the world as it is, to ac-
> knowledge its limits, to recognize its weaknesses, irrationalities,
> and evil forces, and to disbelieve any promises that the world is
> now or ever will be transformed into the City of God. If Jesus
> could not effect that, how shall we? If the tears of six million
> victims pleading for their loved ones could not effect that, how
> shall we? The world is not going to become—ever—a kingdom
> of justice and love.[24]

In all likelihood, God will abandon us just as God abandoned Jesus. We
may hope for some marginal improvements from time to time, but no
utopias, no new ages, no radical Kingdom of God emerging in this world.
With this one bit of Johannine theology, Novak sweeps away virtually
any sense that God might act in history. Jesus does not represent God's
liberation of humanity, but God's abandonment.[25]

> The single greatest temptation for Christians is to imagine that
> the salvation won by Jesus has altered the human condition.
> Many attempt to judge the present world by the standards of
> the gospels, as though the world were ready to live according
> to them. Sin is not so easily overcome. A political economy for
> sinners, even Christian sinners (however well intentioned), is
> consistent with the story of Jesus. A political economy based
> on love and justice is to be found beyond, never to be wholly
> incarnated within, human history. The Incarnation obliges us to
> reduce our noblest expectations, so to love the world as to fit a
> political economy to it, nourishing all that is best in it.[26]

In one of his most sustained biblical arguments, Novak contends
that competition is mandated by the gospel and necessary for the functioning of political economy. While it may be acceptable for religious-
types to repudiate competition, political and economic leaders must be
driven by competition in order for societal advancement to be made.
"The will-to-power must be made creative, not destroyed."[27] This is confirmed by the biblical narrative. Life is a series of choices between good
and evil, or as Novak puts it: "Judaism and Christianity . . . envisage human life as a contest. The ultimate competition resides in the depths of

---

24. Novak, *Spirit of Democratic Capitalism*, 341.

25. See also Rieger, *No Rising Tide*, 6. Novak's Incarnation insists that "the economic status quo should not be challenged since this is the way God intends things to be."

26. Novak, *Spirit of Democratic Capitalism*, 343–44.

27. Novak, *Spirit of Democratic Capitalism*, 344.

one's own heart."[28] King David, the rich young ruler, and Paul, along with the parables of the wise and foolish virgins (Matt 25:1–13), the prodigal son (Luke 15:11–32), the talents (Matt 25:14–30; cf. Luke 19:11–27), and the workers in the vineyard (Matt 20:1–16),[29] are all invoked to prove that God desires competition and eschews equality. God calls for competition: "many are called, few are chosen" (Matt 22:14).[30] Novak is careful to make clear that worldly success and divine aims are not always the same, quoting "the last will be first . . ." (Matt 20:16; cf. Mark 10:31; Luke 13:30), "what does it profit a man . . ." (Mark 8:36; cf. Matt 16:26; Luke 9:25), and the camel through the eye of a needle (Matt 19:24; cf. Mark 10:25; Luke 18:25). And yet he also wants to be clear that they often do coincide; good, clean, Christian living often results in worldly success, and vices like "lewdness, profligacy, laziness, gluttony, intemperance, pride, envy"[31] often result in ruin. Competition is a virtue quite consistent with the gospels, while noncompetition supports the *status quo*, and the competition found in socialist systems is more destructive because it takes place in a zero-sum game of limited good. In the capitalist system, competition generates new wealth and is therefore good for all; in the socialist system, competitive gains must always come at the expense of others.

The Doctrine of Original Sin proves for Novak both that humans are incapable of living by the utopian moral codes of the Bible and that sin is always individual and never systemic. Since humans cannot avoid sin, it is cruel to expect them to do so. It is more important to prevent the tyranny of moralism than to prevent sin. While sin may well be on display in capitalist societies, trust in the freedom of human choices offers hope that, most of the time, humans will make the right and moral choice.

Novak quotes "Give unto Caesar the things that are Caesar's, and to God the things that are God's" (Matt 22:21; cf. Mark 12:17; Luke 20:25) as the key biblical proof for his doctrine of the separation of realms.[32] With

28. Novak, *Spirit of Democratic Capitalism*, 344.

29. The inclusion of the parable of the workers in the vineyard (Matt 20:1–16) as proof that God does not desire equality is particularly remarkable in light of the fact that in it every worker is paid the same amount regardless of how long they have worked. The obvious reading seems to be the polar opposite of the point Novak is trying to make.

30. Novak incorrectly cites this verse as Matt 20:16.

31. Novak, *Spirit of Democratic Capitalism*, 346.

32. Novak, *Spirit of Democratic Capitalism*, 351. However, Horsley and others are correct to point out that the saying does not suggest separate realms. In light of the second commandment, it says that Caesar's empire is illegitimate because it demands

it, he explicitly argues that there can be no Christian economic system because the ideal of liberty is paramount; Christianity cannot impose its morals on the separate realm of economics. Christians can seek to persuade others to just economic practices but must respect that each person will, in their liberty, have their own moral code concerning the market.

> To try to run an economy by the highest Christian principles is certain to destroy both the economy and the reputation of Christianity. Each Christian can and should follow his or her conscience, and cooperate in coalitions where consensus may be reached.[33]

Finally, Novak relates the concept of *caritas* (compare with Hebrew אָהַב or Greek ἀγάπη)—as a form of "love of the other as other," a realistic love—to the liberty one grants to the other in the democratic capitalist system. *Caritas* is the highest, most selfless form of love. It is, in fact, the name and nature of God. When one desires for another what is good for them, one participates in the life and love of God in its most profound form.

> To love humans as they are is to accept them in their sinfulness, while seeking a way to transform such sinfulness into creative action for the commonweal. Some argue that the best way to do this is to appeal to social solidarity and high moral ideals. They erect economic systems accordingly. Others hold that the common good is better served through allowing each individual to work as each judges best and to keep the rewards of such labor. For them, the profit motive is designed to inspire a higher level of common benefit by respecting the individual judgment of economic agents. The more the latter risk and invest, the greater return they may gather in. Most will not be selfish with this return; most will share it liberally. If they bury their talent, or squander it, that is their choice; they will hardly be thought to be good stewards. The idea is that greater incentives will stimulate greater economic activism. The more economically active most citizens are, the greater should be the common prosperity.[34]

Novak claims that wanting others to fully embrace the profit motive is a higher and purer form of Godly love than is any other form of compassionate action. The thing the world needs most is economic activity, because economic activity generates wealth, and wealth benefits all of

---

fealty and honors that are due only to God. Horsley, *Covenant Economics*, xvi, 83.

33. Novak, *Spirit of Democratic Capitalism*, 352.

34. Novak, *Spirit of Democratic Capitalism*, 356.

humanity. Thus, the most selflessly loving thing that one can do is to desire that others seek their own profit to its fullest extent in the capitalist marketplace. Novak grounds this reading in all of the great love commandments: "'Love your neighbor as yourself' (Matt 22:39). 'Love your enemies' (Matt 5:44). 'Love is the highest law' (Rom 13:10). 'The greatest of these is love' (1 Cor 13:13)."[35]

Questioning the Spirit at the Heart of Capitalism

Much of Novak's vision is actually quite beautiful. It envisions a world in which all people respect and love each other, a world in which everyone's economic lot grows steadily better. It appeals to our modern ideals of liberty, freedom, and mutual respect.

Even so, it fails adequately to deal with many of the greatest sources of suffering in our world. It fails to take seriously much of the Bible's economic message. It distorts the biblical concepts of salvation and liberation.

In this section, I will levy a critique on Novak's vision based on the radical economic message of Luke's gospel. In particular, I will show how Novak completely dismisses the biblical theme of God's liberating action in the world. I will question the assertion that the details of biblical morality can be suppressed because democratic capitalism has the pragmatic effect of achieving those moral ends more efficiently. I will deal with the sort of market idolatry to which Novak's thinking leads. Finally, I will question whether Novak's goal of continual economic growth can be justified in light of current environmental degradation and the biblical mandate that humans be good stewards of God's creation. In this critique, my three primary conversation partners are Elsa Tamez, Daniel Finn, and Joerg Rieger.[36]

Liberation

The first problem is that Novak completely dismisses one of the major themes of the Bible, a theme that is particularly strong in Luke: that God acts on the side of the oppressed. That is to say, he ignores or minimizes

35. Novak, *Spirit of Democratic Capitalism*, 353.

36. Tamez, *Bible of the Oppressed*; Finn, *Christian Economic Ethics*; Rieger, *No Rising Tide*.

the entire message of liberation. The covenant code of the Torah that works to ensure fairness and a basic sense of economic equality, the Prophets that take the rich to task for extracting wealth from the poor and vulnerable, the apocalyptic material in which believers expect God to set right the wrongs of the world, the core gospel message that God's Empire is near, Jesus's mission to bring good news to the poor and freedom to the oppressed: none of these are of particular import to Novak. There is no good news for the poor. Instead, Novak leaves us with a highly spiritualized gospel in which God's only saving action is in the promise of an afterlife.

We have seen above how Novak's understanding of incarnation fits into this overall sense of a hands-off God. His primary takeaway from the Incarnation is that it proves God will not intervene in the world to help humans. If God would not act to save the Son from death, then certainly God would not act to save some normal human being. While he insists his vision is not hopeless, it certainly is bleak. It quite baldly states that the Incarnation proves that God's most likely response to human children is abandonment.[37]

Most traditional theologies of incarnation would take away quite a different lesson: that incarnation proves God's interest and investment in our worldly existence. Jesus is Immanuel, God-with-Us, a proof that God does not think human existence is something too trivial or too polluted to get involved in. God, in fact, makes a home among us, pitches a tent among us (John 1:14).

What is more, the particulars of Jesus's incarnation tell us something important about what God's priorities are for humanity. God comes into the world in order to show solidarity with and liberate the oppressed, as Joerg Rieger suggests:

> God does not become human just anywhere, but in a family of construction workers and day laborers, located on the underside of a small part of the powerful economy of the Roman Empire.[38]

Jesus's incarnation was in a context of economic and political marginalization. The lesson of this incarnation is that God is in solidarity with the poor, the oppressed, and the marginalized.[39]

---

37. Novak, *Spirit of Democratic Capitalism*, 341–42.

38. Rieger, *No Rising Tide*, 31–32.

39. This is a basic tenant of most liberation and many liberal theologies. It is important not only that God becomes human, but more so that God becomes a particular

The incarnation is but one instance of the larger theme, though. Running throughout the Bible is the ever-repeating motif of God intervening on the side of the poor and oppressed. The Exodus, the Covenant Code, the Prophets, the Magnificat, the preaching of Jesus: they all testify not only to God's action in the world, but also to God's action on behalf of the oppressed. We have already seen how this message permeates the Gospel of Luke. God calls on people to live justly, and God acts to bring about justice where it is lacking.[40]

For Novak, none of it is important. Either these texts are simply moral expectations that are too utopian and don't account for Original Sin, or they are empty expectations that God will act in history. People are sinners who cannot be expected to live up to the high ideals of the Bible, and God displays a near-Deist indifference to what is happening in the world. God's call to love the neighbor, to renounce wealth, to look out for the widow, orphan, and stranger: they are the unrealistic fantasies of utopians. God bringing slaves out of bondage, God tearing down the mighty from their thrones and lifting up the lowly, God oppressing the oppressors: these things will never happen in the real world. The world must be accepted how it is, and God can be counted on only in heaven.

For Elsa Tamez, one of the key points of the Bible's liberative corpus is the relation of oppressed to oppressor and of rich to poor. In her reading of the Bible, the oppressed are oppressed because they are oppressed by oppressors, the poor are poor because they are oppressed by the rich. The rich are the cause of the poverty of the poor; poverty is not just a natural occurrence.

> For the Bible oppression is the basic cause of poverty, but I want also to introduce a middle term that sheds some light: despoliation, or theft, in other words, the oppressor steals from the oppressed and impoverishes them. The oppressed are therefore those who have been impoverished, for while the oppressor oppresses the poor because they are poor and powerless, the poor have become poor in the first place because they have been oppressed. The principal motive for oppression is the eagerness to

---

kind of human: a marginalized human. For example, De La Torre, *Politics of Jesús*. Also Peters, *Solidarity Ethics*, 52.

40. For extensive catalogues of such texts, see, for example, Ringe, *Jesus*; Horsley, *Covenant Economics*; Gutiérrez, *Theology of Liberation*.

pile up wealth, and this desire is connected with the fact that the oppressor is an idolater.[41]

For this reason, the rich are responsible for poverty; oppressors are responsible for oppression. It is not that poverty exists because of a lack of resources. Poverty exists because the rich take away the resources that properly belong to the poor.[42]

And because they are responsible, they can be held to account by God. God can and will act in history to set things right, to tear the mighty from their thrones. "In order to secure equity and justice for the oppressed, God must 'oppress' the mighty, the proud, the oppressors."[43] Contra Novak, God intervenes in the world and does so in order to rescue the oppressed from their oppressors.

According to Tamez, oppressors do not oppress because they take pleasure in being oppressive. They oppress because of greed:

> Oppressors do not oppress because they are cruel or enjoy it. They do not act violently because they have an aggressive temperament; they do not rob for the sake of robbing. Their primary purpose is to accumulate wealth, and it is possible to accumulate wealth only by robbing one's neighbor and committing acts of violence and injustice.[44]

Greed is thus clearly identified as a source of injustice and violence. It is not productive. It is not secret altruism. It does not mysteriously raise the prosperity of all. Greed causes despoliation. Greed causes injustice. The piling up of resources always comes at the expense of the poor and is therefore always indicted by the Bible.[45]

This is the case not just in the past of biblical narrative, but also in the present day. Wealth comes at the expense of the poor. As Rieger puts it:

> That our neighbors are part of ourselves today often means, first of all, that we are developing our own economic advantages on their backs; they are part of us because we benefit directly or indirectly from their exploitation—if only because we can buy certain goods very inexpensively and because certain services

41. Tamez, *Bible of the Oppressed*, 3.

42. This is the same argument made centuries before by the *De divitiis*. See chapter 5.

43. Tamez, *Bible of the Oppressed*, 13.

44. Tamez, *Bible of the Oppressed*, 24.

45. Tamez, *Bible of the Oppressed*, 32.

are cheap since labor costs are being pushed lower and lower. In these very particular ways, our neighbors are always part of us, even though we may never know them and even though we often prefer not to get to know them.[46]

The biblical tradition, and Luke in particular, indicts the wealth of the wealthy and insists that it comes at the expense of the poor, whether or not the wealthy make a conscious choice to oppress. God takes a side in such circumstances. So also Finn:

> The God of Israelites and Christians is a God who sides with the oppressed, the ignored, and the outcast. Concern for these marginalized people is not simply an ethical principle; it is a religious principle, rooted in the nature of the God we worship. For this reason, the treatment of the poor becomes the central test—the gold standard—for how well a society conducts its economic life.[47]

Of course, Novak rejects this in the strongest of terms. In fact, he devotes two chapters solely to discrediting Gustavo Gutiérrez and liberation theology. With a clearly paternalistic tone, Novak lays blame for the poverty of poor Latin Americans at the feet of Latin American culture, which is not sufficiently developed to have fully adopted democratic capitalist forms of production. Most important for us here, he rejects completely the notion that the wealth of the rich comes at the expense of the poor:

> Secondly, Gutiérrez seems to think that progress and riches in one place must subtract from what is available in another place. In fact, the world economy, since the industrial revolution, has become expansive and dynamic. There is today far more wealth than there was two hundred years ago.[48]

He feels confident in rejecting this biblical principle because he believes the world has changed. He believes the economic strictures of the Bible no longer apply. With the advent of capitalism, wealth can be multiplied, and the greater overall wealth of a society does more good for the poor than any divinely mandated redistribution ever could. The Market, in its providence, is able to supply what the God of the Bible is unwilling to provide.

46. Rieger, *No Rising Tide*, 161–62.

47. Finn, *Christian Economic Ethics*, 48.

48. Novak, *Spirit of Democratic Capitalism*, 304.

In short, Luke's strong message of good news for the poor (A) makes no sense to Novak. God has no material salvation to offer to the poor. God will not lift up the lowly or drag the mighty off their thrones. It is, instead, the Market that must be trusted to bring about material salvation.

Pragmatism

Central to Novak's case is the idea that capitalism grows the economy, and a growing economy helps all members of society. A rising tide lifts all boats. Consequently, greed is not to be discouraged, it is meant to be harnessed. Greed drives economic growth, which in turn helps the poor more than charities or activism or any other intervention can. This is why Novak is able to feel comfortable leaving behind biblical mandates like the prohibition of usury or the gleaning rights of the poor. After the transition to capitalist growth, they actually do more harm to the poor than good, and Novak's stated goal is to benefit the poor most efficiently. Capital development becomes *caritas*, the highest form of Godly love.

But that raises the question of whether capitalism really does improve the lot of all people. If it really is the best way of lifting the poor out of poverty, then perhaps Novak is right that it is worth leaving the biblical call for economic justice to collect dust alongside its prohibitions on women preachers, bacon cheeseburgers, and blended fabrics.

Novak was writing just at the beginning of the neoliberal revolution of the 1980s, led by Ronald Reagan and Margaret Thatcher. In other words, he was writing at a time before our faith and dependence on the Market to achieve the highest social good had been realized. It was a time when the post WWII economic boom had convinced Americans that rapid economic growth was something that could be sustained indefinitely, not the result of a rare set of economic circumstances.[49]

However, as Rieger points out, the world is not the same as it was in 1982. Specifically, the economic crisis and downturn that began at the end of the George W. Bush presidency has given us new perspective on the power of markets to bring about societal welfare.

> The so-called trickle-down theory, according to which wealth accumulated at the top inevitably trickles down, could not be corroborated even during the economic boom of the 1990s. When the global economy has produced growing wealth, this

---

49. See Elliott and Atkinson, *The Gods That Failed*.

wealth has not even moved laterally, for the most part. If anything, economic production has aggregated into a flood of profit and wealth upward.[50]

When one looks at the real-world effects of the financial crisis, it is clear that the Invisible Hand has not been doing what Adam Smith claimed it would. It doesn't work for the benefit of all; it creates new lines of imbalance and exploitation. This is, of course, what liberationists were already claiming.

> The ruling class, as in first-century Palestine, collaborates in the expansion of the wealthy nations. Latin American countries governed by the military receive weapons from abroad in order to put down the discontented masses. In some Latin American countries governments favor the entrance of the multinational corporations on the pretext that this will foster industrial development. At the international level, the economies of the Latin American countries are dependent on foreign nations and are structured according to the interests of the wealthy nations of the world. As everyone knows, these nations see Latin America as a source of raw material and cheap labor. In such a situation the poor feel oppressed; they are hard put to breathe and stay alive. Extreme poverty and exploitation are killing them. They are forced to rise up and fight for the life of the masses.[51]

But now that despoliation is affecting the American "middle class," such claims are harder to ignore. Faith in the Market is so entrenched that not only theologians but also economists can characterize it as a sort of religious fundamentalism that continues to believe in the providence of the Invisible Hand even in the face of clear evidence to the contrary.[52]

Two factors that hurt Novak's case here are that he is presenting an idealized form of capitalism and that he can envision only one modern alternative to democratic capitalism: totalitarian socialism. He admits that he is dealing in ideals, and this is a fair thing to do. It is fair to lay out the ideal form to which a system strives.[53] But on this particular point—that democratic capitalism actually, pragmatically produces a better condition for the poor—we must look not just at ideals but at practice. The assumption that wealth generation is always good for the poor is what allows

50. Rieger, *No Rising Tide*, 5.

51. Tamez, *Bible of the Oppressed*, 67.

52. Rieger, *No Rising Tide*, 17; Elliott and Atkinson, *The Gods That Failed*.

53. Novak, *Spirit of Democratic Capitalism*, 358–60.

Novak to side-step the liberationist voice of the Bible. If that assumption is proved false, then the liberationist voice must be addressed again.

Novak also contends that the only modern alternative to capitalism is totalitarian socialism. Part of what he seems to be doing is marginalizing self-styled socialists by shouldering them with the sins of Stalin and Mao. He says that what most current socialists call socialism is really just a variation on democratic capitalism. Democratic capitalism is very flexible, and it can operate with a more libertarian bent or with a system that includes a robust welfare state.

Of course, this is not how the terms are used in the modern world. And to be fair to Novak, the definitions may have shifted a bit since 1982. The form of capitalism that we have now—neoliberalism—is far more aggressive, far more unchained from state intervention, far more triumphant over the forces of unionization and protectionism than was the capitalism of the 1970s. If Novak's definition of capitalism can encompass income taxes over 50 percent and the nationalization of healthcare and other industries, then it begins to lose meaning. You cannot simultaneously define capitalism as, on the one hand, any system that contains a market, every system that is short of centralized, state-run, planned economies, and, on the other hand, a system that is built on the unintended benefits of profit-seeking and the right of each individual to choose what the good is for themselves. Novak's claim that one can advocate for universal healthcare, for example, without appealing in some way to socialism is nonsensical. If one argues that individualism and the profit motive are the defining characteristics of capitalism, then any limits on individualism and profit-seeking must be understood as something other than capitalism.[54]

In its current, neoliberal form—a form that was anticipated but not yet realized in Novak's time—capitalism is a totalizing force that infuses competition into absolutely every aspect of life. Julie Wilson summarizes,

> Generally speaking, neoliberalism is a set of social, cultural, and political-economic forces that puts competition at the center of social life. According to neoliberalism, government's charge is not the care and security of citizens, but rather the promotion of market competition. In the neoliberal imagination, public social infrastructures (such as social security, unemployment benefits, public education) are believed to squash entrepreneurialism and individualism and breed dependency and bureaucracy.

54. Novak, *Spirit of Democratic Capitalism*, 111–12.

> Competition, on the other hand, is heralded to ensure efficiency and incite creativity. Spurred by competition, individuals, organizations, companies, and even the government itself, will seek to optimize and innovate, creating a truly free social world where the best people and ideas come out on top. Put a little differently, neoliberalism aims to create a market-based society, where there are only competing private enterprises. . . . In a neoliberal society, the capitalist market is no longer imagined as a distinct arena where goods are valued and exchanged; rather, the market is, or ideally should be, the basis for *all* of society. Thus, neoliberalism works aggressively to infuse competition into the nooks and crannies of who we are and the environments we inhabit. Every aspect of our lives, even those facets that do not necessarily have anything to do with money or the economy, become geared toward market competition, from our education to our friendships to our very sense of self and self-worth.[55]

Under neoliberalism, Mammon is no longer god only of the market, Mammon becomes a universal god with power over every part of life. It encourages people to make every decision based on market efficiency. It turns everything into a commodity. Government's function is no longer to protect and serve its citizens, but to protect and serve the Market and the corporations that dominate it. Democracy and public speech are turned over to the Market. Those people and organizations that cannot compete in the marketplace are treated as disposable.[56]

Even my very self becomes a commodity, and I must seek to maximize its value. Education, experience, and relationships are primarily a means of increasing my market worth. The way I present myself in the world and in social media is not about personal expression, but is rather a marketing campaign to help me sell myself. As Jia Tolentino warns:

> Capitalism has no land left to cultivate but the self. Everything is being cannibalized—not just goods and labor, but personality and relationships and attention. The next step is complete identification with the online marketplace, physical and spiritual inseparability from the internet: a nightmare that is already banging down the door.[57]

55. Wilson, *Neoliberalism*, 2–3.

56. Wilson, *Neoliberalism*, 74–75.

57. Tolentino, *Trick Mirror*, 32.

Market logic has taken hold to a degree that Novak could have scarcely imagined, but rather than lifting the poor out of poverty, it has increased wealth inequality, eroded democratic institutions, and transformed every part of human life into something that can and should be sold.

One further note about the holes in Novak's pragmatic case before we move on. Novak trusts that capitalism is safe for the poor because he thinks most people can be counted on to behave in decent, moral ways in their business affairs.[58] Can we have that trust in a neoliberal world? Can we have that trust in relation to corporate persons, who are in control of an ever-growing part of the economy? Corporate persons have no moral code other than profit. The corporation must fulfill its promise to its stockholders by producing the maximum amount of profit possible. If Novak is counting on the crueler effects of the market being checked by individuals who will act in accordance with their own moral code, can that work when the most powerful persons have no morals but profit?

If we grant that Novak cannot simply dismiss the liberative message of the Bible on the grounds that the market does a better job for the poor when it is left completely to itself, then we must determine what to do with a biblical code that ill fits the modern world. Finn suggests that while the specific injunctions of the Bible may no longer apply, the biblical tradition implies that

> we must find structures that will accomplish the same underlying goals, both to assist those whom the market leaves with unmet needs and to enable each able-bodied worker to support self and family through gainful employment.[59]

Finn meets Novak closer to his own ground than Tamez or Rieger. He suggests that there are parts of the market system that work quite well and generally do work for the benefit of most people. For example, he says that the Third World is not poor primarily because of exploitation from the First World, but because the means of production there are not as advanced and efficient. He believes that self-interest has an important and positive role to play in markets, so long as they are properly regulated. He believes prices can be used to encourage desired ethical behavior. Economic incentives can often be the best way of encouraging

58. Novak, *Spirit of Democratic Capitalism*, 92–93, 356.
59. Finn, *Christian Economic Ethics*, 384.

ethical behavior. By making it in a person's self-interest to do the right thing, we do not have to rely on a person's good will.[60]

At the same time, Finn also insists that there are aspects of capitalist markets that are clearly detrimental to human flourishing. Markets tend to dehumanize people, to reduce them to selfish calculators of utility. Economics has no way to talk about good and evil, only different preferences. Markets do not just facilitate human goals, they create them: the quest for greater profit leads marketers to actually create desires where they weren't before. And the growth of markets is not a good measure for the increase of human welfare. People can spend resources on things that decrease their welfare, contrary to the assumptions of capitalist economists. There are ways in which economic markets do not actually allow freedom to all people, especially the poor.[61] These must be addressed by the state. Checks must be placed on the Market in order for it to produce just results. The economic message of the Bible must be followed in spirit, if not in letter. Markets can be good, but they must be closely controlled, because they do not mysteriously create the greatest good for all people. "Markets simultaneously help and hinder morality."[62]

The question is this: Is Novak right that the Invisible Hand of the Market can be trusted, on its own, to bring about the best pragmatic results for all people, including the poor? If it can, then perhaps we can be justified in ignoring the critiques that the Bible levels on capitalism. If the Market can most effectively produce the ends that the Bible envisions (justice for the poor), then why not leave the means to the Market? But if the market is lacking in producing justice for the poor, then we must consider whether our faith in the Market's Invisible Hand is not a rather dangerous form of idolatry.

Idolatry

Jesus's warning against Mammon in Luke 16:13 is arguably more relevant now than it ever was in the first-century Mediterranean world.[63] Then it could refer only to greed that acted as a motivator of individuals. To have more money is to be safe, and so one begins to put their faith in

60. Finn, *Christian Economic Ethics*, 219–23.

61. Finn, *Christian Economic Ethics*, 223–28.

62. Finn, *Christian Economic Ethics*, 232.

63. Schertz, "Shrewd Steward," 19.

the pursuit of money rather than in God. But now Mammon has grown into something so much more than individual greed. Mammon is now an economic engine that demands economic growth; in fact, for Novak, this is its great virtue. Mammon has become the sole god of corporate persons, whose only moral code is the pursuit of profit. Mammon has become a Market whose rises and falls can be consulted, like the entrails of goats or the flights of birds, to determine whether the divine hand approves or disapproves of whatever political proposal is being considered today.

Novak would deny that trust in the Invisible Hand of the Market to produce common welfare amounts to idolatry. "Far from making riches a god, democratic capitalism promotes a pluralism of interests and purposes."[64] It is nothing more than the freedom of individuals to make their own choices about what is moral and what is good.

But Mammon is not just riches. Mammon is a system that drives a particular type of behavior. The Market does not just allow freedom, it encourages a particular behavior: the maximization of profit. As we learned from Friedman, it does not actually have to be a god in order for it to function *as if* it were a god.

As Rieger correctly notes, it does not matter whether people think of the Market as some kind of transcendent being. It does not matter whether people think that there is something mystical about the Invisible Hand. It is the fact that people trust the Market to work things out for the common good that makes the Market like a god. It is the belief that the Market can regulate itself, that it can be trusted to bring prosperity, equilibrium, and the general welfare of humanity. What is more:

> Faith in a regulating invisible hand, as it were, makes efforts to stage corrective interventions in the market appear like unfaithfulness or even blasphemy. It is the principle of the invisible hand of the market, which guarantees that human self interest—considered to be one of the strongest sources of energy of the free market—is transformed into common interest, thus benefitting the community as a whole. This does not necessarily have to be called a transcendent factor or an invisible hand—what matters is the common and unfaltering conviction that this is the way the world works. What is most telling is that no alternative vision is allowed—this one point is not negotiable—and anyone

---

64. Novak, *Spirit of Democratic Capitalism*, 84.

who dares to question this assumption risks being discredited by the guild, which amounts to a form of excommunication.[65]

The Market is an idol because it demands the faith of all people. It demands that we all pursue the profit motive. To try to do otherwise would be to break the system, would be to distrust the Market.

Novak is actually clear that faith must be put in the Market rather than in God. As we saw above, God cannot be counted upon to act in the interests of humanity. This is the message of the Incarnation. God has and will abandon us here on earth. What is more, the Bible simply does not understand the power of capitalism. Since the discovery of the multiplication of wealth, we are in a new epoch in which the old rules do not apply. "Now that the secrets of sustained material progress have been decoded, the responsibility for reducing misery and hunger is no longer God's but ours."[66] And by our responsibility, he really means the Market's responsibility.

The belief that God is no longer active in human history leads to this kind of Mammonist faith. While Novak would resist the emphasis on corporations as a stand-in for profit-seeking, Daniel Bell's description of the faith implied by Novak's position is still quite apt:

> The capitalist vision of providence endows corporations with a significance that is almost messianic and suggests that they should be revered as the church. Moreover, Adam Smith is not infrequently elevated above Jesus Christ when it comes to guidance regarding the economic order, because, it is said, Jesus appreciated neither the power of production nor the ability of money to make money. That the corporation would be elevated to almost messianic standing makes sense if one begins with the premise that God is not active in sanctifying us now and so we are left to our own devices.[67]

For someone like Tamez, who is comfortable applying biblical economic ethics directly to today's world, there is no question that oppressors, those who seek profit, are idolaters. By definition any act of profit-seeking hurts the poor, is against God, and is a form of idolatry.

---

65. Rieger, *No Rising Tide*, 65–66.

66. Novak, *Spirit of Democratic Capitalism*, 28.

67. Bell, *Economy of Desire*, 181.

And it is an idolatry that God is working against, that God will punish. God and Mammon are in combat, and we should choose God.[68]

For Rieger, the idolatry of the Market is problematic because it distorts our image of what and who God should be. If the providence of the market has gained the status of *habitus*, the danger is not so much that the Market becomes our god but that God must behave like the Market. The theology of Market begins to seep into our understanding of who and what God is. Achieved most perfectly in the Prosperity Gospel, this theological shift leaves us worshipping at the altar of Mammon all the time thinking we are worshipping God.[69] Capitalist ideals begin to affect every part of our theology: how we understand God, what salvation is, how we relate to other people.[70]

Bell also contends that market ideology distorts religious devotion. Because the claim of the market is so complete, it frames the way we understand every other part of life. Capitalism is able to absorb any critiques of itself and repackage them as products to be sold.[71] Religion, too, becomes a product, one of many that the market offers.

> Like the vast array of exotic cultural products from around the world that appear side by side on the shelves of the import franchise at the mall, in a consumer culture, beliefs tend to become free-floating cultural objects. These objects do not require anything of me; they entail no particular commitment or engagement. They do not bind me to any particular people or community. Rather, they function only to serve the end(s) or purpose(s) I choose, which, in the case of religious choices, might include shoring up my self-image as "spiritual," or providing meaning amid the stresses of my middle-class life or the right values for my children, and so on. (Consider the popular standard for evaluating worship: "Does it meet my needs?") Reduced to a religious commodity, Christian beliefs can be held in the midst of a political economy that runs counter to those beliefs without any tension at all.[72]

---

68. Tamez, *Bible of the Oppressed*, 33–35.

69. For a history of the prosperity gospel, see Bowler, *Blessed*. For a critique, see Fee, *Disease*.

70. Rieger, *No Rising Tide*, 18–19. For more about how contemporary economy affects other religious practice, see: Turpin, *Branded*; Miller, *Consuming Religion*; Bell, *Economy of Desire*.

71. Bell, *Economy of Desire*, 20.

72. Bell, *Economy of Desire*, 21.

Market capitalism not only replaces religious ideology as the primary means through which Christians understand the world, it also reduces Christian practice to the status of a commodity, thus denying it the power to resist the over-arching framework.

For Finn, a moderate, the warning against idolatry may not be directly relevant to the modern world. It should, nevertheless, inspire us toward moral action. It should warn us against the totalizing claims of the Market. While the Market can do some things well, it cannot be trusted always to do things well. Biblical critiques, like those found in Luke, should inform the ways we place checks on the Market to keep the Market from demanding human sacrifice.

Whether we label it as idolatry or not, it is clear that Novak imputes to the Market the power to save. He is explicit that market-driven profit-seeking is the best possible way to save the poor from poverty. He defines it as *caritas*. Whether or not Novak understands the Market as mystical, there can be no doubt that his devotion to the Market has overruled for him the biblical imperative, found strongly in Luke, for economic justice. This preference for the gospel of economic growth leads inevitably toward environmental destruction.

Sustainability

As we have seen, Novak believes that the best hope for the world's people lays in continual economic growth driven by the Market. With more and more people in the world, we need more and more wealth to sustain them, and the best producer of wealth for the good of the world is profit-seeking through democratic capitalism. Not to seek for one's own profit would be not to love the poor.

The call for continuous economic growth presents a problem, though, one that was not as apparent in 1982. The case is made well by Naomi Klein. Capitalism drives economic growth and economic growth drives climate change. The market creates a literal rising tide. It may or may not raise boats, but it will certainly flood and drown. Novak's magic bullet of economic growth is sure to bring devastation to vast areas of the world, sparking resource wars and human migration on a scale we have not seen in recorded history. It will certainly negatively affect the poor most of all.[73]

73. Klein, *This Changes Everything*.

As Finn points out, in the current economy, no one pays the price for pollution. Polluters do not pay an economic cost for the harm that is being done to the planet. The self-regulative power of the market is short-circuited because no one charges polluters for the externalities they produce. A market solution could be possible, but it would have to be through a worldwide coordination of political power.

In any case, the nonhuman world demands respect as it has a relationship with God independent of us. We must "use creation with respect for its integrity, in accord with our responsibilities as stewards for the natural world." How we treat the environment affects us, and it effects most acutely the poor and vulnerable.[74]

As we have seen above, Tamez talks about environmental issues in the context of despoliation. Environmental degradation hurts the poor, and it is thus an assault against God, the defender of the poor. It is one of the many ways the rich extract wealth while forcing the poor to bear the cost.

Rieger, too, identifies neglect of the environment as one of the gaps between the ideal of capitalism and its actual historical instantiation. Economists tend simply to avoid the issue. This is one of the many ways that the Market's claims to create, by its own self-regulation, the maximum good for the maximum number of people rings hollow. We suffer when we put our faith in a market god that has no concern whatsoever for the state of the environment.[75]

Pope Francis, in his encyclical on climate change, highlights the ways that market logic is oblivious to the environmental impacts of economic growth and the ways that those impacts disproportionately hurt the poor.

> Once more, we need to reject a magical conception of the market, which would suggest that problems can be solved simply by an increase in the profits of companies or individuals. Is it realistic to hope that those who are obsessed with maximizing profits will stop to reflect on the environmental damage which they will leave behind for future generations? Where profits alone count, there can be no thinking about the rhythms of nature, its phases of decay and regeneration, or the complexity of ecosystems which may be gravely upset by human intervention. Moreover, biodiversity is considered at most a deposit of economic resources available for exploitation, with no serious

74. Finn, *Christian Economic Ethics*, 342.
75. Rieger, *No Rising Tide*, 85.

> thought for the real value of things, their significance for persons and cultures, or the concerns and needs of the poor.[76]

A "deified market" cares only for the short-term maximization of profit, treats everything like a commodity, and leaves a trail of despoiled landscapes and impoverished people in its wake.[77]

To these analyses can be added the simple biblical proposition that the world belongs to God. "The earth is the Lord's, and everything in it" (Ps 24:1). Humans do not hold ultimate ownership over the planet. We are meant to be caretakers of its resources. We are meant to show the same care for the world that God would show for the world, and to do it in God's stead. The planet is a creation of God, and in God's good grace, it provides the things we need to survive. But we have the power to destroy it and its life-giving potential.

In light of the increasing evidence of climate change, we must question whether continual economic growth is a responsible goal. Economic growth cannot be the only answer to world poverty if it creates wealth in some places only to destroy it in others. Increased economic investment that produces more consumer goods more efficiently at lower prices is hardly life-giving if it creates desertification in the world's most vulnerable farm and ranch lands. Lower prices for building materials are not life-giving if they result in higher sea levels that destroy the homes of hundreds of millions. Lower prices for food are not life-giving if they result in more frequent tropical storms that kill and destroy. These changes always hurt the poor more than they do the rich.

The "miracle" of capitalism is that it creates wealth; under capitalism people do not need to compete over fractions of a fixed amount of resources, because capitalism can grow the pie. Regardless of the will of the people within the Market, the Market will produce growth. As Novak well knows, growth is the unintended consequence of the seeking of self-interest. In light of the economic externality of climate change, we can see that the unintended consequences are not always blessings, as Adam Smith predicted; sometimes the unintended consequence is a curse.

76. Francis, *Laudato Si'*, §190.
77. Francis, *Laudato Si'*, §56.

Conclusion

As we have seen, Novak claims that capitalist markets, through the law of unintended consequences, transform the sin of greed into the virtue of economic growth which benefits not only the capitalist, but all people. Capitalism lifts more people out of poverty than any other force, we are told, and capitalism does more to promote equality than any redistribution of resources. However, Novak's claims on the market's behalf can now be seen to have been false. The market does not, on its own, promote the maximum good for the poor. Profit-seeking is not *caritas*. Because of this, Novak's dismissal of the liberative message of the Bible cannot be justified. While we may not choose to implement every economic provision in the Bible literally, we must at the very least take heed of the injustices it warns against. To continue to have faith in the Market to be the savior of the poor is a form of idolatry. What is more, the Market's creed of economic growth is driving an environmental change that will likely affect human livelihood for the worse within our lifetimes.

Novak's theological claims cannot stand. Trinity cannot be an excuse to replace community with market relationships. Incarnation is not proof that God has abandoned the world; it is proof that God cares for humanity, and especially for the poor. Competition cannot be held up as a virtue in itself simply because we suppose that it might produce good. Original Sin cannot be a justification to stand by in apathy while some humans gain wealth by oppressing others. The idea that the Bible recommends a separation of realms is quite simply a misreading of the gospel. And most of all, profit-seeking can never be the highest form of Godly love. Self-interest is not *caritas*, and to suggest that it is is a perversion of the gospel and a betrayal of the God whose nature and name is love.

Two Parables of Market

In chapter two I identified two parables as the most problematic in the gospel of Luke: the Parable of the Shrewd Manager and the Parable of the Pounds. In chapter four we struggled with how to incorporate them into Luke's radical economic message of liberation for the poor and resistance to wealth. We return to them now at the close of chapter seven because, in their traditional readings, they are near perfect parables of capitalism. They show better than any other material in Luke just where Market theology leads.

We began this chapter with the well-known apothegm that closes the Parable of the Shrewd Manager: "No slave can serve two masters. . . . You cannot serve God and Mammon" (Luke 16:13 NRSV). For some, it is the words that come immediately before this that unlock the parable:

> Whoever is faithful in a very little is faithful also in much; and whoever is dishonest in a very little is dishonest also in much. If then you have not been faithful with the dishonest wealth, who will entrust to you with the true riches? If you have not been faithful with what belongs to another, who will give you what is your own? (Luke 16:10–12 NRSV)

Aggressive profit-making on behalf of the capitalist becomes both the model and necessary precursor for discipleship. If you do not grow the wealth that is entrusted to you by the owner, then God will never trust you with heavenly wealth. The good disciple creates wealth for the master.

But we must remember what Jesus says dishonest Mammon is of use for: namely, for making friends who will one day welcome you into eternal homes. As Daniel Bell suggests, "In the midst of a political economy where wealth attracts friends and is a source of influence, this is an important clarification."[78] In Luke's gospel, it is not the rich who own eternal homes, it is the poor. The Christian is not to use worldly wealth for the benefit of the rich but for the benefit of the poor. Wealth is to be used for precisely the opposite of its usual use, and it is best managed by working against the interests of the owner. Mammon's economy squeezes wealth from clients in order to promote capital accumulation; God's economy disperses the money of the wealthy in order to make friends of the poor.

But the greatest parable of capitalism is the Parable of the Pounds, as Spiros Zodhiates argues. In this parable, Jesus preaches the very values of capitalist accumulation. It is "a parable on capitalism and profit-making."[79] The Christian is compelled to put money to work, to multiply it. God created humans to seek ever-growing yields, and Jesus confirms that desire with the teachings of this parable.[80] The clear capitalist message can be seen most clearly in the way that the master takes the pound from the unproductive slave and puts it into the hands of the most profit-making. Zodhiates revels in the fact that this part of the story rankles more liberal interpreters:

78. Bell, *Economy of Desire*, 216.

79. Zodhiates, *Did Jesus Teach Capitalism?*, vii. See also a more moderate Christian defense of capitalism: Brat, "God and Advanced Mammon," 176.

80. Zodhiates, *Did Jesus Teach Capitalism?*, 22–23.

In verse twenty-four the Lord now turns to those around Him and says, "Take from him the pound, and give it to him who has ten pounds."

"Unjust, unjust, a capitalist God! He takes from the one who has nothing and gives it to the one who has ten." This is what the radicals in our society would shout. But isn't it better to give the pound to the one who has ten, than to leave it in the hands of the one who will never produce anything, so that when the one with ten gains the eleventh, he can produce another ten or twenty? If our governments and our societies were as wise as the Lord who made this world, we would be far better off. . . .

It makes no difference how much one has, as long as he multiplies what he has. For if we give something to a person who has nothing, and he buries it and does nothing with it, that is where waste occurs. These are fundamental laws of economics. . . . The person who produces is the one who can be trusted with more. Greater productivity brings the greatest good for all.[81]

Jesus explicitly teaches capitalist principles, principles which are part of God's laws. Those who put their money to work to make more are blessed by God. Those who are poor are only poor because of their laziness and lack of attention to God's capitalist principles. Any form of relief for the poor encourages laziness and violates God's laws. Jesus preaches profit-seeking. Jesus wants *homo economicus* as a disciple. Those who find themselves poor now should seek to learn from and emulate those who have struck it rich.[82]

Carrying the traditional interpretation of the parable to its logical capitalist conclusion makes clear just how foreign it is to the rest of Luke's economic message, and just how absurd such an interpretation seems when placed in the context of the full gospel. To read the parable as a parable of capitalism is to replace the God of the Bible with the Market, to replace the message of good news for the poor with a false gospel of wealth.

What the Parable of the Pounds shows is just how faithless a god like Mammon is. The nobleman-king, whom we see now as a capitalist owner, works for no one's benefit except his own. He seeks to parlay his wealth into political power. He entrusts his managers with making profit for him while he is away. Once he has captured political authority, he calls back his slaves to see what profit they have wrought for him. The first has made

81. Zodhiates, *Did Jesus Teach Capitalism?*, 62.
82. Zodhiates, *Did Jesus Teach Capitalism?*, 65–66.

record gains—a 1000 percent increase—and is rewarded by the master. In return for the wealth the manager has got for him, the ruler gives a position of great authority in his administration. Likewise, the second manager is given a position of public authority commensurate with the amount of personal enrichment he has given the ruler. But the last manager, who did not want to participate in the acknowledged theft of his ruler, returns back precisely what the ruler had given him. Angered that the last manager would not steal for him, the ruler dismisses him, giving the money he was managing to his most ruthless manager, saying "When I find someone with money, I figure out how to get them more. When I find poor people, I figure out how to take what they have left." Finally, with his newfound political authority, the ruler imprisons or executes all of his political rivals and everyone who has ever criticized him. At no point does he ever show any concern for his citizens. He is interested only in his own wealth and power. He rewards the people who get him more of it. He uses his money to get more power. He uses his power to get more money. He destroys anyone who gets in his way.

Surely this is *homo economicus*. This is the man who works zealously for his own self-interest. And he uses his market power in order to get political power, which in turn he can use to further enrich himself. His actions create more wealth, but that wealth benefits only him and his cronies. As for the people whose welfare is in his hands, he cares not at all. "Bring them here and slaughter them in my presence" (Luke 19:27 NRSV). Zodhiates is right that the Parable of the Pounds can function well as a parable of capitalism. And it shows where unregulated capitalism leads: to economic exploitation, political corruption, and the destruction of any persons who stand in the way of the unfettered accumulation of wealth and power by the very few. This is the rule of Mammon. Is this what Jesus teaches? No! This is what Jesus warns against.

Conclusion

There is a wide gap between the culture and economy of the Roman Empire and the culture and economy of the present-day United States of America. And yet, despite that gap, we have found it fruitful to use an ancient model of god as a metaphor for the forces of capitalistic markets. Both theologians and economists have acknowledged that markets can function as if they were gods. People put faith in the market to providentially sort out the many competing demands of society, to create wealth and decrease poverty, to provide oracular pronouncements about the events of the day. The market provides a code of conduct and creed: that each seek to maximize their own utility. And there is belief that if that creed is followed, the market will in turn maximize the utility of all.

Michael Novak gives a spirited Christian defense of capitalist markets. He argues that the market does a better job of achieving the aims of biblical wealth ethics than do those ethical codes themselves. If you want to lift people out of poverty, Novak argues, then choose the market. It will increase wealth and drive away poverty better than a set of utopian commandments.

And yet Novak's argument falls short. One can only put the kind of faith he does in the market if one is willing to completely ignore much of the economic message of the Bible, including that part of it which is embodied in Luke. One must reject the notion that God has a mission to liberate the poor. One must overlook all of the ways that market leaves and hurts the most vulnerable members of society. One must truly acknowledge that God either can not or will not save people from oppression in the real world, that one's faith is better put in the Market. And one must ignore the mounting evidence that continual economic growth creates serious externalities that are not addressed by the market, externalities like environmental degradation and climate change created by rich corporations but disproportionately paid for by the poor and marginalized.

Market does function like a god, and it demands a different kind of devotion than does the God revealed by Luke's gospel. Luke's message reveals capitalist and corporation not as salvific benefactors, but as avaricious actors that will exploit others for profit to whatever extent the law allows. The unfettered quest after utility and profit maximization does not universally promote the benefit of all, it creates ever-widening chasms between those who have and those who do not. In the guise of freedom, it concentrates both economic and political power into the hands of those who can afford to pay for it.

In light of this, how is the faithful reader of Luke to live? How might one resist devotion to Mammon and instead live a life faithful to the God of the gospel? It is to this question that we now turn.

CHAPTER 8

Reclaiming the Radical

There was a certain rich man who clothed himself
in purple and fine linen, and who feasted luxuri-
ously every day. At his gate lay a certain poor man
named Lazarus who was covered with sores. Lazarus
longed to eat the crumbs that fell from the rich man's
table. Instead, dogs would come and lick his sores.

—LUKE 16:19–21 CEB

WE HAVE IDENTIFIED TWIN ideals in Luke's economic material: that God favors the poor and that wealth is to be resisted. But how can a modern Christian live in light of these ideals? Should we try to take Luke's message literally? Or if we do not, how can we still take it seriously?

There are several very clear, and very hard, instructions in Luke. For several centuries, Luke 6:35 was interpreted as a prohibition on any kind of lending at interest. Should that continue to be the ideal? Much more pointedly, Luke 14:33 insists that every disciple must give up all possessions in order to follow Jesus. Is that the standard for all Christians?

Making things more complicated are the nearly two millennia and massive cultural difference that stand between us and Luke. Advanced capitalism bears little resemblance to the agrarian economy of ancient Rome. It would be extraordinarily difficult to apply the provisions of

Luke in a fundamentalist fashion to the modern world. The Luke 6:35 ban on interest would make even the most basic of financial transactions impossible. Luke's ethics would also allow the practice of slavery. It would be hard to find a Christian of any persuasion who would be keen to level every modern financial institution while at the same time reinstituting slavery. Blindly applying the rules of the past to the modern economy would likely not be possible without a complete rejection of the technological and social advances of the last two thousand years.

However, it is also problematic to simply pick and choose which provisions to enforce and which provisions to ignore. Daniel Finn warns, it is unacceptable:

> that Christians today can simply reject any part of the tradition they find inconvenient. Such an approach grants the tradition little or no authority in our lives and thinks of tradition simply as a museum where we might choose a piece to put on display— or not—depending on whether our preexisting view of what should occur in life is helped or hindered by it. All too many scholars writing on Christian economic ethics engage in this sort of irresponsible "cherry picking" of the tradition.[1]

As I have argued, many recent influential interpreters of Luke have found Luke's wealth ethic to be simply inconvenient. When faced with provisions that seem challenging to modern systems, they try to ignore them. They find ways to marginalize the more radical parts so that they can be rendered inapplicable, so that Luke loses its bite.

So how can we take seriously the full breadth of Luke's message even if we know that we cannot always apply it literally? Finn suggests a reasonable approach:

> Our task is a difficult one, but it is the only responsible one left to us: to read carefully the views of our spiritual ancestors about economic life, to compare those views with the ones held in our culture today, and to discern carefully what those ancient texts mean for our life now.[2]

Rather than bracketing off those parts of Luke's economic ethic that seem radical, we can interrogate them more closely, hold them in tension with the modern world, suss out the intention behind the provisions, and seek to apply them as wisely and faithfully as we can.

---

1. Finn, *Christian Economic Ethics*, 383.
2. Finn, *Christian Economic Ethics*, 28–29.

In fact, the function that Luke's economic message should have for us is well-stated by Luke Timothy Johnson, though he does not carry it out to its full implications. Johnson argues that Luke-Acts should have a prophetic function in the church, that it holds up a utopian ideal that should challenge and guide the church and every Christian in their economic dealings. He says that Luke-Acts "reveals a prophetic vision of both Jesus and the church. Indeed, the church of Acts is, if anything, even more radically prophetic than Jesus in the Gospel." Furthermore, "it does not simply report past events; it imagines a world that challenges the one that humans in every age construct on their own terms." Finally, Luke's challenge necessitates that Christians "think of the church in more explicitly prophetic terms and find ways of embodying and enacting God's vision for humans."[3] Exploring this prophetic vision is the task of this chapter, though Johnson's conception of the vision is far too narrow. Lukan wealth ethics is not best confined to the practice of small religious communities, as Johnson suggests.[4] It must address the systems that create poverty and wealth.

It is not my goal in this chapter to make an exhaustive application of the whole of Lukan economic material. Instead I will highlight a few key Lukan themes and explore their modern import. These are the preferential option for the poor, the idolatry of the market, the call to solidarity with the poor, and the environmental implications of Luke's message. Even though Luke comes from a very different cultural context, it still holds a radical message of liberation and solidarity for us today.

Primacy of the Poor

The first and most important lesson to take from Luke's economic ethic is that God has a particular concern for the poor. It is all the more important because it is so often overlooked. But it is quite clear within the text of Luke. God has good news for the poor. That is, at its simplest, to say that God has real concern for the real poor. The poor are a key part of the audience for God's good news. It is unjust to exclude the poor from God's message or to cast them as mere props for discussing the interests of the wealthy. The fact that Luke came from a more affluent background only intensifies the seriousness with which we should regard Luke's message

3. Johnson, *Prophetic Jesus*, loc. 19–25.
4. Johnson, *Prophetic Jesus*, loc. 1076–78.

of liberation for the poor. Even through the lens of the elite classes, the message of good news for the poor manages to shine through.

Dario López Rodriguez is among the best at highlighting God's liberative message for the poor and marginalized. It is a message that must be lived out concretely in the world.

> The poor and the marginalized are both subjects and agents of God's mission. . . . God's special love for the poor and the marginalized is one of the key theological themes that Luke outlines and proposes as an inescapable agenda item for the church's mission. In this sense, even though we interpret the missional demands of Luke's gospel in different ways according to our theological and political perspectives, we cannot ignore that one of the central emphases of this gospel is the affirmation of God's special love for the poor and the marginalized. Luke stresses that believers must be like the Good Samaritan and like the poor widow. The disciples of Jesus of Nazareth are not called to be indifferent or to pass by on the other side when faced with real needs of human beings of flesh and bone (Luke 10:31–32). Nor are they called to selfishly accumulate things thinking that one's life "consist[s] in the abundance of possessions" (Luke 12:15). Consequently, they should individually and collectively be like their Lord and Master, "a friend of tax collectors and sinners" (Luke 7:34), proclaiming the good news of the kingdom of God everyday in cities and villages (Luke 8:1). According to Luke no other missional path exists. As Jesus indicated in the synagogue of Nazareth, compelled by the power of the Holy Spirit, we are called "to proclaim the year of the Lord's favor" (Luke 4:19) in our particular historical context. This is how it must be. We do not have another alternative.[5]

God desires that the sufferings of the poor and marginalized be remedied. God also desires that the poor be the agents of that remedy.

As we have seen, though, many interpreters of Luke downplay its material concerning the poor. While some do this because they are seeking a more moderate reading, others do so because they think that Luke is not radical enough. Notable among these are Craig Nessan, Itumeleng Mosala, Roland Boer, and Christina Petterson.[6] All four of these scholars make some version of the argument that what we have in the Gospel of

---

5. López Rodriguez, *Liberating Mission*, 25–26.

6. Nessan, "Luke and Liberation Theology"; Mosala, *Biblical Hermeneutics*; Boer and Petterson, *Time of Troubles*.

Luke is a message that has been co-opted by the rich and powerful, a domestication of the gospel of Jesus. Nessan warns that Luke has deformed
the radical message of Jesus, that "in the process of reinterpreting them
for a new context, the radicality of Jesus' call to discipleship is tamed."[7]
Mosala identifies a similar problem, that "by turning the experiences of
the poor into the moral virtues of the rich, Luke has effectively eliminated the poor from his Gospel."[8] Boer and Petterson argue that Luke
re-inscribes the economic status quo rather than providing meaningful
resistance to it.[9]

And yet, despite the deficiencies pointed out by these scholars, Luke
contains the clearest expression of God's good news for the poor found in
the New Testament. The answer to these criticisms cannot be to abandon
the radical message of Luke as hopelessly subverted, because there is no
purer form of the gospel for us to turn to. Luke, as imperfect as it is, is
the best we have. The fact that it is mediated for us by the voices of the
elite makes it all the more important for us to take seriously its message
of good news for the poor. It makes it all the more important for us to
take seriously the ways that it can speak to the poor and marginalized in
our world. And in fact, this is the course of action that both Nessan and
Mosala recommend to us.[10]

We have a name for interpretations that take seriously the perspective of the poor: theologies of liberation. And it seems quite clear that a
liberationist approach is the approach called for by the message of God's
good news for the poor found in Luke. Luke portrays God as the champion of the poor and hungry who has a clear preference for those who are
dispossessed (Luke 1:52–53; 6:20–21, 24–25; 16:19–31). Jesus's mission
and the very nature of the gospel are defined by good news for the poor
(Luke 4:18–21; 7:22). God's championing of the poor rises to the level of
proclaiming Jubilee (Luke 4:18–19).[11] In Luke, God undoubtedly has a
preferential option for the poor.

This preferential option for the poor manifests in two ways: a special
focus on the voices of the poor and a special concern for the welfare of
the poor. The first of these should not be neglected. Everything about the

---

7. Nessan, "Luke and Liberation Theology," 137.

8. Mosala, *Biblical Hermeneutics*, 163.

9. Boer and Petterson, *Time of Troubles*, 177–78.

10. Nessan, "Luke and Liberation Theology," 137; Mosala, *Biblical Hermeneutics*, 193.

11. Ringe, *Jesus*, 36.

way that we study the Bible—from its composition to its canonization to its interpretation—gives priority to the voices of the rich. We know from Nessan and Mosala that this is a problem at the level of the text of Luke, and it is no less a problem in our modern scholarship. Professional biblical interpretation is dominated by the relatively wealthy. It takes incredible resources to defer working for a living and instead devote more than a decade of full-time study just to receive the doctoral degree that grants one access to the academy. It takes incredible resources to travel to the conferences of the academic guilds that are necessary to establish one's credentials as a scholar. The resources to engage in scholarly study of the Bible are simply unimaginable for the majority of the world's people, including the majority of the world's Christians. As Miguel De La Torre notes,

> All too often, ethical structures are based on the experience of those who write books, preach at influential churches, or teach at prestigious academic centers whose social location differs from the poor of the earth. The experience of religion professors, professional ethicists, and clergy ministering in economically privileged congregations or seminaries usually becomes the norm for the construction of what is moral.[12]

Even when there is discussion about the needs of the poor and marginalized, the voices that have influence are still the voices of the rich and powerful.

Because of this, it is incumbent upon us to privilege the voices of the poor and marginalized whenever they can be heard. At every level of the conversation, we have a tendency to use the poor as little more than a backdrop for ethical discussions about the behaviors of the rich. And I admit, this study suffers from the same fault. But I can at least confess clearly here that our interpretation suffers from the absence of voices from the margins and that such voices should be treated with the utmost respect and care, not only because they are disproportionally missing from the conversation, but because Luke makes clear that they are preferred by God. Again, De La Torre writes:

> Because Jesús put on the flesh of the marginalized, I argue for an ethics rooted in the experiences of the marginalized, an experience that was, and continues to be, shared by God. Those marginalized in Jesús' time occupied the privileged position of being the first to hear the Good News. Not because they were

12. De La Torre, *Politics of Jesús*, loc. 1435–38.

holier, nor better Christians, but because God chooses sides.
God makes a preferential option for those who exist under the
weight of oppression, demonstrated by God's physical solidarity
with the disenfranchised through the incarnation. Jesús willingly assumed the role of the ultra-disenfranchised, becoming the
paragon for disciples to emulate. Followers of Jesús are called
to imitate God, an imitation that excludes those who hold onto
power and privilege, those who lord over humans.[13]

As we have clearly seen in Luke, the poor and the ones who are most
likely to receive and accept the gospel message. The poor are also the ones
who are most likely to speak with the voice of God.

One such voice of the poor that has passed through the gauntlet of
academic study is that of a Nicaraguan peasant named Felipe, who says
of the parable of the rich man and Lazarus:

> What I think is that neither the rich nor the poor ought to suffer
> the fate of those two guys in the Gospel. The rich man damned
> for having squandered selfishly, the poor man screwed all his life
> even though afterwards he's saved. Which means there shouldn't
> be rich or poor, nobody should be screwed in this life, nobody
> should be damned in the next life. All people ought to share the
> riches in this life and share the glory in the next one.[14]

Surely this is as clear a synopsis of the economic ethic of Luke as any
scholarly one. Though we do run the risk of commodifying the words
of the poor, mining lives shaped by hardship for sayings that can be collected and deployed in the esoteric theological battles of scholars, the
point still stands that priority should be given to the voices of those who
for so long have been kept voiceless.

God prioritizes not only the voices of the poor, but also the welfare
of the poor. This is not to say that God does not care for those who are
not poor, nor that Christians should not care for those who are not poor.
Gustavo Gutierrez eloquently clarifies:

> The universality of Christian love is, I repeat, incompatible with
> the exclusion of any persons, but it is not incompatible with a
> preferential option for the poorest and most oppressed. When
> I speak of taking into account social conflict, including the ex-
> istence of the class struggle, I am not denying that God's love
> embraces all without exception. Nor is anyone excluded from

13. De La Torre, *Politics of Jesús*, loc. 1438–44.

14. Cardenal, *The Gospel in Solentiname*, 422; quoted in Miller, "Bridge Work," 426.

our love, for the gospel requires that we love even our enemies; a situation that causes us to regard others as our adversaries does not excuse us from loving them. There are oppositions and social conflicts between diverse factions, classes, cultures, and racial groupings, but they do not exclude respect for persons, for as human beings they are loved by God and are constantly being called to conversion.[15]

God has a preferential option for the poor because their needs have been disproportionately neglected. It is because of the suffering of the poor that God needs to step in as their champion. It is because society is disproportionately responsive to the needs of the rich that God is disproportionately responsive to the needs of the poor.

It may appear obvious by now, but it is important to state clearly that Luke does not fetishize poverty. To say that the poor are blest by God is not to say that God wishes crushing poverty for people. Rather, God is the one who lifts up the poor, who elevates them out of poverty. Elsa Tamez makes the case well:

It is clear that these many passages of the Bible in favor of the poor are in serious danger of being subjected to another kind of spiritualization: that of calling upon the poor to be satisfied with their state, not of poverty as such, but of privilege in God's sight. This would be disastrous because then even the rich would feel tempted to experience certain wants in order that they too might be God's favorites. Then the situation of injustice that God condemns would be alleviated in the eyes of the world. We must always keep in mind, therefore, that poverty is an unworthy state that must be changed. I repeat: poverty is not a virtue but an evil that reflects the socioeconomic conditions of inequality in which people live. Poverty is a challenge to God the Creator; because of the insufferable conditions under which the poor live, God is obliged to fight at their side.[16]

The deprivation of basic subsistence is not a blessing. Rather, God blesses those who experience deprivation by championing their cause.

God's care for the poor calls for concrete changes in society to reverse the oppression of the poor. An unmaterialized spiritual response is not enough. De La Torre warns: "While the dominant culture asks, 'How does one remain ethical in a corrupt society like this?' those who are

15. Gutiérrez, *Theology of Liberation*, 160.
16. Tamez, *Bible of the Oppressed*, 73–74.

marginalized ask, 'How does one make a corrupt society like this just?'"[17]
A Lukan economic ethic cannot be merely personal; it must include the
systems that produce poverty.

Does this dictate a particular form of political economy in which
all injustice is wiped away? Unfortunately, not one that can be easily
achieved or maintained. What it does do is insist that we keep striving
toward a more just society, both through personal action and through
societal change.[18] Without delineating a particular set of policy changes,
let me state the simple guiding principle that God is on the side of the
poor. If there is a situation in which the needs of the poor are held in
the balance with the desires of the rich, God is on the side of the poor.
God desires that all be lifted out of poverty, that the world's resources be
distributed justly, that all have the dignity of being able to supply their
basic needs. As Sharon Ringe says,

> We cannot, from our human perspective, design structures and
> social organizations that will be eternally appropriate, and that
> will always and everywhere support concerns of justice and lib-
> eration. Such structures are appropriately referred to as *God's*
> realm, not a realm of human construction. But we are called
> by the imagery of the Jubilee to respond to that larger vision
> as it breaks into the institutions, systems, and world views that
> characterize life in our own time and place. Coming genera-
> tions, in turn, will respond for themselves (if only we leave them
> a world in which to live), perhaps around issues and in ways
> that would astound us, even as our concerns and ways of acting
> seem foreign to the particular images of the biblical Jubilee tra-
> ditions. These images . . . challenge us to live with the rhythms
> of liberation and to proclaim good news to the poor at the par-
> ticular points of pain, oppression, and alienation in our society
> and world. In doing that, we continue to confess Jesus as the
> Christ who is the herald of the Jubilee, messenger and enactor
> of liberation.[19]

Though not an exhaustive list, the welfare of the poor would certainly
include access to adequate food, water, shelter, and health care. It would
include just working conditions and compensation. It would include
the agency to make meaningful choices about one's destiny. It would

17. De La Torre, *Doing Christian Ethics*, 41.

18. Rieger, *No Rising Tide*, 54.

19. Ringe, *Jesus*, 98.

include remedy for crippling debt, both personal and national. It would include provision for migrants fleeing violence, hopelessness, and environmental disaster.

Ultimately, though, those who can best understand the welfare of the poor are the poor themselves.

> How can the affluent evaluate social and economic activity in our world from the viewpoint of the poor and the powerless? The uncomfortable truth is that we cannot. Only the poor and the powerless can do that. Thus, the only hope for a reversal comes from their being empowered to act on their insights. It is when we recognize the force of "the moral economy" of black women in the United States, of miners in South Africa, or of Indian peasants in Latin America, to name only a few examples, that we really understand the force of Luke's narratives.[20]

When the poor are empowered to seek liberation, though, it is not only the poor who are saved. Like Felipe says, a just world benefits not only Lazarus, but also the rich man. De La Torre imagines how that kind of empowerment of the poor might transform both poor and rich.

> What if, instead of sitting by the gate dreaming about scraps, Lázaro had been proactive? What if Lázaro had organized with other homeless folk and demanded food, shelter, and clothes? What if Lázaro had confronted the rich man for his sin of greed and hoarding? What if the rich man, upon hearing Lázaro's demands, repents? Then salvation would have also come to the rich man, and he too could have found comfort in the bosom of Abraham.[21]

Without falling into the trap of blaming the poor for the systems that create poverty, we can still acknowledge that when the poor are empowered to seek justice and liberation, it is not only the poor who are liberated from the destructive forces of Mammon, it is all.

The Gospel of Luke clearly expresses a special concern for the situation of the poor. It identifies God, Jesus, and the faithful disciples with that preference for the poor. It highlights poor and marginalized persons as the proclaimers and agents of God's liberative mission. It calls to relatively privileged Christians to listen closely to the voices of the poor, and it calls on all Christians to act in concrete ways to bring justice for the

20. Moxnes, *Economy of the Kingdom*, 168–69.
21. De La Torre, *Politics of Jesús*, loc. 1984–87.

poor, with the poor leading the way. Especially since biblical interpretation has a clear bias toward those of means, it is imperative to respect God's preferential option for the poor.

Words on Wealth

Luke does not only talk about poverty; it also talks about wealth. It warns against the acquisition of wealth and against a reliance on wealth for one's security. It advises followers of Jesus to renounce their possessions in order to aid the poor and follow Jesus more closely. It contrasts faith in God with faith in Mammon. It proposes a radical reconception of the place and usefulness of wealth.

In this section we will explore three possible contemporary implications of Lukan resistance to wealth. First is a healthy distrust of the benevolence of markets. While Luke may not suggest a ready replacement for capitalist markets, it clearly warns against having blind faith in them. Second, Luke suggests a renunciation of possessions characterized by solidarity with the poor. Christians of means are called to continuous conversion away from Mammonist faith. Finally, in light of the drive of capitalist markets toward unending growth, Luke suggests a concern for the environment that is jeopardized by such growth. Especially since the environmental effects of economic growth are experienced most profoundly by the poor, Christians are called to seek economic patterns that are both just and sustainable.

Questioning the Benevolence of Markets

We spent a great deal of time in the last chapter on the tendency of the capitalist market to function as if it were a god. It inspires faith in its devotees, it can be consulted for oracular pronouncements about the news of the day, it is seen as a hand of providence that acts mysteriously to facilitate the greater good of all. We also explored some of the limitations of the market and its tendency to supplant the place of God.

As Daniel Bell suggests, the market has a totalizing effect that leads people to think of every aspect of life in economic terms.

> Instead of being a place where you can buy some extra item that you do not produce yourself, markets become the only means by which you can obtain anything. Not only is the market central,

but it is (or aspires to be) "free" as well, that is, free from external constraints and obstacles to its full and uninhibited functioning. Thus capitalism marks the advent of a world where, as Deleuze will argue, not only is the market central to everything, but everything is also subject to the rule of the market.[22]

This totalizing effect needs to be resisted. It dangerously distorts our very conception of God and our religious practice while it normalizes the conditions of poverty and oppression.[23]

For Luke, the stakes are absolute. One must make a choice. God or Mammon. There can be no in between.

And such absolute stakes call for a radical response. It suggests the need for a thoroughgoing shift away from market capitalism and provides justification for the reform agendas of liberationist movements. It does not, unfortunately, dictate an alternative economic system that is free from the corruption and oppression of human actors.

Even if we do not have the stomach for a radical revision of the economic system, there is much that can be done short of that. For example, the principle of Jubilee might be employed to deal with crippling debt that imprisons the poor in perpetual poverty.[24] The message of Luke might be employed against the pernicious message of a gospel of prosperity.[25] Or we might take the practical suggestions of economists like

22. Bell, *Economy of Desire*, 22–23.

23. Rieger, *No Rising Tide*, 79.

24. DeConto, "The People's Interest"; DeConto, "Lending with Grace."

25. Fee, *Disease*. However, Rhee makes an interesting point that some elements of the so-called prosperity gospel function to help the poor be lifted out of poverty. "On the one hand, there is no doubt that this gospel of health and wealth is fraught with hermeneutical, theological, and ethical abuses, and with the problems of commercialized 'anti-gospel of greed' and egotism, and that these ultra-mega-prosperity churches and preachers have exploited the poor and vulnerable with magical formulas, manipulation, and business schemes while amassing their own kingdoms and family enterprises. They distort the gospel of the Christ crucified and reduce the mysterious workings of God to a predictable giant vending machine, and their embarrassing scandals and failures of expectations are too numerous to count. On the other hand, within the specific socioeconomic and cultural situations in which these movements spread among the disinherited (in the global South), these prosperity movements could be and have been the agents of social and economic transformation in a qualified sense. . . . Prosperity gospel preachers, in their promotion of worldly success and material blessings, rather than 'pie-in-the-sky-in-the-sweet-by-and-by,' raise the hope and expectations of the hopeless about the possibility of a better life with the fight against a 'demon of poverty' and 'provoke people to think in new ways, and while members may be disappointed if they are expecting a quick fix, they may also start

Larry Elliott and Dan Atkinson to put in place simple regulations—such as limits on exotic financial instruments and the breaking up of giant financial institutions—that show some skepticism of the market's providence and protect against its most obvious abuses.[26]

Luke warns against faith in Mammon. Faith in markets has become the primary framework by which people structure their lives. Luke reminds us to be skeptical of what markets can do and to resist the tendency of the market to take the place of God.

Solidarity with the Poor

But what is a rich person to do?! This is the question it always seems to come back to. Do I really have to give up everything in order to follow Jesus? Isn't that provision just for certain people (not me!)? Wasn't that just for a particular time (not now!)? Who really counts as rich, anyway? And isn't it impractical? If everyone gave up everything then fields would lay unplanted and everyone would starve to death.

As we have seen so many times in this study, there is a very powerful impulse to try to bracket off Jesus's call for disciples to leave all to follow him (Luke 14:33; 18:22; also Luke 5:11, 28; 9:3; 10:4–8; 18:28). It is such a radical claim on our lives that most find it simply too difficult to face. Especially in our modern consumer culture, it is anathema. And so it must be explained away. It must be circumscribed, limited to a circumstance that is rare and not our own.

Once the radical demand for total renunciation is safely quarantined, the overwhelming tendency is to overlook or ignore any call to renunciation whatsoever. Give something to charity, yes, but don't do anything crazy. Do not give so much that it changes your social standing.

I want to encourage us not to ignore Jesus's radical words. I want to encourage us to hold them in tension with our lives, with every economic choice that we make. No, not many are likely to come close to the kind of release of possessions that Jesus suggests. That does not mean that Jesus's call should not have a place in our ethics. Not many are likely to achieve absolute love of their enemies as Jesus commands in Luke 6:27. That does

---

organizing their lives in ways that allow for upward social mobility.' . . . Thus, while liberation theology advocated a preferential option for the poor, the poor themselves opted for the prosperity gospel (and Pentecostalism) in Latin America and elsewhere." Rhee, *Loving the Poor*, 216–17.

26. Elliott and Atkinson, *The Gods That Failed*, 266–68.

not mean that we bracket that command off as something that is clearly meant for someone else but not for me. Yes, it is a utopian ideal, but utopia has its use. A utopian ideal can at the very least bend us toward justice.

So with that in mind, how might Luke's radical economic message bend those of means toward justice? Not only for those who are fabulously wealthy, not only for the upper middle class, but for all who have an excess of possessions, how might we respond to the call of Luke? Remember, Jesus spoke words of uplift to the poor, those who were at subsistence level (ES6–7), but his warnings against wealth were directed to the full spectrum of those who had more than enough (ES1–5).

One of the most fruitful models is an ethic of solidarity with the poor that models itself on the example of Jesus. Gustavo Gutierrez writes of Jesus's appearance in the circumstances in which he is found in Luke:

> But he does not take on the human sinful condition and its consequences to idealize it. It is rather because of love for and solidarity with others who suffer in it. It is to redeem them from their sin and to enrich them with his poverty. It is to struggle against human selfishness and everything that divides persons and allows that there be rich and poor, possessors and dispossessed, oppressors and oppressed. Poverty is an act of love and liberation. It has a redemptive value. If the ultimate cause of human exploitation and alienation is selfishness, the deepest reason for voluntary poverty is love of neighbor. Christian poverty has meaning only as a commitment of solidarity with the poor, with those who suffer misery and injustice. The commitment is to witness to the evil which has resulted from sin and is a breach of communion. It is not a question of idealizing poverty, but rather of taking it on as it is—an evil—to protest against it and to struggle to abolish it. As Ricoeur says, you cannot really be with the poor unless you are struggling against poverty. Because of this solidarity—which must manifest itself in specific action, a style of life, a break with one's social class—one can also help the poor and exploitated to become aware of their exploitation and seek liberation from it. Christian poverty, an expression of love, is solidarity with the poor and is a protest against poverty. This is the concrete, contemporary meaning of the witness of poverty. It is a poverty lived not for its own sake, but rather as an authentic imitation of Christ; it is a poverty which means taking on the sinful human condition to liberate humankind from sin and all its consequences.[27]

27. Gutiérrez, *Theology of Liberation*, 172.

Clearly, this is still a difficult calling. However, it provides some definition for understanding the purpose behind choosing to give up possessions. It is for the purpose of eradicating poverty.

Rebecca Todd Peters provides an important contribution, from a first world perspective, on how the relatively privileged might live an ethic of solidarity in the midst of a globalizing world that effectuates inequality and suffering.[28] She too grounds her theology in the example of Jesus. Jesus came from humble means and lived his life in connection with and in service to those who were economically and socially marginalized. He preached reversal, he offered healing, he challenged the social and economic patterns of his day.

> His commitment to an alternative worldview and his uncompromising attitude toward seeing God's will done on earth as it is in heaven was a radical witness to a life of solidarity that can serve as a model for understanding solidarity as a contemporary Christian ethic that offers first-world Christians a pathway for living with integrity in a globalizing world.[29]

Peters offers a three-part prescription for first-world Christians. First, we must do the work to understand the ways that we are benefitted by our social location, the sorts of privilege that we have simply by being born into our particular position in society. It is easy to think that everything we have is purely on account of our own work if we don't make the effort to see that we disproportionally benefit from societal structures that are largely invisible to us, that we assume must be available to all people. Second, we must make affirmative efforts to develop relationships with people outside of our social contexts, with people who are normally divided from us by barriers of difference. The work of solidarity is not charity or paternalism. It cannot be effectively done without the benefit of relationship. Finally, we must work for social change. We have to strive for a more just society, not only in our own nation, but within the global community.[30]

An ethic of solidarity is a call to downward mobility. It is a call to simplicity of life. But it does not end there. It is not enough to sell our possessions and give the money to the poor. We must also follow Jesus, follow Jesus into relationship with the poor. We must take the risk of

28. Peters, *Solidarity Ethics*.
29. Peters, *Solidarity Ethics*, 52.
30. Peters, *Solidarity Ethics*, 10.

making a connection with the very people who put our privilege into stark relief. We cannot stop with charity but must work for a change to the conditions that produce poverty.[31]

> The task of changing the direction of where we are headed as a global community is not simply a call for a new direction for public policy in our world; it is also a radical call for people living in the first world to change the direction that their own lives are headed. And getting to a place where we are able to join together with our compatriots in the two-thirds world in ways that move us toward a true partnership that honors each of our unique gifts and strengths is a journey that requires much work. For first-world citizens, developing relationships of solidarity across lines of difference requires acknowledging complicity in contemporary forms of globalization and examining the forms of privilege that shape life in the developed world.[32]

However, as George Tinker points out, there is a danger of self-delusion when people of privilege seek to be in solidarity with the poor and marginalized. The first reaction to the realization that one benefits from systems that oppress others is a feeling of guilt. This sense of guilt, while perhaps a necessary part of consciousness-building, can often become counterproductive.

> White guilt in the U.S. over the past thirty years and more has accomplished very little in terms of the reduction of poverty and injustice in the world. To the contrary, a response to poverty and injustice rooted in guilt eventually shifts to denial, blaming the victim, and even anger at the victim. Alternatively, guilt functions to romanticize the poor and leads white North Americans to act on behalf of the poor, characterized most commonly by a rescuing behavior that perpetuates the co-dependency so typical of addictive patterns of behavior.[33]

We must resist the temptation to swoop in as saviors or think that we know best. We must also resist the trap of being caught in cycles of guilt that prevent any action whatsoever. When we are best living out the call to solidarity, we are "working toward the empowerment of the poor,

---

31. Peters, *Solidarity Ethics*, 88.
32. Peters, *Solidarity Ethics*, 67.
33. Tinker, "Blessed Are the Poor," 52.

standing in solidarity with the poor to enable the poor to act in their own best interests."[34]

And yet, none of this is possible if we are not able to put up some resistance to our devotion to Mammon. Katherine Turpin effectively describes the ways that consumer culture constitutes a complete religious belief system.[35] Her particular concern is for Christian youth navigating faith in a consumerist culture, but the lesson is equally pertinent to older Christians. Turpin describes consumer religion as the dominant religious expression in America, a religion from which youth must convert as they affirm Christian faith.

Conversion from consumer culture is not only necessary because it produces systemic injustices, it is also necessary because it is inadequate for nourishing the spiritual needs of its devotees.

> The desires that are created by consumerism are ultimately artificial desires. Their fulfillment does not bring true human joy and flourishing, and they require endless repetition and escalation to sustain their religious power. The word of grace found in the invitation to conversion recognizes that consumer culture is not a gracious god to serve; its cultivated desires are not easy to fulfill. Consumer capitalism demands from even its most successful adherents regular sacrifices of relationship, rest, and community. The word of grace indicates that there are more life-giving ways to make sense of the world and one's role in it.[36]

And yet, consumerist culture is absolutely foundational to how we understand ourselves. It is much more deeply ingrained in many of us than any biblical faith. It is so prevalent and pervasive that it goes unnoticed; it is simply the way things are. "Consumer culture provides the deeply held images that sort information and provide categories of meaning that are signposts for the direction and purpose of life."[37]

Consequently, there can be no single conversion; there must be a process of continuous conversion. It is not enough just to realize that we are in thrall to Mammon. It is not enough to become aware of the ways that we are enslaved to consumption and possession. Because we have already been indoctrinated into the religious practice of consumption, any effort to resist it is not just a matter of changing one's mind. It isn't even

34. Tinker, "Blessed Are the Poor," 53.
35. Turpin, *Branded*, 41.
36. Turpin, *Branded*, 46.
37. Turpin, *Branded*, 57.

as easy as struggling against the long-practiced habit of consumption. No, it is even more difficult than that. Resisting consumer culture challenges our very sense of identity and our understanding of the world around us. Breaking free from the grasp of Mammon requires ongoing conversion.[38]

I am in need of ongoing conversion from the faith of Mammon. Even as I am elucidating the wealth ethic that I find in Luke, I am well aware that I fall dreadfully short of it. As I consider my own hypocrisy, I am mindful of Jesus's warning in Luke 11:46, "Curses to you Bible scholars, for you shoulder people with impossible burdens, but you yourselves don't exercise even a finger to lift them" (my translation). The radical message of Luke convicts me strongly. It implicates the way I earn, the way I spend, and the way I possess. I am well aware of how hard it is. But I also know that there is good news in it. I know that I have been changed by the Lukan ideal. I have been led to spend less, to change the uses to which I put the money I have, to dispossess myself of possessions for the benefit of the poor, to participate in ministries with the poor, and to develop relationships across difference. I still have a long way to go, but I have experienced the grace that comes through Luke's radical message. Without that radical message, I would not have been led in those directions.

The Gospel of Luke offers a utopian ideal for the disposition of possessions. It is a useful utopia that calls people of means to resist the lures of wealth and practice solidarity with the poor. This task involves identifying our participation in systems of oppression, working to correct those systems, and participating in ongoing conversion from the prevailing practice of consumer capitalism.

Our Common Home

In light of the global reach of capitalism and capitalism's perpetual drive for economic growth, a consideration of economic ethics cannot be complete without attention to the natural environment. As Naomi Klein has so convincingly argued, left to its own market forces, the capitalist economy will continue to advance growth at the expense of the environment because market has no means of assigning the cost of environmental degradation.[39] Mammon is fast gaining the power to destroy life, and its effects are disproportionately experienced by the poor.

38. Turpin, *Branded*, 57–59.
39. Klein, *This Changes Everything*.

These issues of environment, market, and faith are comprehensively addressed in Pope Francis's 2015 encyclical, *Laudato Si'*, or *On Care for Our Common Home*.[40] He approaches the problem as a scientist, as a theologian, and as a pastor. It is remarkable for its scientific attention to the details of environmental change, its erudite analysis of global economic factors, its seamless integration of theological concepts, its advocacy of a joyful simplicity, and its thoroughgoing insistence on the welfare of the poor. It is not some detached theological screed abstractly arguing that because God created the world humans are obliged to take care of it. It speaks cogently to the world at large, to climate scientists, economists, corporate officers, politicians, consumers, and persons of varying religious convictions.

Francis opens the discussion with a look at his namesake, Francis of Assisi, who is known both for his voluntary poverty and for his deep connection to the natural world. Francis approached the created world with a sense of wonder and kinship. He delighted in the beauty of nature and thought of himself as part of one family with it. The pontiff suggests that unless we approach the world with the same openness, "our attitude will be that of masters, consumers, ruthless exploiters, unable to set limits on their immediate needs."[41] Saint Francis's simplicity and his love of nature are intimately connected in a way that has a profound meaning for us today. "The poverty and austerity of Saint Francis were no mere veneer of asceticism, but something much more radical: a refusal to turn reality into an object simply to be used and controlled."[42] Pope Francis suggests this as a spiritual foundation for approaching issues of climate change.

While Francis is outlining the scientific reality of climate change and its varied effects on the natural world, he is quick to tie things back to economic issues and a concern for the poor. In one example among many, he says:

> Climate change is a global problem with grave implications: environmental, social, economic, political, and for the distribution of goods. It represents one of the principal challenges facing humanity in our day. Its worst impact will probably be felt by developing countries in coming decades. Many of the poor live in areas particularly affected by phenomena related to warming, and their means of subsistence are largely dependent on natural

40. Francis, *Laudato Si'*.
41. Francis, *Laudato Si'*, §11.
42. Francis, *Laudato Si'*, §11.

reserves and ecosystemic services such as agriculture, fishing, and forestry. They have no other financial activities or resources which can enable them to adapt to climate change or to face natural disasters, and their access to social services and protection is very limited. For example, changes in climate, to which animals and plants cannot adapt, lead them to migrate; this in turn affects the livelihood of the poor, who are then forced to leave their homes, with great uncertainty for their future and that of their children. There has been a tragic rise in the number of migrants seeking to flee from the growing poverty caused by environmental degradation. They are not recognized by international conventions as refugees; they bear the loss of the lives they have left behind, without enjoying any legal protection whatsoever. Sadly, there is widespread indifference to such suffering, which is even now taking place throughout our world.[43]

Environmentalism is intimately connected with concern for the most vulnerable in the human family. It is an issue of economy, and it is an issue of social justice.

Francis places much of the blame for climate change on rampant consumerism in the first world. No matter what else may be at play, there can be no denying that the problem cannot be fixed without a drastic change in consumer habits. If every person consumed the way that first world people consume, "the planet could not even contain the waste products of such consumption."[44] The grotesquely unbalanced consumption of the first world reveals that "some consider themselves more human than others," having a birthright to possess and consume in a way that robs from the poor while simultaneously destroying the already meager resources on which the poor depend for survival.[45] A few feast sumptuously like the rich man, their crumbs never making it to the many who languish like Lazarus, except that now the rich man's trash is also poisoning the street where Lazarus lives. The problem cannot be blamed on population growth, nor can it be fixed merely with technological solutions.[46] It can only be remedied with a decrease in consumption. And

---

43. Francis, *Laudato Si'*, §25.

44. Francis, *Laudato Si'*, §50.

45. Francis, *Laudato Si'*, §90.

46. It is important to note, though, that population growth plays a larger role than Francis allows for, and the Roman Catholic Church's position on birth control no doubt exacerbates matters.

such a decrease in consumption must be done with special attention to the most vulnerable.

> In the present condition of global society, where injustices abound and growing numbers of people are deprived of basic human rights and considered expendable, the principle of the common good immediately becomes, logically and inevitably, a summons to solidarity and a preferential option for the poorest of our brothers and sisters.[47]

In order to address consumption, it is not enough just to convince a few people to choose to consume less. The power of the deified Market must be resisted.

> Politics must not be subject to the economy, nor should the economy be subject to the dictates of an efficiency-driven paradigm of technocracy. Today, in view of the common good, there is urgent need for politics and economics to enter into a frank dialogue in the service of life, especially human life. Saving banks at any cost, making the public pay the price, foregoing a firm commitment to reviewing and reforming the entire system, only reaffirms the absolute power of a financial system, a power which has no future and will only give rise to new crises after a slow, costly, and only apparent recovery. The financial crisis of 2007–8 provided an opportunity to develop a new economy, more attentive to ethical principles, and new ways of regulating speculative financial practices and virtual wealth. But the response to the crisis did not include rethinking the outdated criteria which continue to rule the world. Production is not always rational, and is usually tied to economic variables which assign to products a value that does not necessarily correspond to their real worth. . . . Once more, we need to reject a magical conception of the market, which would suggest that problems can be solved simply by an increase in the profits of companies or individuals. . . . Where profits alone count, there can be no thinking about the rhythms of nature, its phases of decay and regeneration, or the complexity of ecosystems which may be gravely upset by human intervention. Moreover, biodiversity is considered at most a deposit of economic resources available for exploitation, with no serious thought for the real value of things, their significance for persons and cultures, or the concerns and needs of the poor.[48]

47. Francis, *Laudato Si'*, §158.
48. Francis, *Laudato Si'*, §§189–90.

Francis gives a thoroughgoing critique of personal greed, of patterns of consumption, and of the forces of the market that drive us toward ever more economic growth, ever more production, ever more (unequal) consumption, and ever more despoliation of the limited resources of planet earth. No environmental fix is possible without a change in economic forces; if economic forces continue as they are, it will inevitably lead to even greater environmental crisis. And while the benefits of a growing economy are enjoyed by the relatively wealthy, its environmental costs are borne disproportionately by the poor. Inequality, consumption, and environment must all be addressed together or there can be no improvement in any of them.

This is the radical economic message of Luke put to work as a prophetic call for concrete change in the world. Preferential concern for and solidarity with the poor, a rejection of accumulation and overconsumption of possessions, resistance to faith in market as Mammon—they all come together here in a cogent appeal for radical change at every level of society, from the personal to the global. *Laudato Si'* embodies the values of the Lukan wealth ethic and shows clearly how the radical economic message of Luke can function prophetically in the twenty-first century world.

Conclusion

Much more could be said about the ways Luke's radical economic message could be applied to modern life or how its specific provisions might be translated to contemporary economy, but this is, I hope, a good beginning. Luke's message of liberation for the poor and resistance to wealth has profound relevance today, even if the specific context that gave birth to it is quite different from our own. Hampered as it is by the upper-class perspective of its author, Luke still delivers important good news: God has a preferential option for the poor, while faith in wealth is to be countered with faith in God. Whatever else it might say, Luke clearly preaches liberation from poverty and liberation from the destructive thralldom of wealth.

CHAPTER 9

Conclusion

Sell your possessions, and give alms. Make purses for
yourselves that do not wear out, an unfailing treasure in
heaven, where no thief comes near and no moth destroys.
For where your treasure is, there your heart will be also.

—LUKE 12:33–34 NRSV

IN THIS STUDY, I have attempted to take seriously the radical economic message of Luke. I have tried to resist a middle-class bias present in many of the book-length studies on Lukan economic issues that have preceded this one. I have argued for a recovery of the twin themes of Luke's radical economic message: a proclamation of good news for the poor and a resistance to wealth. I have worked to expose the strategies used to temper this radical message, both in modern scholarship and within the world of early Christianity. I have tried to shine light on the ways that Luke's radical message challenges systems of oppression, both ancient and contemporary. I have promoted Luke as a prophetic call for systemic change, a usefully utopian vision of an alternative empire, an alternative economy, that calls people to strive for a way of living that is ever more conformed to the divine ideal. In short, I have called for Christians to reclaim the radical economic message of Luke.

At the same time, I must admit that there is a nagging ambiguity both in Luke and in my ability to interpret it. I am mindful of Miguel De La Torre's warning:

> To understand Jesús from the social location of the poor is to create a sacred space where the marginalized can grapple with their spiritual need to reconcile their God with their struggle for economic justice and human dignity. If Jesús is indeed counted among the least of these, then any reading of the biblical text through the eyes of middle- or upper-class privilege becomes highly problematic. Only the poor have a better chance of understanding the nuances of the Gospels because they share the existential economic space of those who first heard the Gospel.[1]

If I simply offer yet another interpretation mediated by middle-class bias, what does it accomplish? Does it do more harm than good, functioning to silence the voices of the poor in some wayward attempt to honor them? Is this the same thing that Luke itself is doing, using the poor as puppets to proclaim an ideology that actually inscribes and entrenches oppression and inequality?

Perhaps it is not possible to escape the socio-economic ambiguities that are raised by a text like Luke. There is no way that I, as a middle-class white straight cisgender male American am going to reach a point where I have gotten on the "good" side of the oppressive system. I cannot make myself a hero in the story of rich and poor. I cannot transcend my privilege. The author of Luke never did either.

But there is still a question of how I may live in light of the struggle found in Luke. I could proclaim all of the good, progressive theologies that liberate the oppressed and tear down the oppressor, I could claim them as my own, identify myself with the struggle. And by doing this I could attempt to absolve myself of guilt, to free myself from the conviction I feel in relation to the poor. I could wash my hands of that oppression, use my words as a signal of my virtue. But this would be to ignore the struggle found in the text. This would be to use the text as a justification for my own privilege.

Or perhaps I could recognize that even my proclamation of liberation, a proclamation that comes from a position of privilege, is not unproblematic. Perhaps I could realize that, try as I might, I cannot escape responsibility for oppression. I cannot escape the conviction that the text

---

1. De La Torre, *Politics of Jesús*, loc. 1762–65.

places on me, by both its positive and negative examples. It does not wipe away my privilege, just as it did not wipe away Luke's.

And in that knowledge, perhaps I will be led to listen more deeply to the voices of the oppressed and marginalized. Perhaps I will be led to continue questioning my economic choices, to continue questioning my motives, to continue questioning the effects that my actions have, regardless of my motives. Perhaps I will be led to see, again and again, my slavery to Mammon. Perhaps in the knowledge of that slavery, I will be led, again and again, to conversion and repentance.

I have chosen to claim and proclaim the radical economic message that I find in the Gospel of Luke, knowing that I lack the credibility and perspective to offer what would be far more valuable: a comprehensive interpretation of economics in Luke from the perspective of poverty and marginality. I offer my interpretation here not because it comes naturally, but because it resists my nature, not because the words are easy, but because they are hard, not because I am a radical, but because I am not. I offer it because this text will not leave me alone. It demands my attention, my study, my struggle. More importantly, it demands my praxis, and this is what I find hardest of all. Like the rich ruler, I can scarce release my grip on Mammon. Yet, at the same time, God's radical gospel found in and through Luke will not release its grip on me. Some readers may find either Luke or I to be hopelessly compromised vessels for the gospel message, merchants of moderation rather than proclaimers of good news. I hope, at least, that my work serves to remove some of the many barriers that biblical scholars have placed in the way of God's radical gospel of liberation.

Bibliography

Aland, Barbara, et al., eds. *Nestle-Aland Novum Testamentum Graece*. 28th rev. ed. Stuttgart: Deusche Bibelgesellschaft, 2012.

Aland, Kurt, ed. *Synopsis of the Four Gospels: Greek-English Edition of the Synopsis Quattuor Evangeliorum*. 3rd ed. Stuttgart: United Bible Societies, 1979.

Alexander, John F. *Your Money or Your Life: A New Look at Jesus' View of Wealth and Power*. San Francisco: Harper & Row, 1986.

Anderson, Gary A. *Charity*. New Haven: Yale University Press, 2013.

Ando, Clifford. *Imperial Ideology and Provincial Loyalty in the Roman Empire*. Classics and Contemporary Thought. Berkeley: University of California Press, 2000.

Bablitz, Leanne. "Roman Society in the Courtroom." In *The Oxford Handbook of Social Relations in the Roman World*, edited by Michael Peachin, 317–34. New York: Oxford University Press, 2011.

Baker, Derek. *The Church in Town and Countryside*. Studies in Church History 16. Oxford: Basil Blackwell, 1979.

Balch, David L. "Mary's Magnificat (Luke 1:46b–55) and the Price of Corn in Mexico." *JBL* 136 (2017) 651–65.

Barclay, William. *The Gospel of Luke*. Rev. and updated ed. The New Daily Study Bible. Louisville: Westminister John Knox, 2001.

Barr, David L. *New Testament Story: An Introduction*. 3rd ed. Belmont, CA: Wadsworth, 2002.

Barton, Stephen C. "Money Matters: Economic Relations and the Transformation of Value in Early Christianity." In *Engaging Economics: New Testament Scenarios and Early Christian Reception*, edited by Bruce W. Longenecker and Kelly D. Liebengood, 37–59. Grand Rapids: Eerdmans, 2009.

Bell, Daniel M., Jr. *The Economy of Desire: Christianity and Capitalism in a Postmodern World*. The Church and Postmodern Culture. Grand Rapids: Baker Academic, 2012.

Blosser, Joe. "Can God or the Market Set People Free? Libertarian, Egalitarian, and Ethical Freedom." *JRE* 41 (2013) 233–53.

Boer, Roland, and Christina Petterson. *Time of Troubles: A New Economic Framework for Early Christianity*. Minneapolis: Fortress, 2017. Kindle.

Bovon, François. *Luke 1: A Commentary on the Gospel of Luke 1:1—9:50.* Edited by Helmut Koester. Translated by Christine M. Thomas. Hermeneia. Minneapolis: Fortress, 2002.

———. *Luke 2: A Commentary on the Gospel of Luke 9:51—19:27.* Edited by Helmut Koester. Translated by Donald S. Deer. Hermeneia. Minneapolis: Fortress, 2013.

———. *Luke 3: A Commentary on the Gospel of Luke 19:28—24:53.* Edited by Helmut Koester. Translated by James Crouch. Hermeneia. Minneapolis: Fortress, 2012.

Bowler, Kate. *Blessed: A History of the American Prosperity Gospel.* New York: Oxford University Press, 2013.

Boyer, Robert, and Yves Saillard. "A Summary of *Régulation* Theory: The State of the Art." In *Régulation Theory: The State of the Art,* edited by Robert Boyer and Yves Saillard, 36-44. London: Routledge, 2002.

Brat, David. "God and Advanced Mammon—Can Theological Types Handle Usury and Capitalism?" *Int* 65 (2011) 168-79.

Braun, Adam F. "Reframing the Parable of the Pounds in Lukan Narrative and Economic Context: Luke 19:11-28." *CurTM* 39 (2012) 442-48.

Brodine, Marc. "When the Market God Isn't Worshipped." *People's Weekly World* 21 (2007) 14.

Brown, Peter. *Power and Persuasion in Late Antiquity: Towards a Christian Empire.* Madison: University of Wisconsin Press, 1992.

———. *The Ransom of the Soul: Afterlife and Wealth in Early Western Christianity.* Cambridge: Harvard University Press, 2015.

———. *The Rise of Western Christendom: Triumph and Diversity, A.D. 200-1000.* 2nd ed. The Making of Europe. Malden, MA: Blackwell, 2003.

———. *Through the Eye of a Needle: Wealth, the Fall of Rome, and the Making of Christianity in the West, 350-550 AD.* Princeton: Princeton University Press, 2012.

Brown, Raymond E. *The Birth of the Messiah: A Commentary on the Infancy Narratives in the Gospels of Matthew and Luke.* New updated ed. The Anchor Bible Reference Library. New York: Doubleday, 1993.

Burrus, Virginia. "The Gospel of Luke and the Acts of the Apostles." In *A Postcolonial Commentary on the New Testament Writings,* edited by Fernando F. Segovia and R. S. Sugirtharajah, 133-55. The Bible and Postcolonialism 13. New York: T. & T. Clark, 2009.

Capper, Brian J. "Jesus, Virtuoso Religion, and the Community of Goods." In *Engaging Economics: New Testament Scenarios and Early Christian Reception,* edited by Bruce W. Longenecker and Kelly D. Liebengood, 60-80. Grand Rapids: Eerdmans, 2009.

Cardenal, Ernesto. *The Gospel in Solentiname.* Translated by Donald D. Walsh. Rev. ed. Maryknoll, NY: Orbis, 2007.

Carter, Warren. *Matthew and the Margins: A Socio-Political and Religious Reading.* Journal for the Study of the New Testament Supplement Series 204. Sheffield: Sheffield Academic, 2000.

Cassidy, Richard J. *Jesus, Politics, and Society: A Study of Luke's Gospel.* Maryknoll, NY: Orbis, 1978.

Chadwick, Henry, et al., ed. *The Role of the Christian Bishop in Ancient Society: Protocol of the Thirty-Fifth Colloquy, 25 February 1979 / The Center for Hermeneutical Studies in Hellenistic and Modern Culture.* Berkeley, CA: Center, 1980.

CIA. "Country Comparison: Gini Index Coefficient—Distribution of Family Income." https://www.cia.gov/the-world-factbook/field/gini-index-coefficient-distribution-of-family-income/country-comparison.

Clark, Elizabeth A. *Reading Renunciation: Asceticism and Scripture in Early Christianity.* Princeton: Princeton University Press, 1999.

Clement of Alexandria. *The Exhortation to the Greeks, the Rich Man's Salvation, and the Fragment of an Address Entitled to the Newly Baptized.* Translated by G. W. Butterworth. LCL 92. New York: Putman's Sons, 1912.

Coleman, Kathleen M. "Public Entertainments." In *The Oxford Handbook of Social Relations in the Roman World*, edited by Michael Peachin, 336–57. New York: Oxford University Press, 2011.

Coleman, Rachel L. "The Lukan Lens on Wealth and Possessions: A Perspective Shaped by the Themes of Reversal and Right Response." PhD diss., Regent University, 2018.

Connolly, Joy. "Rhetorical Education." In *The Oxford Handbook of Social Relations in the Roman World*, edited by Michael Peachin, 101–18. New York: Oxford University Press, 2011.

Conzelmann, Hans. *The Theology of St. Luke.* Translated by Geoffrey Buswell. New York: Harper & Row, 1961.

Cox, Harvey. "The Market as God: Living in the New Dispensation." *The Atlantic*, March 1, 1999.

Craddock, Fred B. *Luke.* Interpretation: A Bible Commentary for Teaching and Preaching. Louisville: Westminster John Knox, 2009.

Crowder, Stephanie Buckhanon. "Luke." In *True to Our Native Land: An African American New Testament Commentary*, edited by Brian K. Blount, 158–85. Minneapolis: Fortress, 2007.

Daniélou, Jean, and Henri Marrou. *The Christian Centuries.* Translated by Vincent Cronin. London: Darton, Longman, and Todd, 1964.

De La Torre, Miguel. *Doing Christian Ethics from the Margins.* 2nd ed. Maryknoll, NY: Orbis, 2014.

———. *The Politics of Jesús: A Hispanic Political Theology.* Religion in the Modern World. Lanham, MD: Rowman & Littlefield, 2015. Kindle.

———. *Reading the Bible from the Margins.* Maryknoll, NY: Orbis, 2002.

De Ste. Croix, G. E. M. *The Class Struggle in the Ancient Greek World: From the Archaic Age to the Arab Conquests.* London: Duckworth, 1981.

DeConto, Jesse James. "Lending with Grace: Breaking the Cycle of Payday Loans." *ChrCent* 129 (2012) 28–31.

———. "The People's Interest: A New Battle against Usury." *ChrCent* 127 (2010) 20–25.

Degenhardt, Hans-Joachim. *Lukas, Evangelist der Armen: Besitz und Besitzverzicht in den Lukanischen Schriften: eine traditions- und redaktionsgeschichtliche Untersuchung.* Stuttgart: Verlag Kath. Bibelwerk, 1965.

Dinkler, Michal Beth. "'The Thoughts of Many Hearts Shall Be Revealed': Listening in on Lukan Interior Monologues." *JBL* 133 (2015) 373–99.

Donahue, John R. "Two Decades of Research on the Rich and the Poor in Luke-Acts." In *Justice and the Holy: Essays in Honor of Walter Harrelson*, edited by Douglas A. Knight and Peter J. Paris, 129–44. Atlanta: Scholars, 1989.

Dowling, Elizabeth V. *Taking Away the Pound: Women, Theology, and the Parable of the Pounds in the Gospel of Luke.* Library of New Testament Studies 324. New York: T. & T. Clark, 2007.

Dunbabin, Katherine M. D., and William J. Slater. "Roman Dining." In *The Oxford Handbook of Social Relations in the Roman World*, edited by Michael Peachin, 438–66. New York: Oxford University Press, 2011.

Duncan-Jones, Richard. *The Economy of the Roman Empire: Quantitative Studies*. 2nd ed. New York: Cambridge University Press, 1982.

———. *Money and Government in the Roman Empire*. New York: Cambridge University Press, 1994.

Dupuy, Beatrice. "Most Americans Didn't Approve of Martin Luther King Jr. before His Death, Polls Show." *Newsweek*, January 15, 2018. https://www.newsweek.com/martin-luther-king-jr-was-not-always-popular-back-day-780387.

Elliott, Larry, and Dan Atkinson. *The Gods That Failed: How Blind Faith in Markets Has Cost Us Our Future*. New York: Nation, 2009. Kindle.

ERS. "Food Security in the U.S." https://www.ers.usda.gov/topics/food-nutrition-assistance/food-security-in-the-us/key-statistics-graphics.aspx.

Esler, Philip Francis. *Community and Gospel in Luke-Acts: The Social and Political Motivations of Lucan Theology*. Society for New Testament Studies Monograph Series 57. Cambridge: Cambridge University Press, 1987.

Fagan, Garrett G. "Socializing at the Baths." In *The Oxford Handbook of Social Relations in the Roman World*, edited by Michael Peachin, 358–73. New York: Oxford University Press, 2011.

Fairclough, Adam. "Foreword." In *The Domestication of Martin Luther King Jr.: Clarence B. Jones, Right-Wing Conservatism, and the Manipulation of the King Legacy*, edited by Lewis V. Baldwin and Rufus Burrow Jr., loc. 92–152. Eugene, OR: Cascade, 2013. Kindle.

Fee, Gordon D. *The Disease of the Health and Wealth Gospels*. 2nd ed. Vancouver: Regent College Publishing, 2006.

Finley, M. I. *The Ancient Economy*. Updated ed. Berkeley: University of California Press, 1999.

Finn, Daniel K. *Christian Economic Ethics*. Minneapolis: Fortress, 2013.

Fitzmyer, Joseph A. *The Gospel according to Luke I–IX*. Anchor Bible 28. Garden City, NY: Doubleday, 1981.

———. *The Gospel according to Luke X–XXIV*. Anchor Bible 28A. Garden City, NY: Doubleday, 1985.

Foley, Duncan K. *Adam's Fallacy: A Guide to Economic Theology*. Cambridge, MA: Belknap, 2006.

Ford, Richard Q. *The Parables of Jesus: Recovering the Art of Listening*. Minneapolis: Fortress, 1997.

Fortuna, Robert T. "Reading Jesus' Parable of the Talents through Underclass Eyes." *Forum* 8 (1992) 211–28.

Fox, Robin Lane. *Pagans and Christians*. New York: Knopf, 1987.

Francis, Pope. *Laudato Si'*. https://www.vatican.va/content/francesco/en/encyclicals/documents/papa-francesco_20150524_enciclica-laudato-si.html.

Frank, Thomas. *One Market under God: Extreme Capitalism, Market Populism, and the End of Economic Democracy*. New York: Doubleday, 2000.

Fredriksen, Paula. "Christians in the Roman Empire in the First Three Centuries." In *A Companion to the Roman Empire*, edited by David S. Potter, 587–606. Oxford: Blackwell, 2006.

Frend, W. H. C. "The Failure of Persecutions in the Roman Empire." In *Studies in Ancient History*, edited by M. I. Finley, 263–87. Past and Present. London: Routledge, 1974.

———. *Town and Country in the Early Christian Centuries*. London: Variorum Reprints, 1980.

———. "Town and Countryside in Early Christianity." In *The Church in Town and Countryside*, edited by Derek Baker, 25–42. Studies in Church History 16. Oxford: Basil Blackwell, 1979.

Friedman, Milton. *Essays in Positive Economics*. Chicago: University of Chicago Press, 1953.

Friesen, Steven J. "Poverty in Pauline Studies: Beyond the So-called New Consensus." *JSNT* 26 (2005) 323–61.

Funk, Robert W., and Roy W. Hoover. *The Five Gospels: The Search for the Authentic Words of Jesus*. New York: Polebridge, 1993.

Gago, Verónica. *Neoliberalism from Below: Popular Pragmatics and Baroque Economies*. Translated by Liz Mason-Deese. Radical Américas. Durham, NC: Duke University Press, 2017. Kindle.

Garnsey, Peter. *Social Status and Legal Privilege in the Roman Empire*. Oxford: Clarendon, 1970.

Garnsey, Peter, and Richard P. Saller. *The Roman Empire: Economy, Society, and Culture*. Berkeley: University of California Press, 1987.

George, Susan, and Fabrizio Sabelli. *Faith and Credit: The World Bank's Secular Empire*. Boulder: Westview, 1994.

Gillman, John. *Possessions and the Life of Faith: A Reading of Luke-Acts*. Zacchaeus Studies: New Testament. Collegeville, MN: Liturgical, 1991.

González, Justo L. *Faith and Wealth: A History of Early Christian Ideas on the Origin, Significance, and Use of Money*. Eugene, OR: Wipf & Stock, 1990.

———. *Luke*. 1st ed. Belief: A Theological Commentary on the Bible. Louisville: Westminster John Knox, 2010.

Goodman, Martin. *The Roman World, 44 BC–AD 180*. New York: Routledge, 2012. Kindle.

Goodrich, John K. "Voluntary Debt Remission and the Parable of the Unjust Steward (Luke 16:1–13)." *JBL* 131 (2012) 547–66.

Grant, Robert McQueen. *Augustus to Constantine: The Rise and Triumph of Christianity in the Roman World*. Louisville: Westminster John Knox, 2004.

Gutiérrez, Gustavo. *A Theology of Liberation: History, Politics, and Salvation*. Translated by Caridad Inda and John Eagleson. Maryknoll, NY: Orbis, 1988. Kindle.

Gutiérrez, Gustavo, and Richard Shaull. *Liberation and Change*. Atlanta: John Knox, 1977.

Harris, William V. *Rome's Imperial Economy: Twelve Essays*. New York: Oxford University Press, 2011.

Hauerwas, Stanley. "Living on Dishonest Wealth." *Journal for Preachers* 20 (1996) 15–17.

Hawkins, Peter S. "Living by the Word: Reflections on the Lectionary (September 18, 2016)." *ChrCent* 133 (2016) 21.

Hays, Christopher M. *Luke's Wealth Ethics: A Study in Their Coherence and Character*. Wissenschaftliche Untersuchungen zum Neuen Testament 2 Reihe 275. Tübingen: Mohr Siebeck, 2010.

Herzog, William R., II. *Parables as Subversive Speech: Jesus as Pedagogue of the Oppressed*. Louisville: Westminster John Knox, 1994.

Hinkelammert, Franz J. *The Ideological Weapons of Death: A Theological Critique of Capitalism*. Translated by Philip Berryman. Maryknoll, NY: Orbis, 1986.

Hoek, Annewies van den. "Widening the Eye of the Needle: Wealth and Poverty in the Works of Clement of Alexandria." In *Wealth and Poverty in Early Church and Society*, edited by Susan R. Holman, 67–75. Holy Cross Studies in Patristic Theology and History. Grand Rapids: Baker Academic, 2008.

Holman, Susan R. *God Knows There's Need: Christian Responses to Poverty*. Oxford: Oxford University Press, 2009.

———. *The Hungry Are Dying: Beggars and Bishops in Roman Cappadocia*. Oxford Studies in Historical Theology. Oxford: Oxford University Press, 2001.

———, ed. *Wealth and Poverty in Early Church and Society*. Holy Cross Studies in Patristic Theology and History. Grand Rapids: Baker Academic, 2008.

Honoré, A. M. "A Statistical Study of the Synoptic Problem." *NovT* 10 (1968) 95–147.

Horn, Friedrich Wilhelm. *Glaube und Handeln in der Theologie des Lukas*. Göttingen: Vandenhoeck & Ruprecht, 1983.

Horsley, Richard A. *Covenant Economics: A Biblical Vision of Justice for All*. Louisville: Westminster John Knox, 2009.

———. "Paul and Slavery: A Critical Alternative to Recent Readings." *Semeia* 83 (1998) 153–200.

Humfress, Caroline. "Poverty and Roman Law." In *Poverty in the Roman World*, edited by E. M. Atkins and Robin Osborne, 183–203. New York: Cambridge University Press, 2006.

Jessop, Bob, and Ngai-Ling Sum. *Beyond the Regulation Approach: Putting Capitalist Economies in their Place*. Northampton, MA: Elgar, 2006.

Johnson, Luke Timothy. *The Gospel of Luke*. Sacra Pagina. Collegeville, MN: Liturgical, 1991.

———. *The Literary Function of Possessions in Luke-Acts*. Society of Biblical Literature Dissertation Series 39. Missoula, MT: Scholars, 1977.

———. "The Lukan Kingship Parable (Lk. 19:11–27)." *NovT* 24 (1982) 139–59.

———. *Prophetic Jesus, Prophetic Church: The Challenge of Luke-Acts to Contemporary Christians*. Grand Rapids: Eerdmans, 2011. Kindle.

———. *Sharing Possessions: What Faith Demands*. 2nd ed. Grand Rapids: Eerdmans, 2011. Kindle.

Jones, A. H. M. *The Greek City: From Alexander to Justinian*. Oxford: Clarendon, 1940.

———. *The Roman Economy: Studies in Ancient Economic and Administrative History*. Edited by P. A. Brunt. Totowa, NJ: Rowman and Littlefield, 1974.

Karris, Robert J. "Poor and Rich: The Lukan Sitz im Leben." In *Perspectives on Luke-Acts*, edited by Charles H. Talbert, 112–25. Danville, VA: Association of Baptist Professors of Religion, 1976.

Kim, Kyoung-Jin. *Stewardship and Almsgiving in Luke's Theology*. Journal for the Study of the New Testament Supplement Series 155. Sheffield: Sheffield Academic, 1998.

King, David D. M. "Appendix: Luke Economy Statistics." https://www.academia.edu/38648147/Appendix_Luke_Economy_Statistics.

———. "Luke's Good News to the Poor." Paper presented at the Annual Meeting of the Pacific Northwest Region of the SBL, Tacoma, WA, May 12, 2018.

———. "A New Accounting of Wealth and Poverty in Luke." *Conversations with the Biblical World* 37 (2017) 90–107.

———. "The Perplexing Problem of the Parable of the Pounds as Pertaining to a Preferential Position for the Poor." Paper presented at the International Meeting of the SBL, St. Andrews, Scotland, July 8, 2013. https://www.academia.edu/3662974/The_Perplexing_Problem_of_the_Parable_of_the_Pounds_as_Pertaining_to_a_Preferential_Position_for_the_Poor.

King, Martin Luther, Jr. "I Have a Dream." https://kinginstitute.stanford.edu/king-papers/documents/i-have-dream-address-delivered-march-washington-jobs-and-freedom.

Kitchen, Merrill. "Rereading the Parable of the Pounds: A Social and Narrative Analysis of Luke 19:11–28." In *Prophecy and Passion: Essays in Honour of Athol Gill*, edited by David Neville, 227–46. ATF 5. Adelaide: Australian Theological Forum, 2002.

Klauck, Hans-Josef. "Die Armut der Jünger in der Sicht des Lukas." In *Gemeinde, Amt, Sakrament: neutestamentliche Perspektiven*, edited by Hans-Josef Klauck, 161–94. Würzberg: Echter, 1989.

Klein, Naomi. *This Changes Everything: Capitalism vs. the Climate*. New York: Simon & Schuster, 2014.

Kolivakis, Leo. "Sacrifices to Market Gods?" *Pension Pulse* (blog), May 11, 2010. http://pensionpulse.blogspot.com/2010/05/sacrifices-to-market-gods.html.

Kraybill, Donald B., and Dennis M. Sweetland. "Possessions in Luke-Acts: A Sociological Perspective." *PRSt* 10 (1983) 215–39.

Krüger, René. "Conversion of the Pocketbook: The Economic Project of Luke's Gospel." In *God's Economy: Biblical Studies from Latin America*, edited by Ross Kinsler and Gloria Kinsler, 169–201. Maryknoll, NY: Orbis, 2005.

———. "Lucas 16,1–13: la opción decisiva: por la ley de Dios o por la ley del capital." *Cuadernos de Teología* 15 (1996) 97–111.

Krugman, Paul. "The Market Speaks." *New York Times*, March 7, 2013. https://www.nytimes.com/2013/03/08/opinion/krugman-the-market-speaks.html?_r=0.

Lamborn, Amy Bentley. "Stewarding Unrighteousness." *Living Pulpit* 15 (2006) 4–5.

Lehtipuu, Outi. "The Rich, the Poor, and the Promise of an Eschatological Reward in the Gospel of Luke." In *Other Worlds and Their Relation to This World: Early Jewish and Ancient Christian Traditions*, edited by Tobias Nicklas et al., 229–46. Supplements to the Journal for the Study of Judaism 143. Leiden: Brill, 2010.

Lendon, J. E. "Roman Honor." In *The Oxford Handbook of Social Relations in the Roman World*, edited by Michael Peachin, 377–403. New York: Oxford University Press, 2011.

Levine, Amy-Jill, and Ben Witherington III. *The Gospel of Luke*. New Cambridge Bible Commentary. Cambridge: Cambridge University Press, 2018.

Lewis, Lloyd A. "Philemon." In *True to Our Native Land: An African American New Testament Commentary*, edited by Brian K. Blount, 437–43. Minneapolis: Fortress, 2007.

Liddell, Henry George, and Robert Scott. *A Greek-English Lexicon*. Oxford: Clarendon, 1953.

Lieu, Judith. *The Gospel of Luke*. Epworth Commentaries. Peterborough: Epworth, 1997.

Long, Thomas G. "Making Friends." *Journal for Preachers* 30 (2007) 52–57.

Longenecker, Bruce W. "Exposing the Economic Middle: A Revised Economy Scale for the Study of Early Urban Christianity." *JSNT* 31 (2009) 243–78.

———. *Remember the Poor: Paul, Poverty, and the Greco-Roman World*. Grand Rapids: Eerdmans, 2010.

Longenecker, Bruce W., and Kelly D. Liebengood, eds. *Engaging Economics: New Testament Scenarios and Early Christian Reception*. Grand Rapids: Eerdmans, 2009.

López Rodriguez, Darío. *The Liberating Mission of Jesus: The Message of the Gospel of Luke*. Translated by Stefanie D. Israel. Pentecostals, Peacemaking, and Social Justice 6. Eugene, OR: Pickwick, 2012. Kindle.

MacMullen, Ramsay. *Christianizing the Roman Empire (A.D. 100–400)*. New Haven: Yale University Press, 1984.

———. *Roman Social Relations, 50 B.C. to A.D. 284*. New Haven: Yale University Press, 1974.

———. *The Second Church: Popular Christianity A.D. 200–400*. Atlanta: Society of Biblical Literature, 2009.

Mahali, Faustin. *The Concept of Poverty in Luke from the Perspective of a Wanji of Tanzania*. Makumira Publication 14. Neuendettelsau: Erlanger Verlag für Mission und Ökumene, 2006.

Malina, Bruce J., and Richard L. Rohrbaugh. *Social-Science Commentary on the Synoptic Gospels*. Minneapolis: Fortress, 2003.

Marshall, I. Howard. *The Gospel of Luke: A Commentary on the Greek Text*. 1st American ed. The New International Greek Testament Commentary 3. Grand Rapids: Eerdmans, 1978.

Marulli, Luca. "'And How Much Do You Owe . . . ? Take Your Bill, Sit Down Quickly, and Write . . . ' Luke 16:5–6." *TynBul* 63 (2012) 199–216.

Mayer, Emanuel. *The Ancient Middle Classes: Urban Life and Aesthetics in the Roman Empire, 100 BCE–250 CE*. Cambridge: Harvard University Press, 2012.

McGaughy, Lane C. "The Fear of Yahweh and the Mission of Judaism: A Postexilic Maxim and Its Early Christian Expansion in the Parable of the Talents." *JBL* 94 (1975) 235–45.

Meeks, Wayne A. *The First Urban Christians: The Social World of the Apostle Paul*. New Haven: Yale University Press, 1983.

Meeks, Wayne A., and Robert L. Wilken. *Jews and Christians in Antioch in the First Four Centuries of the Common Era*. Missoula, MT: Scholars, 1978.

Metzger, James A. *Consumption and Wealth in Luke's Travel Narrative*. Biblical Interpretation Series 88. Boston: Brill, 2007.

Miller, Amanda C. "Bridge Work and Seating Charts: A Study of Luke's Ethics of Wealth, Poverty, and Reversal." *Int* 68 (2014) 416–27.

Miller, Vincent J. *Consuming Religion: Christian Faith and Practice in a Consumer Culture*. New York: Continuum, 2009.

Morgenthaler, Robert. *Die lukanishce Geschictsschreibung als Zeugnis: Gestalt und Gehalt der Kunst des Lukas*. Zürich: Zwingli-Verlag, 1949.

Mosala, Itumeleng J. *Biblical Hermeneutics and Black Theology in South Africa*. Grand Rapids: Eerdmans, 1989.

Moxnes, Halvor. *The Economy of the Kingdom: Social Conflict and Economic Relations in Luke's Gospel*. Eugene, OR: Wipf & Stock, 1988.

Myers, Ched. "Jesus' New Economy of Grace." *Sojourners* 27 (1998) 36–39.

Nessan, Craig L. "The Gospel of Luke and Liberation Theology: On Not Domesticating the Dangerous Memory of Jesus." *CurTM* (1995) 130–38.

Newport, Frank. "Martin Luther King Jr.: Revered More after Death Than Before: Americans Chose King as Second Most Admired Person of Century in 1999." *Gallup*, January 16, 2006. https://news.gallup.com/poll/20920/martin-luther-king-jr-revered-more-after-death-than-before.aspx.

North, John A. "Religion and Rusticity." In *Urban Society in Roman Italy*, edited by T. J. Cornell and Kathryn Lomas, 135–50. London: Routledge, 1995.

Novak, Michael. *The Spirit of Democratic Capitalism*. New York: Simon & Schuster, 1982. Kindle.

Ó Fearghus, Fearghail. *The Introduction to Luke-Acts: A Study of the Role of Luke 1.1—4.44 in the Composition of Luke's Two-Volume Work*. Rome: Editrice Pontificio Instituto Biblico, 1991.

Oden, Thomas C., ed. *Ancient Christian Commentary on Scripture*. Downers Grove, IL: InterVarsity, 2010. Accordance.

Osborne, Robin. "Introduction: Roman Poverty in Context." In *Poverty in the Roman World*, edited by E. M. Atkins and Robin Osborne, 1–20. New York: Cambridge University Press, 2006.

Oslington, Paul. "God and the Market: Adam Smith's Invisible Hand." *Journal of Business Ethics* 108 (2012) 429–38.

Peters, Rebecca Todd. *Solidarity Ethics: Transformation in the Globalized World*. Minneapolis: Fortress, 2014.

Peterson, Eugene H. "Gospel Rascals: A Puzzling Parable." *ChrCent* 125 (2008) 30–34.

Petracca, Vincenzo. *Gott oder das Geld: die Besitzethik des Lukas*. Texte und Arbeiten zum neutestamentlichen Zeitalter 39. Tübingen: Francke, 2003.

Phillips, Thomas E. *Reading Issues of Wealth and Poverty in Luke-Acts*. Studies in the Bible and Early Christianity 48. Lewiston, NY: Mellen, 2001.

Pickett, Raymond. "Luke as Counter-Narrative: The Gospel as Social Vision and Practice." *CurTM* 36 (2009) 424–33.

Pilgrim, Walter E. *Good News to the Poor: Wealth and Poverty in Luke-Acts*. Minneapolis: Augsburg, 1981.

Pina Polo, Francisco. "Public Speaking in Rome: A Question of *Auctoritas*." In *The Oxford Handbook of Social Relations in the Roman World*, edited by Michael Peachin, 287–303. New York: Oxford University Press, 2011.

Rees, B. R., ed. and trans. "*De divitiis*." In *The Letters of Pelagius and his Followers*, 171–211. Woodbridge: Boydell, 1991.

Rhee, Helen. *Loving the Poor, Saving the Rich: Wealth, Poverty, and Early Christian Formation*. Grand Rapids: Baker Academic, 2012.

Rieger, Joerg. *No Rising Tide: Theology, Economics, and the Future*. Minneapolis: Fortress, 2009. Kindle.

Ringe, Sharon H. *Jesus, Liberation, and the Biblical Jubilee: Images for Ethics and Christology*. Eugene, OR: Wipf & Stock, 2004.

———. *Luke*. Westminster Bible Companion. Louisville: Westminster John Knox, 1995.

Robbins, Gregory Allen. "Luke 18:1–18: Exegetical Perspective." In vol. 2 of *Feasting on the Gospels: Luke*, edited by Cynthia A. Jarvis and E. Elizabeth Johnson, loc. 4810–66. Feasting on the Word. Louisville: Westminster John Knox, 2014. Kindle.

Robinson, Thomas A. *Who Were the First Christians? Dismantling the Urban Thesis*. New York: Oxford University Press, 2017. Kindle.

Rohrbaugh, Richard L. "A Peasant Reading of the Parable of the Talents/Pounds: A Text of Terror?" *BTB* 23 (1993) 32–39.

———. "The Preindustrial City." In *The Social Sciences and New Testament Interpretation*. Edited by Richard L. Rohrbaugh. Peabody, MA: Hendrickson, 1996.

Rostovtzeff, Michael I. *The Social and Economic History of the Roman Empire*. 2nd ed. Oxford: Clarendon, 1957.

Roth, Ulrike. "Paul, Philemon, and Onesimus: A Christian Design for Mastery." *ZNW* 105 (2014) 102–30.

Sanders, Laura L. "Equality and a Request for the Manumission of Onesimus." *ResQ* 46 (2004) 109–14.

Scheidel, Walter. "Demography." In *The Cambridge Economic History of the Greco-Roman World*, edited by Walter Scheidel et al., 38–86. Cambridge: Cambridge University Press, 2007.

Scheidel, Walter, and Steven J. Friesen. "The Size of the Economy and the Distribution of Income in the Roman Empire." *JRS* 99 (2009) 61–91.

Schertz, Mary H. "Shrewd Steward." *ChrCent* 124 (2007) 19.

Schmidt, Thomas E. *Hostility to Wealth in the Synoptic Gospels*. Journal for the Study of the New Testament Supplement Series 15. Sheffield: Sheffield Academic, 1987.

Schottroff, Luise. *The Parables of Jesus*. Translated by Linda M. Maloney. Minneapolis: Fortress, 2006. Kindle.

Schottroff, Luise, and Wolfgang Stegemann. *Jesus and the Hope of the Poor*. Maryknoll, NY: Orbis, 1986.

Schumacher, R. Daniel. "Saving Like a Fool and Spending Like It Isn't Yours: Reading the Parable of the Unjust Steward (Luke 16:1–8a) in Light of the Parable of the Rich Fool (Luke 12:16–20)." *RevExp* 109 (2012) 269–76.

Seccombe, David Peter. *Possessions and the Poor in Luke-Acts*. Linz: Studien zum Neuen Testament und seiner Umwelt, 1982.

Seo, Pyong Soo. *Luke's Jesus in the Roman Empire and the Emperor in the Gospel of Luke*. Eugene, OR: Pickwick, 2015. Kindle.

Smith, Adam. *An Inquiry into the Nature and Causes of the Wealth of Nations*. Edited by C. J. Bullock. Harvard Classics 10. Danbury, CT: Grolier, 1984.

Smith, Mitzi J. "Slavery in the Early Church." In *True to Our Native Land: An African American New Testament Commentary*, edited by Brian K. Blount, 11–22. Minneapolis: Fortress, 2007.

Spencer, Aída Besançon. "Position Reversal and Hope for the Oppressed." In *Latino/a Biblical Hermeneutics: Problematics, Objectives, Strategies*, edited by Francisco Lozada Jr. and Fernando F. Segovia, 95–105. Atlanta: Society of Biblical Literature, 2014.

Stark, Rodney. *Cities of God: The Real Story of How Christianity Became an Urban Movement and Conquered Rome*. New York: HarperCollins, 2006.

———. *The Rise of Christianity*. Princeton: Princeton University Press, 1996.

Steffen, Daniel S. "La justicia del mayordomo injusto (Lucas 16:1–13)." *Kairós* 58–59 (2016) 135–55.

Stegemann, Wolfgang. *The Gospel and the Poor*. Translated by Dietlinde Elliott. Philadelphia: Fortress, 1984.

Stegemann, Ekkehard, and Wolfgang Stegemann. *The Jesus Movement: A Social History of Its First Century*. Translated by O. C. Dean Jr. Minneapolis: Fortress, 1999.

Story, J. Lule. "Twin Parables of Stewardship in Luke 16." *American Theological Inquiry* 2 (2009) 105–20.

Swanson, Reuben, ed. *New Testament Greek Manuscripts: Variant Readings Arranged in Horizontal Lines against Codex Vaticanus: Luke*. Sheffield: Sheffield Academic, 1995.

Talbert, Charles H. *Reading Luke: A Literary and Theological Commentary on the Third Gospel*. New York: Crossroad, 1982.

Tamez, Elsa. *Bible of the Oppressed*. Translated by Matthew J. O'Connell. Limited reprint ed. Eugene, OR: Wipf & Stock, 2006.

Tannehill, Robert C. *Luke*. Abingdon New Testament Commentaries. Nashville: Abingdon, 1996.

Theissen, Gerd. *The Social Setting of Pauline Christianity: Essays on Corinth*. Philadelphia: Fortress, 1982.

———. *Sociology of Early Palestinian Christianity*. Translated by John Bowden. Philadelphia: Fortress, 1978.

Tiede, David L. *Luke*. Augsburg Commentary on the New Testament. Minneapolis: Augsburg, 1988.

Tinker, George. "Blessed Are the Poor: A Theology of Solidarity with the Poor in the Two-Thirds World." *Church and Society* 84 (1994) 45–55.

Tolentino, Jia. *Trick Mirror: Reflections on Self Delusion*. New York: Random House, 2019. Kindle.

Turpin, Katherine. *Branded: Adolescents Converting from Consumer Faith*. Youth Ministry Alternatives. Cleveland: Pilgrim, 2006.

Turrell, James Fielding. "The Dishonest Manager." *STRev* 55 (2012) 415–17.

Udoh, Fabian E. "The Tale of an Unrighteous Slave (Luke 16:1–8 [13])." *JBL* 128 (2009) 311–35.

Veyne, Paul. *Bread and Circuses: Historical Sociology and Political Pluralism*. Translated by Brian Pearce. London: Lane, 1990.

Wallace-Hadrill, Andrew. "Introduction." In *City and Country in the Ancient World*, edited by John Rich and Andrew Wallace-Hadrill, ix–xviii. London: Routledge, 1991.

Weinert, Francis D. "The Parable of the Throne Claimant (Luke 19:12, 14–15a, 27) Reconsidered." *CBQ* 39 (1977) 505–14.

Weissman, Jordan. "Remembering Martin Luther King, Jr.'s Solution to Poverty." *The Atlantic*, January 20, 2014. https://www.theatlantic.com/business/archive/2014/01/remembering-martin-luther-king-jrs-solution-to-poverty/283193/.

Wells, Samuel. "It's the Economy, Stupid." *Journal for Preachers* 30 (2007) 58–60.

White, Hayden. *Metahistory: The Historical Imagination in Nineteenth-Century Europe*. 40th anniversary ed. Baltimore: John Hopkins University Press, 2014. Kindle.

Wilson, Julie. *Neoliberalism*. New York: Routledge, 2018.

Witham, Larry. *Marketplace of the Gods: How Economics Explains Religion*. Oxford: Oxford University Press, 2010. Kindle.

Wohlgemut, Joel R. "Entrusted Money: The Parable of the Talents/Pounds." In *Jesus and His Parables: Interpreting the Parables of Jesus Today*, edited by V. George Shillington, 103–20. Edinburgh: T. & T. Clark, 1997.

The World Bank. "Rural Population (% of total population)." https://data.worldbank.org/indicator/SP.RUR.TOTL.ZS.

Wright, Addison G. "The Widow's Mites: Praise or Lament?—A Matter of Context." *CBQ* 44 (1982) 256–65.

Wright, N. T. *Luke for Everyone*. 2nd ed. Louisville: Westminster John Knox, 2004.

Yang, Yan. "The Warning of and Exhortation to the Rich in the Gospel of Luke: Facilitating the Survival of the Christian Community in Roman Empire." PhD diss., The Chinese University of Hong Kong, 2013.

Zodhiates, Spiros. *Did Jesus Teach Capitalism? An Exposition of the Parable of the Pounds, Luke 19:11–27*. Chattanooga, TN: AMG, 1981.

Made in the USA
Las Vegas, NV
24 May 2022